The New
CAMBRIDGE
English Course

UPPER-INTERMEDIATE

**MICHAEL SWAN
CATHERINE WALTER**

CAMBRIDGE
UNIVERSITY PRESS

Published by the Press Syndicate of the University of Cambridge
The Pitt Building, Trumpington Street, Cambridge CB2 1RP
40 West 20th Street, New York, NY 10011–4211, USA
10 Stamford Road, Oakleigh, Melbourne 3166, Australia

© Michael Swan and Catherine Walter 1993

First published 1993

Cover design by Michael Peters & Partners Limited, London
Typeset by The University Press, Cambridge
Printed by Chase Web, Plymouth, a St Ives plc company

ISBN 0 521 37640 8 Student's Book 4
ISBN 0 521 37652 1 Practice Book 4
ISBN 0 521 37664 5 Practice Book 4 with Key
ISBN 0 521 37668 8 Teacher's Book 4
ISBN 0 521 37672 6 Test Book 4
ISBN 0 521 37505 3 Class Cassette Set 4
ISBN 0 521 37509 6 Student's Cassette 4

Authors' acknowledgements

We are grateful to all the people who have helped us
with this book. Our thanks to:
- The many people whose ideas have influenced our
  work, including all the colleagues and students from
  whom we have learnt.
- Those institutions, teachers and students who were
  kind enough to comment on their use of *The
  Cambridge English Course*, and whose suggestions
  have done so much to shape this new version.
- The Cambridge University Press representatives and
  agents, for their valuable work in transmitting
  feedback from users of the original course.
- Diann Gruber, Clare Moore, Ramón Palencia and
  Lelio Pallini, who were kind enough to read and
  comment on the typescript; their perceptive
  suggestions and criticisms have resulted in substantial
  improvements.
- Desmond O'Sullivan, of ELT Publishing Services, for
  his most helpful advice and criticism at all stages of
  the project.
- The people who agreed to talk within range of our
  microphones: Alwyn Anchors, Elizabeth Bullock, Inge
  Bullock, Jeanette Cabeldu, the children of Class 1 at
  Chilton County Primary School, Jean-Claude
  Desbuisson, Yvonne Dick, Roger Elbourne, Barbara
  Hately-Broad, Vera Hibbert, Gloria Hirst, Michael
  Hirst, Venetia Kay, Antonio López, Basil Mulford, Liz
  Parkin, John Peake, Hilda Perry, Alexandra Phillips,
  Nighat Qureshi, Anthony Robinson, H.A. Swan, Ian
  Thompson, June Walmsley, Mark Walmsley, Helen
  Walter, Mark Walter Swan, Sue Ward, Tom White,
  Alison Whyte, Jane Woods, Keith Woods, Sumiko
  Yamagoto, Annemarie Young and Lindsay
  Zonderhicks.
- Steve Hall of Bell Voice Recordings, and Jonathan
  Dykes and Robert Campbell of International House,
  Barcelona, and all the singers and musicians: for
  doing a wonderful job on the songs.
- Peter Taylor of Taylor Riley Productions Limited,
  Peter and Diana Thompson, Leon Chambers and
  Andy Tayler of Studio AVP, and all the actors and
  actresses: they made recording sessions seem easy and
  created an excellent end product.
- Randell Harris for his exceptional skill, creativity and
  dedication in designing the book and in choosing and
  directing the illustrators; and to the illustrators
  themselves for their talent and their willingness to
  work to an exacting brief.
- Annie Cornford, for her professionalism and skill as
  our sub-editor.
- Gill Clack, for her expertise and dedication in
  proofreading.
- Barbara Hately-Broad, for the thoughtfulness and
  accuracy of her invaluable secretarial assistance.
- Mark Walter Swan, Helen Walter Swan, Inge Bullock
  and June Walmsley for their readiness to be of help at
  all stages of the project.
- Colin Hayes and Peter Donovan of Cambridge
  University Press, whose confidence and support have
  made the author-publisher relationship so
  unproblematic.
- And finally Catherine Boyce and Nick Newton of
  Cambridge University Press, for their efficient, patient
  and unruffled management of a complicated editorial,
  design and production process.

Contents

Map of Book 4

	Grammar	**Phonology**
	Students learn or revise these grammar points	Students work on these aspects of pronunciation
Block A	Non-progressive verbs; reasons for choosing passives; *so is ...*, *so does ...*, etc.; emphasis with *it* and *what* ('cleft sentences'); *-ing* forms and past participles; complex sentences with subject and verb separated; linking with conjunctions and adverbs; prepositions and particles.	Word stress; rhythm and stress in sentences; hearing and pronouncing unstressed syllables; contrastive stress; /ə/ in unstressed syllables; 'dark' *l*; vowel distinctions.
Block B	Reasons for choosing passives; Present Progressive passive; Present Perfect passive; passive of verbs with two objects; *will* in offers; *if ... would have ...*; past structures with other modal verbs.	Rhythm and stress; linking; intonation of questions and statements; spelling and pronunciation (long and short vowels); pronunciation and spellings of /ɔː/.
Block C	Differences between Present Perfect and Simple Past; Future Progressive; Future Perfect; *need ...ing*; *have something done*; *make* and *let* + object + infinitive; *make* + object + adjective; omission of object relative pronouns; reduced relative clauses; common expressions with *make, take, do, have* and *get*.	Word stress; rhythm and stress in sentences; hearing unstressed syllables; unstressed suffixes with /ə/; weak forms; pronunciation and spelling: 'silent *e*', doubling.
Block D	Simple Past and Present Perfect Progressive; Simple Past and Past Perfect; tenses with *I wish* and *if only*; *had better, ought* and modal verbs; identifying uses of prepositional phrases, participle phrases and relative clauses; punctuation in identifying and non-identifying expressions; identifying and non-identifying relative clauses; relative *whose*; relative *that, who(m)* and *which*; omission of object relative pronouns; compound adjectives; prepositions in descriptions.	Rhythm and stress; hearing unstressed auxiliaries; polite and rude intonation; intonation in relative clauses; the vowels /eə/, /ɜː/ and /ɪə/; spellings of /ɔː/; spellings of /ɜː/.
Block E	Simple Past and Past Progressive; Simple Past and Past Perfect; *shall* and *will*; Future Perfect; present tenses referring to the future; tags, short answers and reply questions; relative *what* and *which*; *everything/all/nothing that*; clauses with *although, whether, so that, in case* and *unless*; position of adverbs; position of prepositions in questions.	Contrastive stress; hearing unstressed syllables; pronunciation of the letter *r*; vowel distinctions.

Functions and specific skills

Topics and notions

Vocabulary

In addition to revising vocabulary taught at earlier levels, students will learn 900 or more new words and expressions during their work on Level 4 of the course.

Students learn or revise ways of doing these things

Students learn to talk about

Listening for gist; noting and learning vocabulary; scanning text for specific information; guessing words from context; writing personal letters; writing reports; distinguishing different levels of formality; using dictionaries efficiently; telephoning; giving directions; emphasising and contrasting; asking about English; using the language appropriate to various situations.

Relative position; parts of things; time relations in narrative; similarity, differences and common ground; countries and regions; activities and interests; likes and dislikes; travel; cars.

Dealing with comprehension problems in speech; listening for detail; understanding different accents; evaluating; scanning text for specific information; guessing unknown words; making spoken and written reports; writing economically; connecting sentences into text; summarising and paraphrasing; asking about English; asking for and giving opinions; bargaining; making offers.

Quality; degree; proportion; language learning and language use; money; newspapers and the treatment of news; work; wishes; personality and personal characteristics.

Listening for specific information; reading for gist; using dictionaries efficiently; writing formal letters; making spoken and written reports; making dates and appointments; making, accepting and refusing invitations; giving contradictory, softened and emphatic answers; distinguishing different levels of formality; interviewing.

Time relations; emotions and reactions; charities; Third World problems; job applications and qualifications; news; buildings, repairs and alterations.

Talking about things without knowing the exact words; linking ideas in discussion; listening for gist; giving spoken and written physical descriptions; scanning text for specific information; reading for overall meaning; summarising; using dictionaries efficiently; expanding text from notes; defining and identifying; classifying; making suggestions.

Time relations; spatial relations and position; shape; types and classification; physical appearance of people and places; wishes and regrets; school and education; personal relationships; the animal kingdom.

Sustaining conversational exchanges; listening for gist; listening and note-taking; reading for gist; reading for main ideas; guessing unknown words; reacting to literary texts; summarising; using lexical and syntactic devices to improve a written draft; warning and promising.

Past and future time relations; position relative to the speaker/hearer; concession; precautions; purpose; materials; shapes; numbers and units of measurement; degrees of probability; prediction and the future; travel and exploration; old age; coincidences; art and reactions to works of art; prehistory; geography; animals.

A1 Art, bird-watching, cars, dancing ...

Listening skills: note-taking; listening for specific information; pronunciation (stress); grammar (*so* and *neither/nor*); discussion.

1 Look at the list in the box.
1. Can you find five things that you are interested in?
2. See if anybody else has noted exactly the same things as you.
3. Which things are you not at all interested in?

antiques   art   baby-sitting   bird-watching
cars   collecting children's books   cooking
the countryside   dancing   dogs   drawing
driving   gardening   glass   Handel
harmoniums   history   horticulture
houses   interior design   jazz   music
opera   pool   reading   shooting
sign language   sport   swimming   theatre
travel   walking   watching cricket
worrying about money

2 🔲 You are going to hear short extracts from interviews with nine people. (Their names, in order, are: Liz Bullock, Vera, Basil, 'H-A', Jeanette, Lindsay, Tony, Liz Parkin and Ian.) They are interested in the activities listed in Exercise 1. Write the people's names, and see if you can note down some of their interests as you listen to the recording.

3 🔲 Now work in small groups and see how many of the following questions you can answer. When you have answered as many as possible, listen to the recording again and try to complete your answers.

1. Who is interested in sign language?
2. What are Liz Bullock's interests?
3. How many harmoniums has Ian got?
4. Is Vera interested in history?
5. What interest do Basil and Jeanette share?
6. What interest do Vera and H-A share?
7. Is the person who worries about money interested in antiques?
8. How many people are interested in reading?
9. Who has the most interests?
10. One of the interests in the list is not mentioned in the interviews. Which?

4 🔲 Pronunciation. Some of these words are stressed on the first syllable and some on the second. Can you sort them into two groups? Listen to the recording and check your answers.

antique   collecting   countryside   gardening
harmonium   history   interested   interior
interview   language   pronounce   recording
theatre

5 Grammar revision. Look at the table. Then add some sentences in each of the four groups.

	Sarah	Richard	Oliver	Celia	Mark		
	✓	✗	✓	✓	✗		likes animals
	✗	✓	✓	✓	✗		can swim
	✓	✓	✗	✗	✓		is interested in money
	✗	✗	✗	✓	✓		has got a home computer
	✓	✗	✓	✗	✗		collects antiques
	✓	✓	✗	✗	✗		plays golf
	✗	✓	✓	✗	✓		used to collect stamps
	✓	✗	✓	✗	✓		used to like pop music

1. Sarah is interested in money, and **so is** Richard.
   Oliver likes animals, and **so does** Celia.

   ....

2. Sarah can't swim, and **nor can** Mark.
   Celia doesn't collect antiques, and **neither does** Richard.

   ....

3. Mark has got a home computer, but Sarah **hasn't.**
   Sarah plays golf, but Celia **doesn't.**

   ....

4. Oliver used to like pop music, and **so did** Mark.
   Sarah didn't use to collect stamps, but Richard **did.**

   ....

6 What are your interests? Make a list by completing some of these sentences.

1. I'm very interested indeed in …
2. I'm quite interested in …
3. I'm not very interested in …
4. I'm not at all interested in …
5. I'm bored by …
6. I think … is/are very interesting.
7. I think … is/are quite interesting.
8. I think … is/are very boring.
9. I used to be interested in …
10. At the moment I'm doing a lot of …

Ask for help if necessary.

> What's the English for …?

> How do you spell …?

7 Exchange lists with another student. Do you have any interests in common? What differences are there?

8 Report to the class. Examples:

'Anna's interested in travel, and so am I.'
'Mary thinks Russian literature is interesting, and so do I.'
'John doesn't like classical music, and neither/nor do I.'
'Alex is interested in economics, but I'm not.'
'Peter used to play a lot of football, and so did I.'

9 Do one of the following activities.
EITHER: Give a short talk to the class about one of your interests.
OR: Write 150–200 words about one of your interests.

Learn/revise: antiques; art; baby-sitting; bird-watching; classical music; countryside; design; economics; gardening; gold; home computer; interview; jazz; list; opera; pop music; recording; sign; sport; stamp; collect; draw (drew, drawn); pronounce; shoot (shot, shot); spell (spelt, spelt); worry; Russian; indeed; so; neither; nor.

A2 Focus on systems

A choice of exercises: emphasis with *it* and *what*; hearing and pronouncing unstressed syllables; nouns and adjectives for places and regions.

GRAMMAR: EMPHASIS WITH *IT* AND *WHAT*

1 Look at the three sentences. They mean the same, but in the second and third sentences *travelling* is emphasised (given more importance). Practise pronouncing the sentences with stress on *travelling*.

In my job, I like the travelling.
In my job, it's the travelling that I like.
In my job, what I like is the travelling.

...what I like is the travelling..

2 Here are some things that people said about their work. Change the sentences so as to express the ideas in the other two possible ways (see Exercise 1).

1. I like working with other people.
2. What I like is organising my own work.
3. It's being alone that I like.
4. I like meeting people.
5. What I like is being able to travel on business.
6. It's having my own office that I like.
7. I like having responsibility.
8. What I like is working in a small personal organisation.

3 Say what you like and what you don't like about your present job, your school, the place where you live, or your way of life. Begin *It's ...* or *What ...*

4 Complete these.

1. What I like most about ... is ...
2. What I like least about ... is ...

5 Contradict three or more of these. Use *It isn't/wasn't … that …* Example:

'It isn't cyclists that cause road accidents. It's bad roads.'

Cyclists cause road accidents.
Soldiers cause wars.
Working hard makes you healthy.
Love makes the world go round.
Napoleon discovered America.

Norway won the World Cup in 1990.
The sun goes round the earth.
Books teach you about life.
Grammars tell you what words mean.

PRONUNCIATION: UNSTRESSED SYLLABLES

6 📼 Listen to the recording. How many words are there in each sentence? (Contractions like *I'd* count as two words.)

7 📼 There is one vowel which comes in all of the following five words. What is it?

America   England   Europe   Japan   Belgium

Practise saying the five words, and then see if you can say these.

Germany   Brazil   Malawi   Singapore   Finland   Canada   Lebanon   Morocco

VOCABULARY: COUNTRIES AND REGIONS

8 Can you complete the table? Can you add some more words?

PLACE	PERSON	PEOPLE	ADJECTIVE
America	an	the Americans	American
Australia	an	the ....s	....
....	a Belgian	the ....s	Belgian
....	(a Chinese)	the Chinese	....
....	a Dane	the ....s	Danish
Egypt	an	the ....s	....
England	an Englishman/woman	the	English
France	a	the	....
Ireland	an	the	....
....	an Israeli	the ....s	....
....	an	the ....s	Italian
....	(a Japanese)	the	....
Kenya	a	the ....s	Kenyan
....	a Scot	the ....s	Scottish/Scotch
....	a Spaniard	the	....
Switzerland	(a Swiss)	the	....
Wales	a Welshman/woman	the	....

9 Can you write down the English names of countries in three or more of the following groups?

1. four countries in Western Europe
2. four countries in Eastern Europe
3. four countries in the Middle East
4. four countries in the Far East
5. four countries in America
6. four countries with an Atlantic coast
7. four countries with a Pacific coast
8. three countries with no sea coast
9. four very hot countries
10. two very cold countries

Learn/revise: (road) accident; cyclist; the earth; office; organisation; responsibility; soldier; travel (*noun*); war; discover; mean (meant, meant); meet (met, met); organise; alone; healthy; on business; most; least; *names of countries etc. from Exercises 8 and 9.*

A3 Situations

1 Do you know all of these expressions? All except one are commonly used in telephone calls. Which one is the exception?

Trying to connect you.
His/Her line's busy.
Can you hold?
Do you know his/her extension?
I'll see if I can transfer you.
I'm sorry. I've/You've got the wrong number.
His/Her number's ringing for you.
I'll put you through.
This is (name).
Who are you?
Who is that?
Speaking.
We got cut off.
This is a very bad line.
I'll ring you back.

2 🔲 Listen to the telephone conversations. You will hear all except three of the expressions from Exercise 1. Which three?

3 🔲 Now listen again to the final conversation between Stuart and Margaret. As you listen, look at the map. Stuart tells Margaret how to find a restaurant called Lacy's. Where is the restaurant – at A, B, C or D?

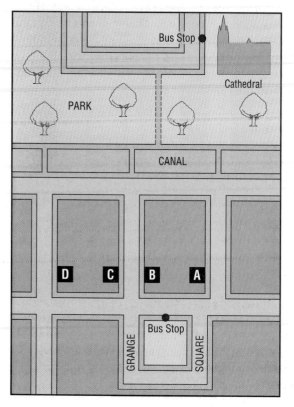

4 Do you know these words and expressions? (They are all used in giving directions.)

across   along   down   in front of   opposite
past   through   towards

roundabout   traffic lights   T-junction   fork
bend

Go straight ahead for … yards/metres.
Take the first/second/*etc.* on the right/left.
Turn right/left at …
It's on your right/left.
You can't miss it.

5 Work in pairs. Imagine that you are standing in the centre of a town or city that you know well. One of you lives there, the other is a tourist asking for directions to somewhere. Act out the conversation.

6 What situations would the following expressions be used in? Choose one of the situations: how many more typical English expressions can you remember?

What would you like to start with?
Three first-class, please, and this one is to be
   registered.
Do you mind if I look round?
Twenty in fives and the rest in tens, please.
Is it direct or do I have to change?
Day return to London, please.
Could you check the oil?
Can I get you another drink?
How long have you been with your present firm?

7 Work in groups of three or four. Prepare and practise a conversation which takes place in one of the situations from Exercise 6. The conversation must involve three or four characters, and must include the following: 1) a problem; 2) a telephone call; 3) directions about how to get to a place. When you are ready, act out your conversation for the class.

Learn/revise:
Expressions used in telephoning: Can/Could I speak to …?; Speaking; One minute/moment; (I'm) trying to connect you; The/His/Her line's engaged/busy; Can/Will you hold?; I'll ring/call again in a minute; Do you know the/his/her extension?; It's ringing for you; I'll put you through; I'll see if I can transfer you; I've/You've got the wrong number/extension; This is …; Who's that?; We were/got cut off; It's a bad line; I'll ring/call you back.
Giving directions: across; along; down; in front of; opposite; past; through; towards; roundabout; traffic lights; T-junction; fork; bend; Go straight ahead for … yards/metres; Take the first/second/*etc.* on the right/left; Turn right/left at …; It's on your right/left; You can't miss it.

A4 The sun was in the north

Reading skills: reading for specific information, guessing words from context, careful reading for details; vocabulary choice; writing skills: writing a personal letter.

1 Read the text and look at the map. If the Phoenician sailors set off in 600 BC, where do you think they were (roughly) in: December 600; May 599; July 599; December 598? You can use your dictionary or ask your teacher about words that are necessary for answering the question, but don't look up or ask about any other words.

THE SUN WAS IN THE NORTH

The Portuguese discovered the west coast of black Africa 500 years ago. But historians believe that, 2,000 years earlier, the Phoenicians may have travelled right round Africa in small boats from Suez to Gibraltar and
5 back to Egypt.

The journey was planned by the Egyptian pharaoh Necho in 600 BC. He was interested in finding a sea route from Egypt's eastern coast on the Red Sea to Alexandria on the Mediterranean. In those days, nobody
10 knew how big Africa was, and he believed it would be easy to follow the African coast round to Morocco and back to Egypt.

Necho hired crews of Phoenicians to make the journey. The Phoenicians lived at the eastern end of the
15 Mediterranean, where Israel, Lebanon and Egypt are today. They were interested in Necho's plan, because their traders wanted to find a new route to their markets in the western Mediterranean, avoiding waters which were controlled by their Greek rivals.
20 According to an old story reported by the Greek historian Herodotus, the Phoenicians set off at the beginning of winter in 50-oared sailing ships, rowed to the eastern tip of Africa at Cape Gardafui, and then sailed south-west on the monsoon winds. Month after
25 month went by, and they sailed further and further south. During their journey, the weather became steadily colder, and the seas rougher, and the Phoenicians were amazed to see that the sun was now in the north at midday. They must have thought that they would never
30 see their homes again. But after six months, the coast turned west; they went round the Cape of Good Hope and at last began to travel north.

While they were sailing up the west coast of Africa they ran out of food, and had to land to collect more supplies.
35 This delayed them, and it was only after another fifteen months that they reached a country they knew – Morocco. From there they went on to Gibraltar and then sailed east to Egypt. When they eventually arrived home, they had been away for over two years,
40 and had travelled 25,000km.

14

2 Guessing new words from context. Match each word or expression in column A with the meaning in column B that comes closest to it. There are some extra meanings in column B.

A	B
1. hired (*line 13*)	a. at last, finally
2. crews (*line 13*)	b. boats
3. traders (*line 17*)	c. competitors, people who wanted their markets
4. avoiding (*line 18*)	d. groups of sailors
5. rivals (*line 19*)	e. had no more
6. rowed (*line 22*)	f. keeping away from
7. monsoon (*line 24*)	g. little by little
8. steadily (*line 26*)	h. moved their boats with long pieces of wood
9. amazed (*line 28*)	i. ordered
10. ran out of (*line 34*)	j. paid (them) to work for him
11. supplies (*line 34*)	k. people who buy and sell
12. eventually (*line 38*)	l. rainy time of the year
	m. terribly cold
	n. things they needed
	o. using, crossing
	p. very surprised
	q. went very fast in the water

3 Look at these sentences. Compare them with the text; write *S* if the sentences say the same as the text and *D* if they say something different from the text.

1. Necho had business reasons for finding a sea route round Africa.
2. He didn't think it would be such a long journey.
3. The Phoenicians traded with countries in the western Mediterranean.
4. The Greek historian Herodotus went with the Phoenician sailors.
5. They started from the eastern Mediterranean.
6. They got lost on the way south, and sailed in the wrong direction.
7. The weather got better after they had gone round the Cape of Good Hope.
8. It took them a long time to get from the Cape of Good Hope to Morocco.
9. One reason for this was that they stopped in West Africa to get more food.
10. Morocco was the first country they recognised on the way north.
11. The whole journey took nearly two years.

4 Look at Exercises 1 and 2 again, and choose some words and expressions to learn. Compare your list with another student's.

5 Imagine you are one of the Phoenician sailors on Necho's ships. You have landed on the west coast of Africa to take on supplies. You are afraid you will never see your home again. Write a letter about your experiences to a relative or friend (you will put it in a bottle and throw it in the sea, hoping it gets to them). Use plenty of the vocabulary from the lesson.

The Phoenicians' sea route round Africa

Learn/revise some of these: boat; business; coast; food; journey; (on) land; market; midday; month; route; ship; supplies; tip; wind; amaze; arrive; avoid; become (became, become); control; delay; discover; follow; land; plan; reach; report; run out of (ran, run); sail; set off (set, set); travel (travelled); away; easy; rough; eastern; western; east; north; south; west; south-west; eventually; further; roughly; steadily; according to; round (*preposition*).

A5 Secret thoughts

Listening skills: listening for detail, prediction; pronunciation; speaking practice; grammar (verbs not used in progressive).

1 📼 Read the text and listen to the recording. The sentences in brackets ( ) are the motorist's secret thoughts.

A motorist comes back to his car. A traffic warden is standing beside it.

TRAFFIC WARDEN: Excuse me, sir.
MOTORIST: Yes?
(Oh, no, not again.)
TW: Is this your car?
M: Yes, it is.
(No, it's the Queen's private aeroplane, you fool.)
TW: I'm afraid you're parked on a double yellow line, sir.
M: Good heavens, am I really? I'm so sorry, I didn't notice.
(She'll never believe that. Let's try flattery.)
I say, what a pretty uniform.
(You look like a camel wearing a tent.)
TW: I'm sorry, sir, but I'll have to give you a ticket.
M: I see.
(If you do, I'll kill you.)
TW: May I have your name, please, sir?
M: James Baxter.
(My name is Tarzan, terror of the jungle. I am going to tear your uniform into little pieces and stuff them down your throat.)

2 📼 Close your book and listen to the recording again. Can you remember any of the secret thoughts?

3 📼 Now read this text. Try to imagine what the shop assistant is thinking. Then listen to the recording: you will hear one possible version of the assistant's secret thoughts.

A customer is trying on shoes in a shoe shop.

CUSTOMER: No, I'm afraid they don't quite fit. Could I try another pair, please?
ASSISTANT: Of course, madam.
C: Yes, these ones fit quite nicely, but I don't think this shade of red really suits me. What do you think?
A: I think the colour suits you very well, madam.
C: I'm afraid I'm giving you a lot of trouble …
A: Oh no, madam, not at all.
C: … but I think I'd like to try that pair over there.
A: But you've already tried those ones on, madam.
C: Well, I think I'll try them again just to make sure.
A: Very well, madam.
C: No, I was right the first time. They suit me very well, but they don't quite fit.
A: No, madam.

16

4 📼 Pronunciation. Listen to the recording, and write the numbers of the sentences that you hear.

1. I'd park on that double yellow line.
2. I'll park on that double yellow line.

3. They never give me a ticket for parking here.
4. They'll never give me a ticket for parking here.

5. I need your name and address, sir.
6. I'll need your name and address, sir.

7. The police tow your car away if it stays there too long.
8. The police'll tow your car away if it stays there too long.

9. Those shoes look great on you.
10. Those shoes'll look great on you.

11. Do you think these suit you?
12. Do you think these'll suit you?

13. I think these colours match your dress.
14. I think these colours'll match your dress.

Now say these sentences from Exercises 1 and 3.

She'll never believe that.
I'll have to give you a ticket.
I think I'll try them again.
I'll kill you!

5 Look at Exercises 1 and 3. Choose some useful words and expressions to learn. Discuss your list with other students and explain your choices. (Do you choose words because they are common, because they are connected with your interests, because you like the sound of them, because they are easy, because they are difficult, …?)

6 Work in groups of three or four. Complete two or more of the following conversations. In each conversation, try to use the *will*-future (*I'll/you'll/he'll* etc.) at least once, and/or one of the verbs *think, feel, hope, want, know, believe, like, love, need, remember, understand, seem, look.* (Note that these verbs are not usually used in progressive forms.) When you have completed the conversations, act some of them for the other students.

FATHER: What are you doing this evening, Sylvia?
DAUGHTER: ....
(SECRET THOUGHTS: ....)
FATHER: ....
(SECRET THOUGHTS: ....)

WIFE: How do you like my hair, darling?
HUSBAND: ....
(SECRET THOUGHTS: ....)
WIFE: ....
(SECRET THOUGHTS: ....)

TEACHER: Do you all understand?
STUDENTS: ....
(SECRET THOUGHTS: ....)
TEACHER: ....
(SECRET THOUGHTS: ....)

BOSS: ....
SECRETARY: ....
(SECRET THOUGHTS: ....)
BOSS: ....
(SECRET THOUGHTS: ....)

POLITICAL SPEAKER: ....
(SECRET THOUGHTS: ....)
(AUDIENCE'S SECRET THOUGHTS: ....)

PATIENT: ....
DOCTOR: ....
(SECRET THOUGHTS: ....)
PATIENT: ....
(SECRET THOUGHTS: ....)

SALESMAN: ....
(SECRET THOUGHTS: ....)
CUSTOMER: ....
(SECRET THOUGHTS: ....)

OFFICER: ....
SOLDIER: ....
(SECRET THOUGHTS: ....)
OFFICER: ....
(SECRET THOUGHTS: ....)

Learn/revise some of these: aeroplane; audience; bracket(s); camel; customer; line; motorist; pair; secret (*noun and adjective*); shade (of a colour); tent; thought; throat; traffic warden; trouble (*uncountable*); uniform; fit; kill; make sure (made, made); notice; park; stuff; suit; tear (tore, torn); try on; wear (wore, worn); political; private; beside; already; just (= only); the (first) time; Good heavens; I'm afraid …

A6 Focus on systems

A choice of exercises: understanding and writing complex sentences; reported speech; contrastive stress; words for parts of things; prepositional expressions.

GRAMMAR: COMPLEX SENTENCES

1 In complex sentences, verbs don't always come immediately after their subjects. Compare:

School was a very happy time.
The year after I left school **was** a very happy time.

A good plan is to do nothing.
The worst solution when you have a problem and can't think of a good plan **is** to do nothing.

2 Here are the ends of some sentences. Look in the box to find the right beginnings.

1. my military service was the best time of my life.
2. children always seem so peaceful.
3. the Cathedral has got a lot of good restaurants in.
4. my first wife had holes in the roof.
5. Fred was the hottest she had ever known.
6. a number 7 bus is really beautiful.
7. my mother works down a coal mine.
8. today's paper looks a bit like you, except for the hair.

Places where there aren't any
That picture of a little girl in a pink dress on the front seat of
The day when she married
The house where I lived with
The photo at the bottom of page 1 in
The second street on the right after you get to
The week before I started
The man in the flat next door to

---

3 Now use the following information to build a sentence. Begin *I think the tin ...*

There's a tin.
It's behind the cookery books.
They're on the top shelf.
The shelf is over the cooker.
I think the tin has got some biscuits in.

Now make a sentence beginning *Anne says that place ...*

There's a place.
It's by the river.
Anne stayed there.
She stayed there with Elaine.
They stayed there last summer.
They stayed there after Anne's exams.
She says it's incredibly beautiful.

4 Here are the ends of three sentences. Can you put suitable beginnings with them, so as to make sensible sentences?

1. the stairs has gone out.
2. the station is a good place to find cheap clothes.
3. the bus stop looks so funny.

PRONUNCIATION: CONTRASTIVE STRESS

5 📼 Look at the sentences. Which of the words in *italics* is stressed in each one? Say the sentences.

1. The American Democratic Party has quite similar policies to the *American Republican Party*.
2. The New Zealand Labour Party is rather different from the *British Labour Party*.
3. Export figures are rising faster than *import figures*.
4. I've never met the President, but I've met the *President's wife*.
5. I don't usually vote in elections, but *this one*'s important.
6. First reports of the crash referred to two cars, but it is now believed that *three cars* were involved.

6 Here are some sentences from a newspaper report, with notes for corrections in brackets. Make the corrections (the first two are done for you). Be careful to stress the right words.

1. The President's husband is forty-eight today. (46)
   'The newspaper said that the President's husband was forty-eight today, but actually he's forty-six.'
2. He is visiting the south of France. (north)
   'The newspaper said he was visiting the south of France, but in fact he's visiting the north of France.'
3. The President is leaving for China on Sunday afternoon. (Monday)
4. She will be accompanied by two senior officials from the Ministry of Technology. (four)
5. While in China, she plans to meet officials from the Ministry of Education. (Foreign Trade)
6. She will rejoin her husband before her visit to China. (after)
7. On her return, the President will take a long holiday. (short)
8. The President is not planning to stand again at the next election. (is planning)

VOCABULARY: PARTS AND RELATIVE POSITIONS

7 What can you see in the pictures? Write sentences.

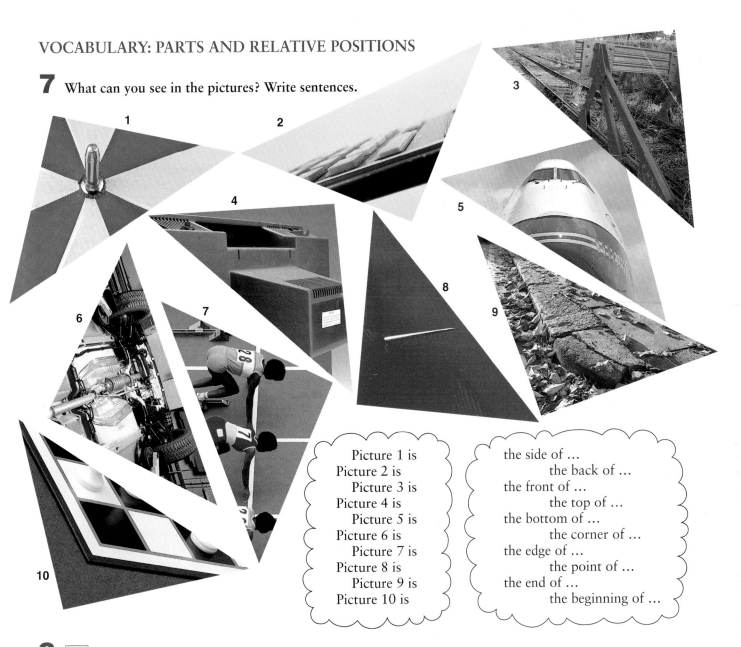

Picture 1 is	the side of ...
Picture 2 is	the back of ...
Picture 3 is	the front of ...
Picture 4 is	the top of ...
Picture 5 is	the bottom of ...
Picture 6 is	the corner of ...
Picture 7 is	the edge of ...
Picture 8 is	the point of ...
Picture 9 is	the end of ...
Picture 10 is	the beginning of ...

8 🔲 Listen to the recording and write answers to the questions, using *at the top/bottom/front/back/side(s).*

9 Read the description of the first picture; complete the description of the second picture; and write the third description yourself.

There's a big circle. Inside the circle at the top there's a small triangle. On the right at the side there are two small circles. On the left at the side there's a dot, and there's a cross at the bottom. In the middle there's a small square.

There's a big .... the triangle at the .... there's a ....
On the .... at the .... there are three .... ; .... the ....
the .... there are four .... Outside the triangle on the ....
.... circle, and there's a small .... near the bottom left-hand ....

Learn/revise: top; bottom; front; back; side; edge; corner; point; end; beginning; circle; square; triangle; dot; cross; at the top/bottom/side *etc.*; in the middle; on the right/left; draw (drew, drawn); describe; description; complete (*verb*); similar to; different from; quite; rather; actually; in fact; *other words of your choice from the lesson.*

10 Draw a simple picture. Describe it to another student and see if he/she can draw it.

A7 Cruelty to cars

> Vocabulary, and techniques for learning vocabulary; reading and writing practice; choosing between active and passive; prepositions; linking words; tenses.

1 Read one or more of these newspaper reports. The first two are to be completed with words from the boxes (there are too many words in each box). In the third, the correct verb forms have to be chosen.

ENRAGED MOTORIST 'KILLS' CAR

A motorist became enraged Tuesday when his car got stuck ....1.... the snow, smashed its windows ....2.... a tire iron then pulled ....3.... a pistol and shot out the tires, police said.

"He killed it. It's a case of autocide," said police Maj. Jack Kellem.

The car got stuck in six inches ....4.... snow.

Police said the driver became so angry that he pulled a tire iron ....5.... the trunk and smashed every window ....6.... the car. Still not satisfied, he pulled ....7.... a pistol and shot all four tires full ....8.... holes, then reloaded and emptied half ....9.... a second clip of bullets ....10.... the car.

When the gun jammed, he threw it ....11.... the snow and returned ....12.... the tire iron.

When police arrived, he was beating ....13.... the hood.

Kellem said the man was sober and rational, but very perturbed.

He was jailed ....14.... discharging a firearm ....15.... the city.

(from *The Houston Post*)

down	for	from	in	in	in	into
into	of	of	of	off	on	out	out
to	up	with				

CRUELTY TO CAR RESULTS IN FINE FOR OHIO MAN

A suburban Cleveland man learned the hard way ....16.... it can be costly to attack one's own unwilling automobile.

A Municipal Court judge fined Jeffrey G. Janor of Cleveland Heights $50 for disorderly conduct ....17.... hearing of ....18.... Janor beat upon his car with a tire iron in a rage.

Janor was on his way to a canoe outing with some friends ....19.... his Oldsmobile stalled in the parking lot of a shopping mall in neighboring Richmond Heights.

He pushed the car into a parking space, grabbed a tire iron ....20.... smashed all the windows. He was picked up by friends, ...21.... transferred the canoe from Janor's car to their own.

....22...., his outburst was witnessed by a Mall security guard, ...23.... alerted police. Janor was arrested in South Euclid.

(from *The Houston Post*)

after	although	and	because	how	
however	that	when	who	who	

BROTHERS DESTROY CAR BESIDE MOTORWAY

Two brothers who (*wrecked / have wrecked*) their car with a sledgehammer and jackhandle and (*left / have left*) it abandoned on a motorway will (*send / be sent*) the bill for its removal.

Ricky and Ronnie Johnson of Cheltenham (*decided / have decided*) to punish their Rover 2000 after it (*broke / was breaking*) down on the M5 in Gloucestershire – the day after they (*have spent / had spent*) £150 on repairs.

Motorists watched in amazement as the two brothers set about destroying the vehicle at the roadside.

Workers (*now moved / have now moved*) it to a depot. "As far as I'm concerned it can (*stay / to stay / staying*) there," said Ricky, a 28-year-old builder.

(from *The Wantage Gazette*)

2 What do you think of the behaviour described in the reports? Have you ever got so angry with something that you destroyed it? Tell the class about it.

3 Look at the following expressions from the reports. Why do you think they are constructed with passive verbs? Would it be easy to rewrite the sentences using active verbs (e.g. ... *jailed him*; *friends picked him up*) instead?

First report:
He was jailed
Second report:
He was picked up by friends
His outburst was witnessed
Janor was arrested
Third report:
Two brothers ... will be sent the bill

4 Look at the following pairs of words. Which word in each pair do you feel is more emphatic ('stronger')? Can you think of any more pairs of words like these?

angry – enraged	hit – beat
smash – break	wreck – destroy
take – grab	

5 Here are some words from the first two texts, with their British English equivalents. Do you know any more US/GB differences?

US	GB
trunk	boot
tire	tyre
hood	bonnet
parking lot	car park
learned	learnt
neighboring	neighbouring

6 Choose some vocabulary to learn from the reports. Compare notes with other students, and talk about the reasons for your choices. How are you going to note the meanings and use of the words? How are you going to memorise them?

7 📼 Pronunciation. One word in each group has a different vowel sound. Which is it?

1. pulled   hood   push   stuck
2. shop   one   costly   watched
3. who   full   threw   two
4. how   broke   snow   so
5. jammed   stalled   grab   smash
6. said   friends   then   break
7. half   hard   car   all
8. jail   rage   their   space

8 Here are some questions about a text that you have not seen. Read the questions, think what the text might say and write the text.

1. What was the weather like when Mrs Dawson started her journey?
2. What happened when she got to the bridge?
3. Why did she decide to destroy her car?
4. Where did her husband go when she started attacking the car?
5. How did the people in the street react?
6. What did she use to try to smash the windows?
7. Why couldn't she smash them?
8. What happened when she tried to drive the car into the river?
9. What happened when she tried to set fire to it?
10. What else did she do to it?
11. What did the policeman want to know?
12. Why did the policeman arrest her?

Learn/revise: amazement; bill; builder; bullet; canoe; city; guard; hole; rage; removal; snow; tyre; vehicle; arrest; attack; beat (beat, beaten); break down (broke, broken); destroy; empty (*verb*); get stuck; grab; jam; learn (learnt, learnt); move; pick up; pull; punish; push; return; shoot (shot, shot); smash; spend (spent, spent); stay; throw (threw, thrown); transfer; wreck; angry; (one's) own; satisfied; sober; although; however; still; on his way.

21

A8 Here is the news

Listening and reading skills: general comprehension, listening for the exact words, guessing unknown words, dictionary use; speaking skills: discussion and reading aloud; the language of news reports.

1 Here are some words and expressions from four radio news items. They have been mixed up. Divide the words and expressions into four groups, and then try to decide what is probably reported in each news item.

a busload of women and children   a woman
at first   drizzle on the hills   dry   figures
fridge door   gunmen   has risen
have opened fire   little hope   picture
'Slimmer of the Year'   temperatures up to 22
the economy   Ulster   unemployment
weight

2 📼 Listen to the news items. Some of the difficult words and expressions are given below. As you listen, try to guess what they mean.

First item:
wound   ambush   Armagh   wreck
suffer   target   Sinn Féin
he apparently had taken the day off

Second item:
recovery   recession   euphoria
the stock market   jobless   Wiltshire
the previous month

Third item:
a 'before' picture   18 stone 5

Fourth item:
Met Office   spell   clouding over

3 📼 Choose one of the items and listen again two or three times. Write down as much as you can of the text. Then work with one or two other students and see if you can get the whole of the text.

4 Read the following news report without a dictionary. Look carefully at the words in *italics*, and write or say what you think they probably mean. Discuss your answers with other students, and then use a dictionary to check. If possible, look in a translating dictionary and an English-English dictionary. Which gives you more useful information?

A *subpostmaster* and his eight-month-old son have been hit by shotgun *pellets* in a *raid* in Sussex. A gunman opened fire when David Halberg set off an *alarm* at his post office in the village of Polegate. He had his baby son in his arms at the time. He was hit in the shoulder. *Stray* pellets *struck* the baby's head. Police say neither, *though*, have been *seriously* hurt. *Armed* police have since *surrounded* the robbers at a house in *nearby* Eastbourne.

5 Work in small groups.

EITHER: Make up a short radio news report about some things (real or imaginary) that have happened in your school, town or country. When you are ready, read your report to the class.

OR: Make up a short radio news report about the story behind one of the newspaper headlines. In your report, try to use some words and expressions that you have learnt in this lesson.

Ex-President starts new job

MP WITH CAT PROBLEMS

10-mile swim for nothing

Flowers for girlfriend cost him £5,000

Blind teenager climbs Everest

Aliens steal Eiffel Tower

PRISON FOR MIDNIGHT FRIDGE THIEF

Learn/revise: alarm; economy; figure; load; post office; raid; recession; recovery; stock market; stone (*British unit of weight = 14 pounds = 6.5 kg*); target; temperature; unemployment; weight; hurt (hurt, hurt); rise (rose, risen); slim (*verb and adjective*); strike (struck, struck); surround; wound; wreck; armed; previous; nearby; though; seriously; a day off; take the day off.

Summary A

Non-progressive verbs

You **look** like a camel wearing a tent.
  (You're looking like ...)
I **think** the colour suits you very well, madam.
  (I'm thinking ...)
I **know** she'll be angry. (I'm knowing ...)
I **don't believe** you. (I'm not believing you.)
Do you **understand**? (Are you understanding?)

> *Other verbs that are not often used in progressive forms:* hope, want, like, love, need, remember, seem, feel *(meaning 'think')*, see, hear, smell, taste.

Using passives to avoid a change of subject

Kellem said the man was sober and rational, but very perturbed. **He was jailed** for discharging a firearm.
  (*Better than* A judge jailed him ...)
He pushed the car into a parking space, grabbed a tire iron and smashed all the windows. **He was picked up** by friends.
  (*Better than* Friends picked him up ...)

so is ..., *so does ...* etc.

Sarah is interested in money, and **so is** Richard.
Oliver likes animals, and **so does** Celia.
Oliver used to like pop music, and **so did** Mark.
Sarah can't swim, and **neither/nor can** Mark.
Celia doesn't collect antiques, and **neither/nor does** Richard.

Emphasis with *it* and *what*

In my job, **it**'s the travelling that I like.
In my job, **what** I like is the travelling.

It isn't cyclists that cause road accidents. **It**'s bad roads.

What I like most about Mary is her sense of humour.
What I like least about Joe is his laugh.

Complex sentences with subject and verb separated

The year after I left school **was** a very happy time.
The worst solution when you have a problem and can't think of a good plan **is** to do nothing.
The tin behind the cookery books on the top shelf over the cooker **has got** some biscuits in.

Irregular verbs in Lessons A1–A8

INFINITIVE	PAST	PAST PARTICIPLE
beat	beat	beaten
become	became	become
break	broke	broken
draw	drew	drawn
hold	held	held
hurt	hurt	hurt
learn	learnt	learnt
make	made	made
mean	meant	meant
meet	met	met
put	put	put
ring	rang	rung
rise	rose	risen
run	ran	run
set	set	set
shoot	shot	shot
speak	spoke	spoken
spell	spelt	spelt
spend	spent	spent
strike	struck	struck
tear	tore	torn
throw	threw	thrown
wear	wore	worn

Present and past participles

Art is **interesting**.
She's **interested** in art. (She's interesting in ...)
I thought the lesson was **boring**.
I was **bored** in the lesson. (I was boring ...)

Linking: conjunctions and adverbs

He learned *that* it can be costly to attack one's own automobile.
A judge fined Jeffrey G. Janor $50 *after* hearing of *how* Janor beat upon his car with a tire iron.
Janor was on his way to a canoe outing *when* his Oldsmobile stalled.
He was picked up by friends, *who* transferred the canoe.
However, his outburst was witnessed by a Mall security guard, *who* alerted police.

Prepositional expressions: relative positions

at the top (of)   at the bottom (of)   at the side (of)
at the front (of)   at the back (of)
in the middle (of)   on the right (of)
on the left (of)   inside   outside   near

Prepositions and particles

stuck *in* the snow
he smashed its windows *with* a tire iron
he pulled *out* a pistol
six inches *of* snow
he pulled a tire iron *from / out of* the trunk
he smashed every window *in* the car
full *of* holes
he emptied half *of* a second clip of bullets *into* the car
he threw it *into* the snow
he returned *to* the tire iron
beating *on* the hood
jailed *for* discharging a firearm *in* the city

Telephoning

Trying to connect you.
His/Her line's busy.
Can you hold?
Do you know his/her extension?
I'll see if I can transfer you.
I'm sorry. I've/You've got the wrong number.
His/Her number's ringing for you.
I'll put you through.
This is (*name*).
Who is that?
Speaking.
We got cut off.
This is a very bad line.
I'll ring you back.

Giving directions

across   along   down   in front of   opposite
past   through   towards

roundabout   traffic lights   T-junction   fork
bend

Go straight ahead for ... yards/metres.
Take the first/second/*etc.* on the right/left.
Turn right/left at ...
It's on your right/left.
You can't miss it.

Asking about English

What's the English for ...?
How do you spell ...?

Emphatic synonyms

angry – enraged
break – smash
take – grab
hit – beat
destroy – wreck

British / United States differences

BRITISH	US
boot	trunk
tyre	tire
bonnet	hood
car park	parking lot
learnt	learned
neighbouring	neighboring

Words for countries and regions: some examples

PLACE	PERSON	PEOPLE	ADJECTIVE
America	an American	the Americans	American
Australia	an Australian	the Australians	Australian
Belgium	a Belgian	the Belgians	Belgian
China	(a Chinese)	the Chinese	Chinese
Denmark	a Dane	the Danes	Danish
Egypt	an Egyptian	the Egyptians	Egyptian
England	an Englishman/woman	the English	English
France	a Frenchman/woman	the French	French
Ireland	an Irishman/woman	the Irish	Irish
Israel	an Israeli	the Israelis	Israeli
Italy	an Italian	the Italians	Italian
Japan	(a Japanese)	the Japanese	Japanese
Kenya	a Kenyan	the Kenyans	Kenyan
Scotland	a Scot	the Scots	Scottish/Scotch
Spain	a Spaniard	the Spanish	Spanish
Switzerland	(a Swiss)	the Swiss	Swiss
Wales	a Welshman/woman	the Welsh	Welsh

The commonest vowel in English: /ə/

America /əˈmerɪkə/   England /ˈɪŋglənd/
Europe /ˈjʊərəp/   Japan /dʒəˈpæn/
Belgium /ˈbeldʒəm/   Maria /məˈrɪə/
Christopher Columbus /ˈkrɪstəfə kəˈlʌmbəs/

Contrastive stress

The American Democratic Party has quite similar
    policies to the American **Republican** Party.
The American Democratic Party has quite similar
    policies to the **Fantasian** Democratic Party.
The Fantasian Democratic Party has very different
    principles from the Fantasian Democratic **Union**.

Vocabulary

Look through the 'Learn/revise' boxes at the end of
Lessons A1–A8.

Revision and fluency practice **A**

A choice of activities.

1 📼 Look at the picture for two minutes. Then close your book and listen to the recording. There are a number of mistakes in the description. Can you say what they are? Example:

'She said the sky was grey, but actually it's blue.'

Dürer: *Piper and drummer*

2 Half-dictation. The teacher will dictate the first half of some sentences; write what you hear, decide how to continue and write the rest.

3 Describe one of the things in the pictures. You must not use its name (if you know it), and you must not use your hands to help you explain. The other students will try to decide which thing you are talking about. Useful structures:

something (that) …
a thing (that) …
something / a thing that you wear when …
something / a thing that you use to … / for …ing
a thing for …ing
a thing with …
a thing that has …
stuff that …
liquid/powder/material that … / for …
you use it to … / for …ing
you use it when you …
you can … it
a kind/sort of …
it happens when you …
you do it …

4 The teacher will give you a card describing an activity and a card describing the weather (e.g. 'You're singing'; 'It's snowing'). Act out what is on the cards so that the class can guess both the activity and the weather.

5 Conversational expressions. Complete the following dialogue and then act it out.

(Alice is waiting in front of the station for Bill.)
CAROL: Hello, Alice. What are you doing?
ALICE: Waiting for Bill.
CAROL: Yeah. He's always late, isn't he?
　　　(Alice agrees.)
ALICE: .... But he's nice.
CAROL: Yes, I know.
　　　(Carol explains why she can't go on talking to Alice, and leaves.)
CAROL: ....
　　　(Steve, a stranger, tries to get into conversation with Alice.)
STEVE: ....
　　　(Alice gets rid of him.)
ALICE: ....
　　　(Joe, another stranger, starts talking to Alice.)
JOE: ....
　　　(He is successful.)
ALICE: ....
　　　(Joe asks Alice about her job.)
JOE: ....?
ALICE: I'm a nurse.
　　　(Joe expresses interest.)
JOE: ....? Do you like it?
ALICE: Well, it's hard work. But it's interesting. I only started –
　　　(Bill turns up. Alice greets Bill, asks Joe's name, and introduces Bill and Joe.)
ALICE: ....?
JOE: ....
ALICE: ....
BILL: ....
　　　(Joe greets Bill and goes back to his conversation with Alice.)
JOE: .... You only started –
ALICE: Yes. I only started six weeks ago –
　　　(Bill apologises for interrupting.)
BILL: ....
　　　(He reminds Alice that they are going to a party.)
BILL: ....
ALICE: Oh, dear. I didn't realise it was so late. Time flies when you're having fun, doesn't it?
　　　(Alice invites Joe to come along with them to the party.)
ALICE: ....? You don't mind, do you Bill?
　　　(Joe accepts.)
JOE: ....
　　　(Bill agrees, not very enthusiastically.)
BILL: ....
　　　(Joe says he's going to get a bottle of wine, and promises to be back shortly.)
JOE: You wait here a minute. I'm just going to get a bottle of wine. ....
ALICE: OK.
　　　(You finish the conversation.)

6 How brave are you? How do you react (or how do you think you would react) to the following experiences? Note your reactions as follows: very frightened 2; frightened 1; not frightened 0. Take away one point from your total for each experience that excites you; take away two points for each experience that excites you very much.

1. being driven very fast
2. driving very fast
3. going on a very fast roller-coaster
4. flying in a big passenger plane
5. flying in a small plane
6. going down in a submarine
7. climbing a high ladder
8. climbing a difficult mountain
9. looking down from the top of a high building
10. being outside in a thunderstorm
11. being in a storm at sea
12. being lost in a dark forest
13. being alone in the dark
14. being in the middle of a big crowd
15. being in a small tunnel
16. being in a lift that has broken down
17. attending a spiritualist séance
18. learning a dangerous sport (e.g. shark-hunting, motor-racing, sky-diving)
19. speaking in public
20. taking an exam
21. getting into a fight
22. being alone with a drunk in a railway carriage
23. being alone with a mentally disturbed person in a railway carriage
24. being alone at night in a house that is said to be haunted
25. seeing a big dog coming towards you
26. touching a non-poisonous snake
27. touching a non-poisonous spider
28. having bats fly over your head
29. hearing a fire alarm in your hotel
30. seeing an injured person pouring with blood
31. having a non-dangerous operation
32. going to the dentist

When you have finished the questionnaire, find out the scores of different people in the class. What are the highest and lowest scores? What is the average score? How does your own score compare with the average? Are you surprised by your result? What kind of scores do you think show that people are: very brave; quite brave; quite nervous; very nervous?

7 Work in groups and make up a questionnaire to find out something else about people – for example how generous they are, or how sociable, or how honest, or how hard-working.

8 ▣ Listen to the song. The words are on page 118.

Test A

LISTENING AND NOTE-TAKING

1 🔊 **Listen to the three weather forecasts. Which forecast corresponds to the postcard?**

> Dear Martin,
> Beautiful sunshine for our sightseeing this morning – a bit cold, but we expected that. We got into the local history museum just before the showers started and spent the afternoon there – you'd love it.
> All the best,
> Jenny
>
> Martin Sullivan
> 15 Church Lane
> Canterbury
> CT4 3DW

GRAMMAR

2 **Complete the sentences.**

1. Angela enjoyed the film, and so .... Ransi.
2. My birthday's in January, and so .... my mother's.
3. Monica's been to China, and so .... Derek.
4. Richard watches a lot of television, and so .... his sisters.
5. I don't like getting up early, and nor .... my children; but my husband ....
6. My father can't swim, and neither .... I.

3 **Choose the best alternatives.**

1. *Don't you think / Aren't you thinking* Michèle *looks / is looking* like Greta Garbo?
2. 'What *do you do / are you doing*?' 'I *wait / I'm waiting* for my sister. I *hope / I'm hoping* she won't be long.'
3. I *don't understand / I'm not understanding* what *happens / 's happening*: the lights keep going off and on.
4. Davenport police are searching for seven-year-old Felix Hinojosa, *who someone last saw / who was last seen* yesterday morning on his way to school.

4 **Here are the ends of three sentences. Put suitable beginnings with them, so as to make sensible sentences.**

1. that big house on the corner have moved to Miami.
2. my boyfriend was built in the year 1843.
3. mathematics in secondary school had beautiful red hair.

LANGUAGE IN USE

5 **Describe the picture as completely as possible.**

6 **Complete the dialogue with appropriate sentences.**

(phone rings)
OPERATOR: Hello, Slade and Lewis, may I help you?
CHRIS: ....?
OPERATOR: One moment please.
(a moment passes)
OPERATOR: I'm sorry, ... hold?
CHRIS: Yes, please.
JENNIFER: Hello, Jennifer Slade speaking.
CHRIS: .... wrong .... I was calling ....
JENNIFER: Oh dear. Well, just a moment, I'll try to transfer you.
CHRIS: Thank you very much.
(a moment passes)
JENNIFER: Sorry, ... message?
CHRIS: No, thank you anyway. .... later.
JENNIFER: All right, then. Goodbye.
CHRIS: Bye.

VOCABULARY

7 **Nouns and verbs: complete the table.**

NOUN	VERB
1. amazement	amaze
2.	describe
3.	travel
4. meeting	....
5.	drive
6.	organise
7. report	....
8. snow	....
9.	supply
10.	think
11.	weigh

8 **Countries: add four more rows to the list.**

	PLACE	PERSON	PEOPLE	ADJECTIVE
1.	America	an American	the Americans	American
2.	....	....	....	....
3.	....	....	....	....
4.	....	....	....	....
5.	....	....	....	....

PRONUNCIATION

9 Look at these words. In each list, are all the underlined letters (or groups of letters) pronounced the same, or is one different? Write *S* if they are the same, or write the word with the different sound.

1. <u>a</u>ccident   j<u>a</u>zz   st<u>a</u>mp   w<u>a</u>tch
2. econ<u>o</u>mics   g<u>o</u>ld   <u>o</u>pera   sh<u>o</u>t
3. can<u>oe</u>   f<u>oo</u>d   sh<u>oo</u>t   thr<u>ew</u>
4. br<u>ea</u>k   coll<u>e</u>ct   del<u>ay</u>   w<u>eigh</u>t
5. comp<u>u</u>ter   m<u>u</u>sic   p<u>u</u>nish   <u>u</u>niform
6. b<u>u</u>llet   g<u>oo</u>d   p<u>u</u>ll   p<u>u</u>sh
7. pron<u>ou</u>nce   r<u>ou</u>nd   surr<u>ou</u>nd   w<u>ou</u>nded
8. c<u>ou</u>ntryside   r<u>ou</u>gh   r<u>u</u>n   tr<u>ou</u>ble
9. <u>ough</u>t   t<u>augh</u>t   th<u>ough</u>   th<u>ough</u>t

10 Mark the stressed syllable in each word.
Example:

accident

Atlantic   avoid   beginning   complete
computer   Denmark   eventually   indeed
interview   Japan   political   recession
recovery   satisfied

11 Circle the vowels that are pronounced /ə/.
Example:

ⓐvoid

alarm   audience   Belgium   figure   previous

READING

12 Read the text and do the tasks that follow.

Helicopter plucks two from jail

ROME: Two gunmen yesterday hijacked a Red Cross helicopter, lifted two inmates from a Rome prison courtyard and flew off in a hail of automatic gunfire. A third prisoner ran to the helicopter, but slipped in the rain.

After taking off from the prison, the helicopter landed in a Rome football field where a match was underway, and the hijackers and escapees fled by car.

Officials said the two hijackers spoke French and that one of the escapees, a Tunisian-born Frenchman, was sought by French authorities for a Paris bank robbery and murder. The other one was suspected of supplying arms to Italian terrorists.

Police said the hijackers walked into San Camilio Hospital in western Rome and cornered the helicopter pilot, Mr Mauro Pompa, aged 42.

They handcuffed the pilot's 10-year-old son to a radiator and forced Mr Pompa at gunpoint to take them to the helicopter, parked across the street.

The white helicopter with red crosses painted on each side then flew across the city to Rebibbia prison in eastern Rome. There, it hovered a yard above the courtyards where about 50 inmates were exercising, deputy warden, Mr Giancarlo Baldassini, said.

As the hijackers fired automatic weapons for cover and lowered a rope ladder, two inmates dashed to the helicopter and jumped in. A guard at Rebibbia prison was slightly injured by flying glass during the gun battle.

Two shots fired by a guard hit the helicopter.

(from *The Guardian*)

1. Write down in order the places where the gunmen went.
2. Write down four or more things that prove that the escape was carefully planned.
3. True, false, or don't know: the escape plan originally included three prisoners.
4. How do you think officials found out that the hijackers spoke French?

WRITING

13 Write a personal letter to a close friend or family member on one of these subjects.

1. Write about how you have spent the past week.
2. Imagine you are one of the other prisoners in the story in Exercise 12. You were exercising in the courtyard when the escape happened. Write about what you were doing, what you saw, heard and did, and how you felt.
3. Choose a famous person from your country's history. Pretend you are that person, writing home about something that has just happened.

SPEAKING

14 Look at the map. Choose three places on it and mark them. Then work with another student. Each of you must tell the other how to get to one or more of the places you have chosen. Don't look at each other's maps or say what the destinations are. Your teacher will tell you how many of the places you must give directions to.

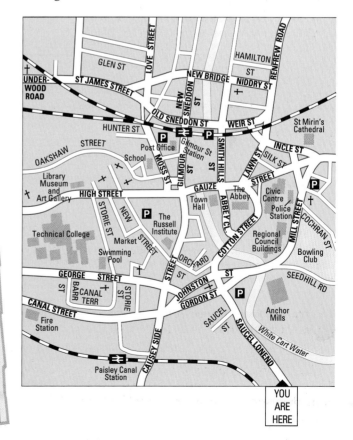

YOU ARE HERE

B1 Learning a language

Language awareness; asking for and giving opinions; vocabulary and idioms; listening skills: understanding different accents, hearing intonation; different grammatical uses of the same words; formal and informal language.

1 Use the words in the box to answer the questions.

consonant   culture   functional language
grammar   intonation   pronunciation
situational language   spelling   stress
vocabulary   vowel

1. A foreigner asks for 'fire' instead of 'a light' for a cigarette. What kind of mistake is he making?
2. A foreigner is asked 'How long are you here for?' She replies 'Since April' (the correct reply would be 'Till November'). What kind of mistake is this?
3. A foreigner tries to buy paper and is given pepper. What is the problem here?
4. The verb *record* is pronounced differently from the noun *record*. Do you know what the main difference is?
5. These two sentences don't sound the same if you hear them. What makes the difference?
   That's Mrs Lewis.
   That's Mrs Lewis?
6. If you don't know whether to write *necesary*, *necessary*, *neccesary* or *neccessary*, you have a problem with – what?
7. Which is the odd one out: *b, m, a, c, f, z*? Why?
8. A foreigner is asked 'How are you?' and replies with a long description of her health problems. She needs to learn more about – what?
9. A foreigner knows a lot of grammar and vocabulary, but doesn't know what to say in a shop or when making a phone call. What does he need to learn?
10. A foreigner knows a lot of grammar and vocabulary, but doesn't know how to apologise, complain, interrupt politely, give warnings or change the subject. What does she need lessons in?

6. What is the most interesting aspect of English, for you?
7. What is the most boring aspect of English, for you?
8. Do you think that musical people are good at learning pronunciation?
9. What do you think is the best way to learn pronunciation?
10. What do you think is the best way to learn grammar?
11. What do you think is the best way to learn vocabulary?
12. How long do you think it takes to get a good working knowledge of a language?
13. Do you prefer British English, American English, or another kind of English? Why?
14. Can you think of one thing in English that you dislike (for example a word, a sound or a grammatical rule), and one that you like?
15. What is the most important job of a language teacher?
16. Would you like to be a language teacher?
17. Do you think your language is easy or difficult for foreigners to learn? Why?
18. Do you think it is possible to learn a foreign language perfectly?

2 Choose one of these questions to ask other students. Make notes of the answers, and tell the class what people have said.

1. What do you think is the most important thing to learn in English?
2. Can you think of something in English that it is not important to learn?
3. How important is it to speak correctly?
4. What is the most difficult aspect of English, for you? Why do you think this is so?
5. What is the easiest aspect of English, for you? Why do you think this is so?

"Phrase-book."

THIS PAGE HAS EXERCISES ON FIVE DIFFERENT ASPECTS OF LANGUAGE.
CHOOSE EXERCISES ON THE ASPECTS OF LANGUAGE THAT INTEREST
YOU MOST.

3 🔲 Understanding different accents: can you understand English spoken with different accents? Listen to each person on the recording. How much can you understand? Do you think English is the speaker's mother tongue? Can you guess where he or she is from?

4 🔲 Intonation and meaning: listen to the recording. You will hear a conversation between an adult and a child. The adult says *OK* three times. Listen again, and decide what *OK* means each time. Choose your answer from this list.

1. I've heard and understood your answer.
2. You're right.
3. Do you understand?
4. I'm going to change the subject.

One of the examples of *OK* has a different intonation from the other two. Which? Does it rise or fall? Can you imitate it?

5 Grammar: different ways of using words. Many words in English can be used in more than one way. For example, *snow* can be a noun (*There's a lot of snow on the ground.*) or a verb (*Do you think it will snow?*); and *warm* can be a verb (*Shall I warm the milk?*) or an adjective (*The house isn't very warm.*). The following words can all be used in at least two ways: can you make sentences with them? Can you think of any other words that can be used in two ways?

cold   empty   land   light   look   open
past   play   rain   walk

6 Style: can you divide these words and expressions into two groups – informal and formal? Can you 'translate' any of them from formal to informal, or from informal to formal? Can you think of any other words and expressions that are very formal or very informal?

Hi!
It's a pleasure to meet you.
What?
Great!
Pass me the bread, would you?
Excuse me, have you got the time?
Sleep OK?
I think you may be mistaken.
I'm afraid I have no idea.
Let's dance.
I don't think we've met before.

7 Vocabulary and idiom: 'language functions'. Here are some language functions – things that we do with language. Do you know how to do all of these things in English? Can you add some more functions to the list?

asking for information
offering something
offering to do something
apologising
inviting
accepting an invitation
asking for something to be repeated
giving reasons
interrupting

8 Language functions and style: work in pairs or small groups. Prepare and practise a conversation which contains three or more of the language functions from Exercise 7, and some of the expressions from Exercise 6.

"Well, really! You'd think by now he'd have picked up English."

> **Learn/revise:** accent; adjective; consonant; culture; foreigner; grammar; meaning; mistake; noun; pronunciation; spelling; stress; style; verb; vocabulary; vowel; accept; apologise; divide; fall (fell, fallen); imitate; invite; learn (learnt, learnt); offer; rise (rose, risen); difficult; formal; informal; correctly; perfectly; according to; change the subject; in your opinion; working knowledge.

B2 Focus on systems

A choice of exercises: reasons for using passives; difficult passive structures; spelling (*k* and *ck* etc.); intonation of questions and statements.

GRAMMAR: PASSIVES

1 Read through the sentences. Then choose the best sentence from each pair to build up a continuous text.

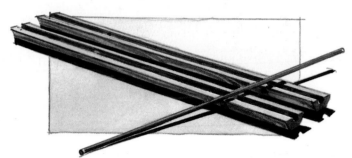

a. HOW PENCILS ARE MADE
b. HOW PEOPLE MAKE PENCILS

a. A well-made pencil looks like a single piece of wood, but actually it is made from two pieces of wood which have been carefully glued together.
b. A well-made pencil looks like a single piece of wood, but actually people make it from two pieces of wood which they have carefully glued together.

a. The workers send strips of wood through a machine which cuts grooves in them.
b. Strips of wood are sent through a machine which cuts grooves in them.

a. They cut pencil lead, which people make from graphite, clay, water and wax, into lengths and insert it into the grooves in one strip.
b. Pencil lead, which is made from graphite, clay, water and wax, is cut into lengths and inserted into the grooves in one strip.

a. A second strip is put on top of the first so that the grooves meet, with the lead inside, and the strips are glued together.
b. They put a second strip on top of the first so that the grooves meet, with the lead inside, and they glue the strips together.

a. Then they cut and shape them into separate pencils.
b. They are then cut and shaped into separate pencils.

2 Present Progressive passive. Imagine you are in a busy hotel kitchen at 11 a.m. Can you mention some of the things that are being done? Examples:

'Coffee is being made.'
'Vegetables are being prepared.'

Can you suggest things that are being done in other parts of the hotel?

3 Present Perfect passive. Imagine that the following newspaper report is about a town or city that you know well. Read the report, and then make up two or three sentences which could appear in the next paragraph, to say what has been done to put things right after the disaster. Use the words in the box to help you.

A few months ago, this town was a smoking ruin. In the volcanic eruption of June 17, most of the houses were badly damaged. The Town Hall, the railway station and a number of other public buildings were completely destroyed. The central library was burnt down, with the loss of all the books. Electricity, gas and water supplies were cut off, and the railway line was buried under tons of rock and earth. Roads and open spaces were covered under 20cm of volcanic ash.
Today, the transformation seems miraculous. The town has been completely restored. A new concrete and glass Town Hall, several times as large as the old one, has been put up in the central square.

Swathes o. suffered th floods in a terday as tial downp ain. South hit, with co both battli flooding a problems. Drivers faced haz with man because o trees. Rai fected, ca With fur pected in today, th

clear away	(re)build	(re)connect	remove
repair	replant		

4 Passive of verbs with two objects. Look at the examples, and then complete three or more of the sentences.

They sent me a letter. → *I was sent a letter.*
The referee gave him a warning. → *He was given a warning by the referee.*

1. I have never been given …
2. I was once given …
3. I have often been told …
4. Last week I was sent …
5. I have just been lent …
6. I would like to be brought …
7. Have you ever been offered …?
8. I have never been bought …
9. I was once shown …

5 Imagine that you are writing a letter to a visitor from another planet. (He/she/it understands English, but knows very little about our world.)

Write a paragraph explaining (very briefly) one of the following things. Use your dictionary, or ask the teacher for vocabulary, if necessary.

When you have finished, exchange letters with another student.

Now imagine that you are the visitor. Read the letter you have received, and write three or more questions asking for more information.

How a house is built.
How coffee or tea is made.
How glass is manufactured.
How a table is made.
How a woollen sweater is made.

SPELLING

6 Some of these words are written with *k*; others are written with *ck*. Why? Can you find a rule?

back	break	sick	look	luck	thank
rock	wake	neck	work	stuck	think
walk	like	sack	week	joke	

Some of these words are written with *ch*; others are written with *tch*. The rule is the same as for *k* and *ck*, but four of the words are exceptions. Which?

catch	reach	coach	rich	fetch	each
much	arch	bench	such	hitch	search
which	couch	brooch	hutch		

Does the same rule work for *ge* and *dge*? Look at the examples and decide.

arrange	badge	bridge	bulge	cage
charge	dodge	edge	hinge	large	lodge
rage	urge				

PRONUNCIATION: INTONATION

7 📼 Look at these two conversations, and listen to the recording.

1. 'Cambridge 31453.' 'Mary?' 'No, *this is Sally*.'
2. '*What's your name?*' 'Mary.'

In the first conversation, *Mary* is a question. The voice goes up: Mary?

In the second conversation, *Mary* is a statement. The voice goes down: Mary.

Now listen to the words and expressions on the recording, and decide whether they are questions or statements. Write *Q* or *S*.

1. three o'clock	6. at the pub
2. London	7. a cigarette
3. Michael	8. two pounds
4. Tuesday	9. Washington
5. a girl	10. trinitrotoluene

8 📼 Write down this conversation. Listen to the recording and decide where to put full stops (.) and where to put question-marks (?).

PETER: John
JOHN: Peter
PETER: Tired
JOHN: Tired   Thirsty
PETER: Drink
JOHN: Beer
PETER: Music
JOHN: Yes
PETER: Good day
JOHN: Terrible
PETER: Problems
JOHN: You know Jake
PETER: Jake
JOHN: Jake Lewis   Friend of Janet's
PETER: Well
JOHN: His wife
PETER: Mary
JOHN: Mary
PETER: Yes
JOHN: More beer
PETER: Yes
JOHN: She's mad
PETER: Mad
JOHN: Mad   Listen

Learn/revise: building; concrete; disaster; electricity; gas; kitchen; length; library; loss; machine; pencil; planet; ruin; supply; ton; burn down (burnt, burnt); bury; cover; cut (cut, cut); cut off; damage; destroy; fix; glue; insert; leave (left, left); meet (met, met); polish; prepare; remove; send (sent, sent); shape; smoke; train; busy; public; separate; carefully; together; on top of.

B3 I'll give you £25 for it

Talking about money; bargaining; listening skills: listening for detail; *will* for making offers; pronunciation: linking words in sentences.

1 📼 Close your book and listen to the conversation. Can you remember any words or expressions? Open your book and read the conversation while listening to it again. Then close your book again, listen to the gapped dialogue, and try to write the missing words.

A: How much do you want for it?
B: Forty.
A: Forty pounds?
B: Yes. It's worth fifty, but I'm in a hurry.
A: I don't know. It's not in very good condition. Look. This is broken. And look at this. I don't think it's worth forty. I'll give you twenty-five pounds.
B: Twenty-five? Come on. I'll tell you what – I'll take thirty-five. Since you're a friend of mine. You can have it for thirty-five.
A: No, that's still too much. To tell you the truth, I can't afford thirty-five.
B: I'm sorry. Thirty-five. That's my last word.
A: Come on, let's split the difference. Thirty pounds.
B: Thirty. Oh, very well. All right, thirty.
A: Can I give you a cheque?
B: Well, I'd prefer cash, if you don't mind.

2 📼 Say these sentences from the dialogue. Remember to link the marked words.

How much do you want for it?
I'm in a hurry.
I don't know.
I don't think it's worth forty.
Since you're a friend of mine.
You can have it for thirty-five.
Come on, let's split the difference.
Can I give you a cheque?
Well, I'd prefer cash, if you don't mind.

3 Work with a partner. Each of you tries to sell something to the other, and you try to agree on a price. But you can't buy or sell until each of you has used at least two of the words or expressions you wrote down in Exercise 1.

4 How much do you know about money? Answer the questionnaire, and then compare answers with a partner. For your score, see the bottom of the page.

money and you

1. **Do you know the price of a daily newspaper?**
   a. *yes, exactly*
   b. *approximately*
   c. *I've got no idea*

2. **Do you know the price of a dozen eggs?**
   a. *yes, exactly*
   b. *approximately*
   c. *I've got no idea*

3. **Do you know how much you or your household spends on groceries each week?**
   a. *yes, to within a few pounds*
   b. *yes, to within ten pounds*
   c. *I've got no idea*

4. **Do you know today's exchange rate of your country's currency against the US dollar?**
   a. *yes, exactly*
   b. *approximately*
   c. *I've got no idea*

5. **How many names of other countries' currencies can you list?**
   a. *ten or more*
   b. *five to nine*
   c. *four or fewer*

6. **Do you know the current rate of inflation in your country?**
   a. *yes, exactly*
   b. *approximately*
   c. *I've got no idea*

7. **Do you know the name and title of the person in the government of your country who is in charge of finance?**
   a. *yes, both the name and the title*
   b. *only the name or only the title*
   c. *no, neither the name nor the title*

8. **How many banks in your country can you name?**
   a. *five or more*
   b. *three or four*
   c. *two, one or none*

5 Now work in small groups to write your own questionnaire to find out about people's attitudes to money: are people mean, careful, generous, reckless? Write about six questions. You can ask your teacher for help with any vocabulary that you need. Then exchange questionnaires with another group.

Learn/revise: bank; banker; cash; cheque; currency; dollar ($); dozen; exchange rate; finance; groceries; household; inflation; pound (£); spend (spent, spent); careful; current; daily; generous; mean; reckless; approximately; reasonably; can('t) afford; Come on; friend of mine; I'd prefer …; I've got no idea; if you don't mind; I'll tell you what; in a hurry; in … condition; my last word; Oh, very well; split the difference (split, split); to tell you the truth; to within (e.g. a few pounds); well informed; *five or more words and expressions from the questionnaires in Exercise 5.*

Give yourself three points for every *a* answer, two points for every *b* answer, and one point for every *c* answer. Then add the points up. Nine points or less: you don't know much about money. Ten to fifteen points: you are reasonably well informed. Sixteen to twenty points: you are very well informed. Twenty-one points or more: are you a banker?

B4 It must be true: it's in the papers

Reading for specific information; reading for exact meaning; guessing unknown vocabulary; writing reports; discussion.

1 Read the following note and reports without a dictionary. Can you find four or more differences between the reports?

(NOTE: One summer night in the 1980s, a man broke into Buckingham Palace. He got through a window into the Queen's bedroom and spent some time talking to her. These are parts of the newspaper reports which appeared the following day; nothing has been changed except the people's names.)

THE PROWLER who had a bed-side chat with the Queen at Buckingham Palace has made at least TWELVE night-time visits to the building, his family said yesterday.

And each time he left his wife in bed, saying "I'm going to see my girlfriend – Elizabeth Regina."

Once he told his wife: "I don't just want to see the Queen – I must talk to her."

The midnight caller, who was found in the Queen's bedchamber, is a "royal fanatic", said his 53-year-old father.

But the 31-year-old intruder – a father-of-four – has had "domestic problems".

(from *The Sun*)

THE FATHER of a man on a Buckingham Palace theft charge said yesterday: "My son is a Royalist."

Unemployed Michael Flynn appeared in court last Saturday accused of stealing a half-bottle of wine from the Palace on June 7.

His 59-year-old father, also called Michael, said: "He would not hurt a fly."

(from *The Daily Express*)

THE QUEEN'S ordeal at the hands of an intruder may have lasted at least half an hour.

I understand from Buckingham Palace insiders that the man found in her bedroom in the early hours of last Friday had been there for "considerably longer than ten minutes".

(from *The Daily Star*)

THE man who terrorised the Queen on Friday was on his second illicit visit to the Palace.

(from *The Daily Star*)

THE father of the man found on Friday morning in the Queen's bedroom said last night that he believed his son had got into Buckingham Palace three times since May 9.

(from *The Daily Mail*)

Jenny and her husband, married for eleven years, have been living in a half-way house with their six children.

Four are from the marriage: Sally, ten, Andy, six, Tracy, five, and Rob, three. Jenny also has two children by a previous marriage – Lucille, sixteen, and Darren, fifteen.

(from *The Daily Express*)

The intruder, revealed yesterday as 30-year-old Michael Flynn, sat on the Queen's bed for ten minutes and chatted to her.

He was arrested after he asked for a cigarette, which enabled the Queen to call a footman.

(from *The Daily Mirror*)

Yesterday Mr Flynn, who is in his fifties and lives in Highbury, insisted that any money he made from the story would go to his son's wife Jenny.

Jenny, who has two children by Michael Junior and two by another man, recently returned to her husband after a separation.

(from *The Daily Mirror*)

---

2 Guessing difficult vocabulary. Look at the way these words and expressions are used in the reports, and choose what you think is the best explanation for each one. Don't use a dictionary. Can you explain the reasons for your choices?

1. prowler (*The Sun*)
   a. person who goes round looking for opportunities to commit a crime
   b. unemployed builder
   c. person who has recently been let out of prison
   d. person whose marriage is in trouble
2. royal fanatic (*The Sun*)
   a. crazy member of the royal family
   b. very strange person
   c. person who is very interested in the royal family
   d. person who hates the royal family
3. domestic problems (*The Sun*)
   a. trouble with his house
   b. trouble with his family
   c. trouble with his servants
   d. trouble with his health
4. ordeal (*Daily Star*)
   a. orders   c. waking period
   b. conversation   d. difficult time
5. intruder (*Daily Star, Daily Mirror*)
   a. person who goes where he/she is not wanted
   b. person who hurts other people
   c. person who talks too much
   d. person who thinks he/she is very important
6. illicit (*Daily Star*)
   a. happy, enjoyable   c. evening
   b. stupid   d. illegal, against the law
7. footman (*Daily Mirror*)
   a. policeman
   b. royal servant
   c. royal shoe-cleaner
   d. person who takes the Queen's dogs for a walk
8. on a ... theft charge (*Daily Express*)
   a. in prison for stealing things
   b. in the habit of stealing things
   c. accused by the police of stealing things
   d. wrongly accused of stealing things
9. He would not hurt a fly. (*Daily Express*)
   a. He likes animals.
   b. He is not very strong.
   c. He is kind and gentle.
   d. He is not very intelligent.
10. half-way house (*Daily Express*)
   a. small house
   b. house between two villages
   c. house that occupies half of a building
   d. place where people in trouble can live

3 Do the reports say this?

1. Michael Flynn went to the Palace to see his girlfriend, but met the Queen instead.
2. He was drunk when he broke into the Palace.
3. He stole some wine while he was there.
4. He spent ten minutes or more in the Queen's bedroom.
5. The Queen was frightened by Mr Flynn.
6. He was arrested by a footman.
7. He was taken to court and charged with breaking into the Palace.
8. He lives in Highbury with his wife Jenny.
9. He doesn't get on well with his wife.
10. His father expected to get money from the newspapers.

4 Work in groups of four. Act out the scene (taking the parts of Michael Flynn, the Queen, the footman and a policeman).

5 Do one or more of these exercises. You can work alone, in pairs or in groups.

A. Look at the following notes (taken from a newspaper report). Add some more details, and write two short reports (as if from different newspapers) with some differences. Read your reports to other students and see if they can find all the differences.

Police station burgled.
Money, policeman's uniform, other things stolen.
Theft noticed a week later. Police called to crash.
Police found thief in uniform directing traffic.

B. Buy several different newspapers on the same day and look at the various reports of the same incidents. Or listen to the news on two different radio/TV channels (record them if possible). Talk to the class about the differences you have found.

C. Interview other people in (or outside) the class about the newspapers they read. Find out the reasons for their choices. Which papers are most popular and why? Give a written or spoken report to the class.

D. Look at several different newspapers and compare them. What do you think is good and bad about each one? Discuss your opinions with the other students.

E. Put together a class newspaper or radio programme, with reports of the things that have happened in your school during the last week.

Learn/revise: chat (*noun and verb*); choice; crime; difference; disturbance; fly; manager; midnight; opinion; problem; programme; report; theft; accuse (sbdy of sth); arrest; bite (bit, bitten); break into (broke, broken); charge (sbdy with sth); enable (sbdy to do sth); expect; frighten; get on (with sbdy); insist; interview; last (*verb*); steal (stole, stolen); certain; domestic; drunk; false; popular; previous; true; unemployed; considerably; instead; on a visit; in court.

B5 Work

Listening, speaking, reading and writing skills; vocabulary study.

1 📼 Listen to the recording (it is part of a discussion about work) and write down a phrase from the box for each blank.

> I'd like to *(three times)*   I'd really like to
> I'd really like   I would like to   I *would* like
> I'd love to   I'd just like to

KEITH: .... work in a museum. *(Mm-hm)*
JOHN: I think .... own me own gardening centre. I'd love that. *(Yeah)* Yeah. .... that.
SUE: .... be a really good potter. *(Mm-hm)* *(Yeah)* Be on my own. *(Yeah)*
JANE: .... be really good at something – anything!
ALEX: Actually with the job I've chosen, the police force, ... go into dog handling in that. That's what ....
KATY: I think .... teach again.
MIKE: What .... spend my time doing isn't really classed as jobs.

2 What job would you really like to do? Use words from Exercise 1 to answer.

3 What job do you do, or what jobs have you done in your life (including part-time or holiday jobs)? Tell other students, and ask what jobs they do or have done. Talk about what you like(d) about your work, and what you don't (didn't) like. Ask the teacher for help with vocabulary if necessary.

> How do you say ... in English?

> What do you call a person who ...?

> How do you pronounce ...?

> What's the English for ...?

4 Look at the 'Job Suitability Questionnaire'. Can you add some more questions in each section?

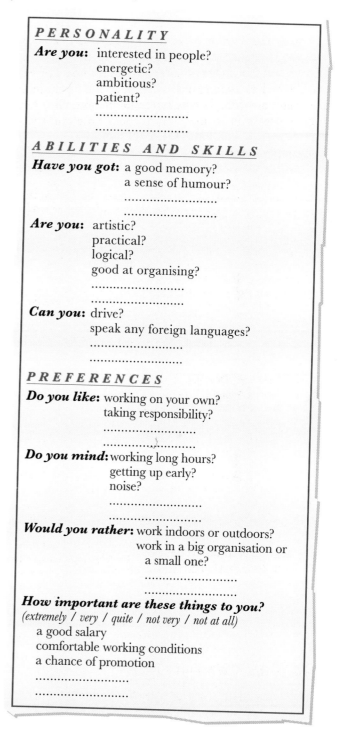

PERSONALITY
Are you: interested in people?
            energetic?
            ambitious?
            patient?
            ....
            ....

ABILITIES AND SKILLS
Have you got: a good memory?
                a sense of humour?
                ....
                ....

Are you: artistic?
            practical?
            logical?
            good at organising?
            ....
            ....

Can you: drive?
            speak any foreign languages?
            ....
            ....

PREFERENCES
Do you like: working on your own?
               taking responsibility?
               ....
               ....

Do you mind: working long hours?
               getting up early?
               noise?
               ....
               ....

Would you rather: work indoors or outdoors?
                    work in a big organisation or a small one?
                    ....
                    ....

How important are these things to you?
(extremely / very / quite / not very / not at all)
    a good salary
    comfortable working conditions
    a chance of promotion
    ....
    ....

5 Work with another student. Ask him or her the questions on the questionnaire. Note his or her answers. Useful expressions:

Sorry, what did you say?
What do you mean?
Could you speak more slowly?

6 Try to suggest a suitable job for your partner.

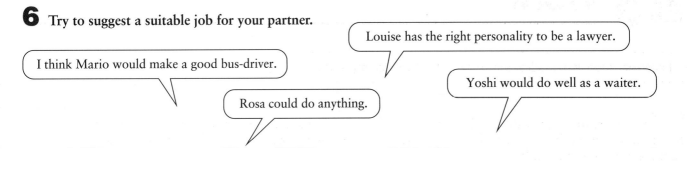

I think Mario would make a good bus-driver.

Louise has the right personality to be a lawyer.

Rosa could do anything.

Yoshi would do well as a waiter.

7 You be the teacher. Choose one of the texts and study it. Use a dictionary or ask the teacher for help if necessary. Then close your book, and tell another student what the text says, *in your own words*. Tell your partner to write down what he/she has understood. Then open the book, look at the text with your partner, and explain anything he/she can't understand. Give him/her some words to learn. Finish by preparing a small test to check how much your partner remembers.

PARKINSON'S LAW

Work expands so as to fill the time available for its completion. General recognition of this fact is shown in the proverbial phrase 'It is the busiest man who has time to spare'. Thus, an elderly lady of leisure can spend the entire day in writing and dispatching a postcard to her niece at Bognor Regis. An hour will be spent in finding the postcard, another in hunting for spectacles, half an hour in a search for the address, an hour and a quarter in composition, and twenty minutes in deciding whether or not to take an umbrella when going to the pillar box in the next street. The total effort that would occupy a busy man for three minutes may in this fashion leave another person prostrate after a day of doubt, anxiety and toil.

(from *Parkinson's Law* by C. Northcote Parkinson)

The Commercial Artist

I am a commercial artist. Many people imagine that artists live a lazy life. Perhaps some do. However, my family get very bad-tempered if there is no food, and I find I have to work quite hard to pay the bills. So I do not simply sleep all morning, stagger out of bed at midday, and go off to the pub for a liquid breakfast. Here is how I spend my day.

I get up at about eight o'clock. I wash, dress, and have breakfast. I look through the mail, hoping to find cheques and commissions. There are never enough of either. When breakfast is over I drive to my studio and spend the morning working. Working, for me, means trying to think of new design ideas, and then working the ideas out in detail when I have found them. This goes on till about twelve-thirty or one o'clock; then I have a quick sandwich lunch, and after that it's back to work. During the afternoon I often have meetings with clients. These tend to be difficult, because many of my clients have strong views about art (although very few of them know what they are talking about). By the time five-thirty comes round I'm more than ready to stop. I close up the studio, drive home, and begin to relax.

(from *How people live* by Jason Taylor)

How much is a housewife worth?

How much is the average British housewife worth? The answer is £600 a week. An insurance company has carried out a survey to find out the value of a housewife's work.

It seems that she is on call for 90 hours in a seven-day week, working as a shopper, waitress, nurse, driver, cook, cleaner and child-minder. Taking employment agencies' standard fees for these jobs, the insurance company has calculated that a housewife's work is worth £32,031 a year – more than the salary of a bishop, a divisional fire service chief or a second division footballer.

(from a newspaper report)

A Twelve-Year-Old Servant

I left school when I was twelve and I had to go into service. I went to a young couple who were farmers, and I had to live in. It was about fifteen miles from home and it seemed to me the back of beyond. It was a big rambling place, and I was the only help they had. I got one and threepence a week. They weren't bad to me, but they used to go out a lot and I'd be in the place on my own. I'd go and look in all the cupboards, under beds, I was literally terrified. I helped the mistress make butter, and sometimes I used to milk the cows as well. Anyway, I didn't last long. I got so lonely. I went to a butcher's wife near Wellingborough. She was a terror. There was another maid there, and fortunately we got on well together. We could laugh and cover up for each other if we did anything wrong. We slept in an attic, and we had to be up at six o'clock in the morning. If we were a minute or two late, she'd be there and want to know why. I reckon she laid awake all night long, just for the pleasure of catching us out in the morning.

I had fifteen places in twelve years, and only at one of them was I treated like a human being. They didn't think of us as people like themselves. We were different. Occasionally my father and brother used to come and see me, and I felt really unhappy when they left. I wanted to say 'Take me with you', but of course they couldn't. You had to work; your parents couldn't afford to keep you. Sometimes, if I'd been home, when the time came for me to go back I used to pray that the train wouldn't come or that it would crash. But it always came.

(*Mrs Webb*, from *Loneliness* by Jeremy Seabrook)

Learn/revise: ability; chance; job; memory; museum; noise; personality; promotion; responsibility; salary; sense of humour; skill; working conditions; drive (drove, driven); organise; spend time ...ing (spent, spent); ambitious; artistic; energetic; foreign; good at ...; logical; (my) own; part-time (job); patient; practical; early; extremely; indoors; outdoors; on your own; would you rather ...?

B6 Focus on systems

A choice of exercises: past structures with *would*, *should* and other modals; spellings of /ɔː/; words that describe personality.

GRAMMAR

1 Past structures with *would(n't)*. Look at the examples and then complete the sentences.

*If I **had known** her name, I **would have introduced** you to her.*
*If his parents **had had** more money, he **wouldn't have left** school at sixteen.*
*She **would have won** the race if she **hadn't fallen** over.*
*His life **would have been** happier if he **hadn't met** Cleo.*

1. If the policeman (*be*) awake, Michael Flynn (*not get*) in to see the Queen.
2. If I (*go*) to University after I left school, I (*study*) physics.
3. She (*probably pass*) her exams last year if she (*study*) harder.
4. If it (*not rain*) yesterday we (*play*) tennis.
5. I (*sleep*) better last night if I (*not eat*) so much.
6. If the traffic warden (*be*) a bit slower, I (*get*) away without a parking ticket.
7. We (*catch*) the train if Alice (*not be*) late.
8. If I (*be born*) in Ireland, perhaps I (*grow up*) speaking Irish.
9. If you (*tell*) me the truth yesterday, I (*be*) more willing to help.

2 Make a sentence about something that changed your past life. Possible structures:

If I hadn't met ..., I wouldn't have ...
If I hadn't gone to ..., I wouldn't have ...
If I hadn't studied ...,
If my ... hadn't ...,

3 Past structures with *could*. Look at the examples.

*Anna works in a shop, but she's very intelligent. If she had gone to university she **could have become** a doctor.*
*Sue **could have got** married at eighteen, but she decided to go abroad and study instead.*
*If Phil hadn't had a car accident he **could have been** an international footballer.*

Now talk about somebody you know who could have had a very different life.

4 Past structures with *should(n't)*. Think of three things that you should have done yesterday, but didn't, and three things that you shouldn't have done, but did. Examples:

*I **should have mended** my bicycle.*
*I **should have phoned** my mother.*
*I **shouldn't have stayed** in bed all morning.*

5 Past structures with *may* and *must*. Look at the examples, then change the sentences in the same way.

*(He's late.) Perhaps he missed his train. → He **may have missed** his train.*
*(She didn't phone this morning.) It seems clear that she forgot. → She **must have forgotten**.*

1. (I don't know where she is.) Perhaps she's gone home.
2. (I can't find my keys.) It seems certain that I left them in my other coat.
3. Perhaps he got into the Palace when the policeman was asleep.
4. I think perhaps we have met before.
5. If you were at Rosemount College in 1988, you certainly knew my friend Len Bright.
6. (All my things have been moved.) Somebody has clearly been in my room.
7. I'm sorry. I think perhaps I took your coat by mistake.
8. (There's water all over the floor.) This can only be because somebody left a window open.
9. Perhaps Shakespeare travelled to Germany – we're not sure.

PRONUNCIATION: THE VOWEL /ɔː/

6 How is *au* usually pronounced? Practise the following words. Which three are exceptions?

Australia authority automatic aunt
autumn because daughter caught fault
sauce taught

7 In standard British English, the following words are all pronounced with the same vowel (/ɔː/). Can you say them? And can you think of ten more words with the same vowel that are written with *or*, *aw*, *wa* or *al*?

although awful call caught corner
draw false fork law north sauce
story towards walk war warm

VOCABULARY: WHAT ARE PEOPLE LIKE?

8 Do you know all these words? If not, use a dictionary or ask your teacher. Can you find words from the list to describe the people in the pictures?

affectionate   aggressive   bad-tempered   calm
cheerful   cold   easy-going   emotional
friendly   generous   honest   kind   mean
moody   nervy   optimistic   pessimistic   polite
practical   reserved   rude   self-confident
sensitive   serious   shy   sociable

Do any of the words in the list describe you? Are there any words that definitely don't describe you?

A

B

C

D

E

F

9 Make up three questions that you could use to find out how aggressive people are. Use some of these structures:

Do you ever ...?
Have you ever ...?
How often ...?
If ..., would ...?

10 Now choose another characteristic from the list in Exercise 8, and make up questions for it. Ask the teacher for help if necessary. When you are ready, go round the class, or talk to people around you, asking your questions. Speak to as many people as possible and note each person's answers. Then report to the class on what you have found out. Use some of these words and expressions:

extremely   very   quite   not very   not at all
(nearly) everybody   most people   some people
several people   a few people   hardly anybody
one person   nobody   the majority
two out of nine, three out of fourteen *etc.*

> **Learn/revise:** *vocabulary from Exercise 8.*

B7 The Lonely One

Writing skills: asking for information, finishing a story; listening skills: listening for detail, for gist; speaking fluency practice.

1 Look at the map and pictures. Three single women, Lavinia, Helen and Francine, went out on the evening of July 20, 1928. At some time that evening, some or all of them were: at Lavinia's house, at Helen's house, at Francine's house, in the ravine, at the cinema, at the drugstore. Work in groups to find out as much as you can about their movements that evening, and about the Lonely One.

– Writing: write to the teacher, asking five questions.

– Reading: when you get your answers from the teacher, compare them with another group's. Did the other group find out anything you didn't?

– Speaking: each group can then ask the teacher another five questions. Don't waste your questions: listen to what the other groups ask.

THE RAVINE

2 📼 You will hear five recordings of people from the story. Who is speaking in each recording? Where does each recording happen?

3 What do you think happens next in the story of the Lonely One? Work in groups to write ten or more sentences to end the story.

4 Read the text on page 118 to see how the original author (Ray Bradbury) ended the story.

LAVINIA

PARK STREET

Elizabeth Ramsell's body

FRANCINE

MAIN STREET

ELITE THEATER

DRUG STORE

HELEN

Learn/revise: author; bridge; drugstore (US); map; movement; purse (US; GB = handbag); stranger; bark; check; compare; cross; find out (found, found); lean (leant, leant); promise; spend (spent, spent); terrify; waste; afraid; lonely; single; against; around; maybe; over (= finished); My God!

43

B8 My heart is too full for words

SKILLS FOCUS
SKILLS FOCUS
SKILLS FOCUS
SKILLS FOCUS
SKILLS FOCUS
SKILLS FOCUS

Listening; economical writing; evaluating.

1 Here are the beginnings of three stories. Choose one of them and then listen to the recording. You will hear some more sentences. Write the sentences which continue your story.

A: 'My heart is too full for words' she whispered,
B: Sally pulled out a gun,
C: Mary brought her horse round

2 Writing economically. Can you shorten four or more of these sentences? Example:

My physical condition is, on the whole, one in which food would be of considerable benefit. *(I'm hungry.)*

1. I am telling no more than the truth when I say that George is a habitual consumer of tobacco. *(Rewrite the sentence in two words.)*
2. In her employment, Mary showed a thoroughly satisfactory degree of energy and efficiency. *(four words or less)*
3. My sister shows a distinct tendency to prefer the company of people who are no longer in the first flower of youth. *(seven words or less)*
4. It is undeniable that the large majority of non-native learners of English experience a number of problems in attempting to master the phonetic patterns of the language. *(eight words or less)*
5. I have had to give up the belief, which I previously held, in the existence of a kind white-haired bearded figure who was accustomed to visit private houses on the anniversary of the birth of the founder of the Christian religion, in order to distribute gifts to young people. *(nine words or less)*
6. Tea, whether of the China or Indian variety, is well known to be high on the list of those drinks which are most frequently consumed by the inhabitants of the British Isles. *(seven words or less)*
7. It is not uncommmon to encounter sentences which, though they contain a great number of words and are constructed in a highly complex way, none the less turn out to contain very little meaning of any kind. *(ten words or less)*
8. One of the most notable phenomena in any big city, such as London or Paris, is the steadily increasing number of petrol-driven vehicles, some in private ownership, others belonging to the public transport system, which fill up the roads and make rapid movement more difficult year by year. *(nine words or less)*
9. 'The main problem with which I am faced is to decide whether it is preferable to continue in existence, or whether it would, on balance, be a more advisable policy to give up the struggle.' (Shakespeare) *(ten words)*

3 Here are some 'mini-sagas' (50-word stories). Read them and say what you think of them. Examples:

'I think the first one is very good.'
'I don't think much of the second.'
'What do you think of the fourth one?' 'There's nothing in it.'
'I think the fifth is better than the fourth.'

1. The Inner Man
Their marriage was a perfect union of trust and understanding. They shared everything – except his desk drawer, which through the years remained locked. One day, curiosity overcame her. Prised open, there was – nothing. 'But why?' she asked, confused and ashamed. 'I needed a space of my own,' he replied sadly.

(Christine M. Banks)

2. Homer's Odyssey in 50 words
Odysseus was a cunning, resourceful man who fought with the Greeks against Troy. Sailing back from the war, he and his crew met with a number of menaces – such as Circe, the witch who turned men into pigs – and overcame them. But it took him ten years to get home.

(C. C. Shackleton)

3. An Exile tries to write a Mini-Saga
Wolverhampton in the winter. Frost on the railway lines. It's so drab. Sometimes I long for the tropics where I came from. The sun at zenith every day. The pleasures of open-air restaurants every evening. But there's work in Wolverhampton. You expect all my feelings in fifty words?

(V. V. Fisher)

4. Love among the Laundry
When Sally found a man's striped sock curled among her clothes at the launderette she returned it to the tall dark young man with a shy smile. They met there every week for several months, then were seen no more. One of their wedding presents had been a washing machine.

(Molly Burnett)

5. Alien Economy
The flying saucer landed in Alf's orchard. Alf's mower had stopped again. The alien pointed to the apples. Alf pointed to the mower. The alien mended the mower. Alf gave him some apples. The alien left. Alf's lawn mower gave no more trouble and never used another drop of petrol.

(Tony Ellis)

CHOOSE ONE OR MORE OF EXERCISES 4–6.

4 Mini-sagas. Work alone or with two or three other students, as you prefer, and write a mini-saga in exactly 50 words. (You can invent a story, or tell a story that you know, or write about something that has happened to you.)

5 Class story. The teacher reads aloud the first sentence: *It was a dark and stormy night.* Students take it in turn to continue the story, in any way they want to.

6 Modernising a story. Work with two or three other students. Take a traditional story (for instance *Romeo and Juliet, Bluebeard, Noah and the Flood*) and change it to bring it up to date.

> **Learn/revise:** apple; ashamed; confused; crew; desk; drawer; expect; feelings; frost; heart; gun; launderette; marriage; perfect; present; railway line; sock; space; trust; washing machine; wedding; invent; mend; prefer (preferred); pull; share; whisper; full; locked; sad; else; up to date.

Summary **B**

Choosing passive verbs to get the right subject

A well-made pencil looks like a single piece of wood, but actually **it is made** from two pieces of wood which have been carefully glued together.
(*Better than* ... but actually **people make it** from two pieces of wood which they have carefully glued together.)

Present Progressive passive

Coffee **is being made** (at this moment).
Vegetables **are being prepared**.

Present Perfect passive

Today, the transformation seems miraculous. The town **has been** completely **restored**. A new concrete and glass Town Hall **has been put up** in the central square. ...

Passive of verbs with two objects

They sent **me a letter**. → I was sent **a letter**.
The referee gave **him a warning**. → He was given **a warning** by the referee.

Past structures with *if* and *would*

If I **had known** her name, I **would have introduced** you to her.
If his parents **had had** more money, he **wouldn't have left** school at sixteen.
She **would have won** the race if she **hadn't fallen** over.
His life **would have been** happier if he **hadn't met** Cleo.

Past structures with other modals

Sue **could have got** married at eighteen, but she decided to go abroad and study instead.
I **should have mended** my bicycle yesterday, but I didn't.
He's late. He **may have missed** his train.
She didn't phone this morning. She **must have forgotten**.

Irregular verbs in Lessons B1–B8

INFINITIVE	PAST	PAST PARTICIPLE
bite	bit	bitten
break	broke	broken
burn	burnt	burnt
cut	cut	cut
drive	drove	driven
fall	fell	fallen
find	found	found
lean	leant	leant
learn	learnt	learnt
leave	left	left
meet	met	met
rise	rose	risen
send	sent	sent
spend	spent	spent
split	split	split
steal	stole	stolen

Asking about English

How do you say ... in English?
What's the English for ...?
What do you call a person who ...?
How do you pronounce ...?

Problems in understanding

Sorry, what did you say?
What do you mean?
Could you speak more slowly?

Evaluating

I think the first one is very good.
I don't think much of the second.
What do you think of the fourth one?
There's nothing in it.
I think the fifth is better than the fourth.

Degrees

extremely   very   quite   not very   not at all

Proportions

(nearly) everybody   most people   some people
several people   a few people   hardly anybody
one person   nobody   the majority
two out of nine, three out of fourteen *etc.*

Different ways of using words

There's a lot of **snow** on the ground. *(noun)*
Do you think it will **snow**? *(verb)*

Shall I **warm** the milk? *(verb)*
The house isn't very **warm**. *(adjective)*

Writing economically

I am telling no more than the truth when I say that
    George is a habitual consumer of tobacco.
    → George smokes.

Spelling: *ck* and *k*; *tch* and *ch*; *dge* and *ge*

After one short vowel: *ck*, *tch* and *dge*

back	neck	sick	rock	luck
catch	fetch	hitch	hutch	
badge	edge	bridge	lodge	

After anything else: *k*, *ch* and *ge*

break	look	week	wake	joke	thank
walk	reach	coach	couch	search	bench
cage	rage	charge	arrange		

Exceptions

which	rich	much	such

Intonation

'Cambridge 31453.' 'Mary?' 'No, this is Sally.'

'What's your name?' 'Mary.'

The vowel /ɔː/: typical spellings

awful   caught   corner   walk   warm

Vocabulary

Look through the 'Learn/revise' boxes at the end of
Lessons B1–B8.

Revision and fluency practice B

A choice of activities.

1 🔲 Read the text for two minutes. Then close your books and listen to the recording. How many differences can you find? Open your books and listen again; see if you can find some more.

Elsie lives in Oxford. She's quite tall, with grey hair, green eyes and a big nose. She's 70, but she looks a lot younger.

When she was a child she lived in a small village in the country not far from Oxford, with her brother Joe and her sister Betty. Her mother was a difficult woman with a very strong, hard personality; her father was a quiet man, completely dominated by his wife.

After Elsie left school she studied to be a nurse, but she didn't finish her studies because she got married. She and her husband went to live in London. However, London was a dangerous place because of the war, and shortly after her first child was born they moved to the country.

Elsie is a very lively woman, and she is the most talkative person I know. She likes music, dancing and making jewellery. She is also a fanatical gardener, and she has a wonderful garden full of beautiful roses and a variety of other flowers. She lives alone with her cat, whose name is Simon, but she spends a lot of time visiting her grandchildren.

2 'Strangers on a train.' Six students are in the same compartment on a long train journey. They don't know each other, but they get into conversation. Each one has a terrible secret; he/she feels a desperate need to tell someone.

3 Reading report. Talk to the class about what you have been reading recently in English.

4 Question box. Each student writes three questions on separate pieces of paper. One of the questions must begin *Have you ever …*, and one must begin *Do you …* The questions are folded up and put in a box. Students take turns to draw out questions and answer them.

5 'For and against.' Prepare a short talk (two – three minutes) for or against one of the following ideas. Students speak in turn for and against each idea; the class must decide who has made the most convincing case.

People should have the right to carry guns.
All town centres should be closed to traffic.
People should not eat meat more than once a week.
Criminals should not be sent to prison unless they are
    really dangerous to society.
Fishing for sport is cruel and should be banned.
People should be allowed to say and write exactly
    what they like at all times.
Children should not be allowed to watch violent TV.
People should not have to wear clothes if they don't
    want to.

6 How good is your memory? The teacher will show you twenty objects for one minute and then put them away. See if you can remember all of them.

7 Here are some questions about a text. You haven't got the text. Imagine what it might say, and write it.

1. Where did Mrs Harris decide to go on holiday?
2. Did she enjoy her unexpected swim?
3. What happened to the dog?
4. Who said 'This is impossible'?
5. Why did the space-ship break down?
6. Do you think Andrew did the right thing?
7. Who or what woke everybody up in the middle of the night?

8 🔲 Listen to the song *Fiddling across the USA*. Try to write down two place names, two forms of transport and two kinds of weather that are mentioned in the song. Then look at page 118 and check your answers.

9 Look at the cartoons. Tell other students what you think about them. Find out which are the most and least popular cartoons. Useful expressions:

I don't see the joke.
What do you think of this one?
This one's really funny.
It isn't funny at all.
I think it's wonderful/stupid.
It makes / doesn't make me laugh.

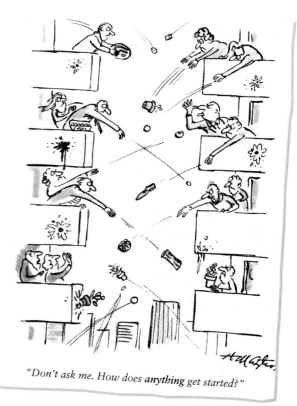

"Don't ask me. How does **anything** get started?"

"Yes?"

"My family's all grown up now – except my husband, of course."

"Agreed, then – no sign of intelligent life on Earth?"

Test B

LISTENING

1 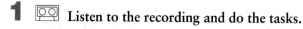 Listen to the recording and do the tasks.

1. Who is who? Match the jobs and the recordings.

    a. antiques dealer
    b. cello teacher
    c. club manager

2. Listen again, and write down one thing each person likes about their job. The first person doesn't dislike anything about her job – write down one thing that each of the others dislikes or finds difficult.

PRONUNCIATION

2 Listen to the words and expressions on the recording, and decide whether they are questions or statements. Write *Q* or *S*.

1. by truck	5. the Queen
2. destroyed	6. tomorrow morning
3. music	7. white
4. six	8. your sister

GRAMMAR AND READING

3 Passives: put each verb into the correct form.

Dear Christine,
This will be my last letter for a while – we are very nearly ready to leave, after all our preparations. All the food (1. *deliver*) to the dock this week, and yesterday evening the crate of medical supplies (2. *bring*) by truck from the nearest airport: let's hope we won't have to open it. Over these past few days the boat (3. *check*) by two teams of people to make sure everything is sound. And while the boat (4. *check*), all the crew members and the stand-by crew (5. *examine*) by the medical officer. thank goodness I got through that OK! The view from the dock now is a beautiful one – for me, at least: the supplies (6. *load*) into the boat under the captain's watchful eye, ready to sail early tomorrow morning. The exact time (7. *not decide*) on yet – it will depend on what the weather looks like at six in the morning. But anyway, sometime tomorrow will see us on the high seas – I can hardly believe it! Meanwhile I must go – we (8. *entertain*) by the mayor this evening, and I have to try and find something clean to wear! I will write as often as I can, but I won't be near a post office for a while! I'll be thinking of you.
Love,
Anna

4 Choose a meaning in column B for each word or expression in column A. There are some extra meanings.

A	B
1. dock	a. large box, usually wooden
2. crate	b. arrange in a sensible manner
3. stand-by	c. begin moving in a boat or ship
4. load	d. far from any land
5. sail	e. in a bad storm at sea
6. on the high seas	f. last and most important bits
	g. person in charge of the boat
	h. place where boats and ships have things put on and taken off
	i. possible replacement (in case of illness, *etc.*)
	j. put

5 Infinitive or *-ing* form?

1. Anna checked what she'd packed three times – she won't be able *run / to run / running* to the local shop if she's forgotten anything!
2. Her parents want Anna *be / to be / being* a research scientist, but she wants *be / to be / being* a teacher so she can spend her summers sailing.
3. I don't know how I would feel about *spend / to spend / spending* such a long time without *see / to see / seeing* land.
4. I've asked Anna *write / to write / writing* every two or three days if she can – that way she'll have a record of her journey.
5. It didn't take Anna long to decide between *buy / to buy / buying* a car and *join / to join / joining* the sailing expedition.
6. Now that Anna's gone, I don't have anyone *talk / to talk / talking* to about music.
7. *Sail / To sail / Sailing* is not just a sport for Anna – it's a passion.
8. The medical officer told them they should *be / to be / being* very careful about drinking water from streams and rivers if they land on any islands.
9. They might *be / to be / being* out of radio contact for days at a time.

6 Past modals: complete the sentences correctly.

1. I (*should phone*) Ann this morning, but I didn't have time.
2. Jake's late: he (*must miss*) the bus.
3. If I (*work*) harder I (*would pass*) my exams last year.

50

LANGUAGE IN USE

7 Some of these expressions are formal and some are informal. Divide them into two lists – formal and informal. 'Translate' them from formal to informal and from informal to formal.

1. Fine, thanks.
2. Good afternoon.
3. Great to meet you at last!
4. I beg your pardon?
5. I think you're wrong.
6. Pass me the bread, would you?
7. Would you like to dance?
8. Excuse me, have you got the time?

8 Write one sentence or question for each situation.

1. You are offered a cup of coffee, but you don't like coffee. How do you ask for tea instead?
2. Someone is speaking English too fast for you to understand.
3. You have seen an old coffeepot that you like in a market stall. The market trader has asked for £20 for it. You want to pay less. What do you say?
4. You owe a friend some money and are ready to pay it back. You want to know whether your friend prefers cash or a cheque (use the word *rather*).
5. You want someone to repeat what they have just said.
6. You want to ask your teacher for the translation of a word from your language into English.
7. You want to ask for the pronunciation of this word: *thorough*.

VOCABULARY

9 Write opposites for these words. The first one is done for you as an example.

1. calm ..*nervy*...
2. careful
3. fall
4. formal
5. generous
6. indoors
7. polite
8. send
9. shy
10. teach

10 Divide this list into five groups of words and expressions according to meaning.

accent   accuse   adjective   affectionate
arrest   bad-tempered   banker   break into
cash   consonant   crime   currency
emotional   exchange rate   finance   honest
job   part-time   promotion   reserved   salary
sensitive   serious   skill   spelling   steal
theft   vocabulary

WRITING

11 Shorten two of these sentences.

1. It is not untrue for me to say that Annie is in the habit of consuming far more food than can reasonably be considered good for her health. *(Rewrite the sentence in five words or less.)*
2. Pasta, in all of its many forms, is well known to be high on the list of those foods which are most frequently consumed by the inhabitants of the Italian peninsula. *(seven words or less)*
3. My brother's membership in the great army of the unemployed is caused in large part by the fact that he is not able to spend the first three or four hours of the morning in any way except lying down in his bedroom with the lights off and the curtains closed. *(fourteen words or less)*
4. I find it is almost entirely impossible for me to put pen to paper with the intention of communicating with someone without spending a very long time and covering several sheets of paper. *(six words or less)*

12 Write the story of a film or TV programme you have seen, or a book you have read, in 100 or more words.

SPEAKING

13 Work with another student. Each of you must talk about one of the subjects listed below. Speak for about two minutes while your partner listens carefully. Then the partner will ask three or more questions to get further information.

1. What do you find attractive and unattractive about the English (or American) way of life?
2. What newspaper do you read regularly? Why? Talk about the main newspapers in your country and what sort of people usually read each one.
3. Describe how you usually spend your day. What is enjoyable about your daily routine? What is unpleasant?
4. Tell a traditional story (it can be a children's story) from your country or another country; or tell a modern version of a fairy tale.

C1 It makes me want to scream

Talking about emotions; emphatic, contradictory and 'softened' answers; *make* and *let* + object + infinitive without *to*; listening skills: listening for gist.

1 Work with a partner. Make sure you know the meanings of the words and expressions in the table (use a dictionary or ask your teacher). Then look at the pictures, and make five or more sentences (make sure you make sentences from both parts of the table).

… make(s) me		… make(s) me	
	laugh		sick
	cry		cross
	smile		angry
	want to scream		unhappy
	want to hide		miserable
	see red		nervous
	feel uncomfortable		proud
	feel calm		glad
	…		…

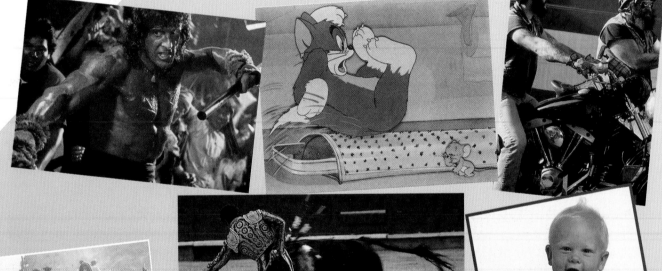

2 Strong words. In each of these pairs, one word or expression is a more emphatic ('stronger') version of the other. Which are the emphatic versions?

angry – furious
delighted – pleased
frantic – worried
terrified – nervous
unhappy – miserable

3 📼 Make sure you understand the words in the box, and practise their pronunciation. Then listen and write down how you think each person feels.

afraid	amused	angry	cross	delighted
disgusted	embarrassed	frantic		furious
glad	happy	lonely	miserable	nervous
pleased	proud	relaxed	surprised	
terrified	uncomfortable	unhappy		upset
worried				

4 Look at the three answers to the question.

'My brother's just told me he's getting married next week.'
'Are you pleased?'
(−) 'Well, no, actually, I'm not.'
(±) 'Quite pleased, but he could have told me earlier.'
(++) 'I'm absolutely delighted.'

Which category do these answers go in: −, ± or ++?

1. 'Was she pleased?'
   'Actually, she was a bit embarrassed.'
2. 'Is he happy?'
   'Quite happy, but he misses his family.'
3. 'Was she worried?'
   'She was frantic!'
4. 'Are they unhappy?'
   'They're miserable.'
5. 'Weren't you afraid?'
   'We were too busy to be afraid.'
6. 'Is he uncomfortable?'
   'Well, a bit, but I think he'll get used to it.'
7. 'Were you pleased?'
   'Well, no, I was a bit cross, actually.'
8. 'Were you lonely?'
   'Yes, very lonely. But what could I do?'

5 Work with a partner. Use each of the sentences to begin a three-sentence dialogue:
a. announcement
b. question about feelings
c. answer (−, ± or ++)
Example:

'My daughter doesn't want to go on holiday with us this year.'
'Are you upset?'
'No, actually, I'm quite pleased.'

1. I have to give a speech in front of 1,000 people tonight.
2. My boss has just said I have to work on New Year's Day.
3. My cousin's girlfriend has been transferred to New Delhi.
4. My mother has been named Businesswoman of the Year.
5. My sister is going to have a baby.
6. There was a robbery while I was in the bank this morning.

When you have worked out and practised dialogues for all the sentences, change partners. Practise the dialogues together – you may get some surprises.

6 📼 Make sure you understand the questions. Then listen to the recording. Which question is being answered by each person? There is one extra question.

a. Do you often let small things upset you very much, or are you usually easy-going?
b. Do you ever let emotions build up inside you and then express them too strongly?
c. Do you usually let the people around you know how you feel about things?
d. Can you think of a time when you were very upset but didn't let anyone know?
e. Would you let your children know if you were very worried about something?
f. Would you let your parents know if you were very worried about something?

7 Now choose one of the questions from Exercise 6 to ask other students. Note the answers and report to the class.

Learn/revise: emotion; parent; build up (built, built); cry; express; feel (felt, felt); hide (hid, hidden); laugh; scream; see red (saw, seen); smile; afraid; angry; calm; cross; frantic; furious; glad; happy; lonely; miserable; nervous; proud; sick; uncomfortable; unhappy; amused; delighted; disgusted; embarrassed; pleased; relaxed; surprised; terrified; upset; worried; a bit; absolutely; actually; quite; strongly; too (+ *adjective* + *infinitive*); inside.

C2 Focus on systems

A choice of exercises: suffixes pronounced with /ə/; weak forms of *have* and *for*; Future Progressive and Future Perfect tenses; common expressions with *make*, *take*, *do*, *have* and *get*.

PRONUNCIATION

1 📼 Do you know how to pronounce the ends of the words in each group? Practise them. Can you add another word to some of the groups?

1. pleas*ure*   nat*ure*   furni*ture*
2. preposi*tion*   organisa*tion*   examina*tion*
3. profe*ssion*   posse*ssion*
4. deci*sion*   divi*sion*
5. religi*ous*   delici*ous*

2 📼 How do you think *have* and *for* are pronounced in the following sentences? Practise saying them, paying special attention to rhythm.

1. By next July I'll have been here for eight months.
2. When they get married they'll have known each other for three years.
3. When I retire I'll have been working for nearly 50 years.
4. Next summer we'll have been married for 30 years.

GRAMMAR: FUTURE PROGRESSIVE TENSE

> **Future Progressive tense**
>
> I will (I'll) be working/seeing/...
> you will (you'll) be working/seeing/...
> *etc.*
>
> will I be working/seeing/...?
> *etc.*
>
> I will not (won't) be working/seeing/...

3 Make sentences as in the examples. Use the words in the box to help you.

eight o'clock tomorrow morning / in the bathroom
'*At eight o'clock tomorrow morning I'll be brushing my teeth.*'

half past eight / in the car
'*At half past eight tomorrow morning I'll be driving to work.*'

1. ten o'clock tomorrow morning / in a meeting with the Sales Director
2. one o'clock tomorrow / in a restaurant
3. four o'clock tomorrow / on the tennis court
4. five o'clock tomorrow / in the swimming pool
5. six o'clock tomorrow / in the pub
6. eight o'clock tomorrow / in front of the TV
7. ten o'clock tomorrow evening / on the night train to Glasgow

drive	have a drink	have lunch	play
swim	talk	travel	watch	

4 Ask as many people as possible what they will be doing at a particular time tomorrow. (You decide what time.)

GRAMMAR: FUTURE PERFECT TENSE

> **Future Perfect tense**
>
> I will (I'll) have worked/seen/...
> you will (you'll) have worked/seen/...
> *etc.*
>
> will I have worked/seen/...?
> *etc.*
>
> I will not (won't) have worked/seen/...
> *etc.*

5 Fill in the gaps in the text.

Professor Horsebrush is writing a book on the love life of the mosquito. She is writing ten pages a day. She started yesterday. By yesterday evening she had written ten pages. Now she has written fifteen pages. When she goes to bed tonight she will have written ... pages. By tomorrow night she ... have written ... pages. By the end of the day after tomorrow she ... thirty pages. By the night after that she ... By next Tuesday night she ... By the end of the month ... By the end of August ... In ten years from now she ... about ... pages.

6 Change the sentences as in the examples, so as to use the Future Perfect tense.

By the end of the year I'll be famous. *(become)*
'By the end of the year I'll have become famous.'

July 17th will be our tenth wedding anniversary. *(be married)*
'On July 17th we'll have been married for ten years.'

1. By the time I'm 70 I won't be working. *(retire)*
2. By next summer I expect I'll be fully qualified. *(pass all exams)*
3. I suppose in another few weeks the ice won't be there. *(melt)*
4. You say you love me, but a year from now I expect you won't even know my name. *(forget)*
5. We can't phone him at 11 o'clock. He'll be in bed. *(go to bed)*
6. Our house will be ready by next Thursday. *(the builders; finish)*
7. By the end of the week I won't have any more money left. *(spend)*
8. When I see her again, I'm sure she'll be very different. *(change)*
9. In a couple of years her life will be very different. *(get married; settle down)*

7 Choose one of the following questions, and ask as many people as possible in two minutes. Then tell the class what you have found out.

By next summer, how long will you have been at school / married / living in the same house / learning English?
Will you have finished studying English by next summer?
Ten years from now, will you have forgotten me?
When you're 70, do you think you will have changed a lot?
How many hours will you have worked by the end of this week?

VOCABULARY

8 Put the words from the box into the right lists. (Some words can go in more than one list.) Can you add some words of your own to the lists?

MAKE	TAKE	DO	HAVE	GET
coffee	train	work	supper	dressed
...	...	...	...	...

> bath   bed   breakfast   bus   changed
> coffee   decision   dressed   holiday
> housework   lost   medicine   mistake
> nothing   phone call   photo   plan   rest
> size 9 shoes   something stupid   soup
> supper   tea   train   work

Learn/revise: builder; decision; examination; furniture (*uncountable*); month; nature; organisation; pleasure; tennis court; wedding anniversary; change; melt; pass an examination; retire; settle down; famous; *expressions from Exercise 8.*

C3 I'm a bit short of time

Making appointments by telephone; invitations, acceptances and refusals; pronunciation (weak forms); conversational expressions; speaking practice.

1 Choose one of the telephone conversations. Work in pairs: fill in the gaps and practise the conversation.

SUE: Hello. Marketing Department.
JOE: Hi. Is that Sue?
SUE: (1) ....
JOE: This is Joe. How are you?
SUE: (2) ....
JOE: Listen, Sue. Are you doing (3) .... this evening?
SUE: I'm not (4) .... Why?
JOE: Well, I thought we might go out for a meal somewhere.
SUE: Oh, dear. I've just (5) .... It looks as if I'm not (6) .... this evening after all. I'm (7) ....ing.
JOE: Well, how about tomorrow?
SUE: No. I really ought to stay in tomorrow. It's ages since I washed my hair.
JOE: What (8) .... the day (9) .... tomorrow?
SUE: No, I'm away then. Look, Joe. I'm really a bit short of time (10) .... days. I've got a whole lot of work to finish by the end of the month. It's because of the reorganisation at the office. You know how it is. I'll (11) .... you a ring when things get easier. OK?
JOE: OK. Bye.
SUE: Bye.

TOM: Hello. Accounts Department.
SUE: Hello. (12) ....?
TOM: Yes, (13) ....?
SUE: (14) .... is Sue.
TOM: Oh, hi, Sue. (15) ....?
SUE: Fine. What about you? Still working (16) .... the same place?
TOM: Yes. They haven't found out about me (17) .... In fact, they even say they're (18) .... to give me a rise next month.
SUE: Look, Tom, I haven't seen you (19) .... ages. (20) .... this evening?
TOM: Don't think so.
SUE: (21) .... to come out for a drink? That is, unless you're too (22) ....
TOM: No, I'd love (23) .... Where (24) .... we meet?
SUE: How (25) .... the King's Arms?
TOM: OK. (26) ....?
SUE: Say, about (27) .... o'clock?
TOM: Eight o'clock's difficult. I don't get home (28) .... half past seven. Could we make it a quarter past?
SUE: OK. Quarter past eight at the King's Arms. (29) .... you then.
TOM: See you. Bye.
SUE: Bye.

2 🔲 How are the words in *italics* pronounced? Listen to the recording and check your answers. Practise saying the expressions, with particular attention to rhythm.

Are you doing anything this evening?
I haven't seen you *for* ages.
a whole lot *of* work
the end *of* the month
Still working *at* the same place?
Would you like to come out *for* a drink?
Where *shall* we meet?
at the King's Arms

3 🔲 Imagine that you are going to invite a friend of yours, Ann, to go out with you. Decide where you want to go, and where and when you want to meet. Then answer the tape-recorder as follows.

ANN: Hello. Rainbow Hill 8180.
YOU: *Ask if it's Ann speaking.*
ANN: ....
YOU: *Answer.*
ANN: ....
YOU: *Answer. Ask how Ann is.*
ANN: ....
YOU: *Ask if Ann is doing anything this evening.*
ANN: ....
YOU: *Invite Ann to go out somewhere with you.*
ANN: ....
YOU: *Answer what Ann says. If she accepts, continue the conversation. If she refuses, keep trying (ask her out for tomorrow, the day after tomorrow etc.) until she accepts or ends the conversation.*

4 Work in pairs. Prepare and practise phone conversations in which one person asks the other out. You can be: yourselves; yourselves in twenty years; you and the king / queen / president / prime minister; you and a famous singer / film star *etc.*; two famous people (you choose). Use some of the following expressions.

Are you free this evening?
Are you doing anything this evening?
I thought we might …
unless you're too busy/tired.

I'm not sure.
It depends.
Maybe, maybe not.
I can't remember.

Just a minute.
Let me just look in my diary.

It looks as if I'm not free.
I'm not free after all.
I've just remembered.
No, I'm afraid I'm baby-sitting / washing my hair / going to the theatre / working / playing bridge / …ing.
I really ought to wash my hair / write letters / …
I'm away tomorrow.
I've got a terrible headache.

What/How about tomorrow / the day after tomorrow?

I'm really a bit busy at the moment / for the next few weeks.
You know how it is.

It's ages since I …
I haven't … for ages.

I'll give you a ring one of these days / some time / when things get easier.

That would be lovely.   I'd love to.

Where shall we meet?
What time?
What time were you thinking of?

I'll come round to your place.
I might be a bit late.

That's difficult.
Could we make it a bit later?

See you then.

> **Learn/revise:** diary; headache; meal; office; reorganisation; rise; accept; baby-sit; continue; give sbdy a ring; go out; keep …ing (kept, kept); meet (met, met); ought (to); refuse; busy; free; sure; terrible; not … yet; till; short of time; somewhere; the day after tomorrow; these days; one of these days; it's ages since …; for ages; a whole lot of …; say, …; What about …?; See you; *other expressions from Exercise 4.*

57

C4 We regret …

Writing skills: formal letters; speaking skills: interviews, discussion.

1 Here are the interviewer's notes on a job applicant, together with three possible letters to the applicant. Which letter do you think is the best? Why?

Post: bilingual secretary/receptionist
Applicant: Alice Prior, age 23
April 13, 2.30
nervous, unconfident; silly laugh
physically unattractive – spots
French not very good
slight stutter
lacks experience

No!

BATSFORD & STAPLETON

17 Mews Lane
Cosfield
DO7 6AJ

Tel: 9162 34455

April 16, 1993

Ms A Prior
10a Silver Street
Cosfield DO7 4BQ

Dear Ms Prior

Thank you for coming for interview on April 13.
We have considered your application carefully,
but regret that we are unable to offer you the
post.

Yours sinc____

A. Lon

Alan Lom
Personn

BATSFORD & STAPLETON

17 Mews Lane
Cosfield
DO7 6AJ

Tel: 9162 34455

April 16, 1993

Ms A Prior
10a Silver Street
Cosfield DO7 4BQ

Dear Ms Prior

Thank you for coming for interview on April 13.
We regret that neither your linguistic
qualifications nor your interpersonal skills are
up to the level we require. We are therefore
unable to offer you a post.

__ sincerely

BATSFORD & STAPLETON

17 Mews Lane
Cosfield
DO7 6AJ

Tel: 9162 34455

April 16, 1993

Ms A Prior
10a Silver Street
Cosfield DO7 4BQ

Dear Ms Prior

Thank you for coming for interview last Tuesday.
We have considered your application carefully,
but regret that we are unable to offer you the
post. While your secretarial skills are well up
to the standard required, I did not feel that
your command of French was sufficiently good for
our purposes. In addition, you appear to lack
confidence in dealing with people, which would
certainly be a handicap if you were to work as a
receptionist. May I suggest that you might do
better to look for a job involving routine office
work?

With kind regards.

Yours sincerely

A. Lomas

Alan Lomax
Personnel Director

2 Here are some informal expressions. In the letters, can you find more formal expressions with the same meanings?

We have thought about
(We) are sorry
(We) can't
job
good enough (*three versions*)
need
you don't seem to have

3 Job interviews. Work in groups of six or so: three interviewers and three applicants.

1. The group chooses a job for which applicants will be interviewed.
2. Interviewers prepare their questions; applicants prepare details of their qualifications and experience.
3. Applicants are interviewed in turn.
4. Each group of three interviewers chooses the best applicant and writes letters to all three.

4 Discuss one of the following questions with two or three other students. At the end of your discussion, write a brief note of the group's opinion and report to the class. Useful expressions:

> I would/might lie   On the other hand
> I wouldn't/mightn't tell the truth   It depends
> I think it would be wrong to …

1. Imagine that you have been in prison. Should you tell the interviewer when you apply for a job?
2. Would you want to know if you only had a short time to live?
3. A married person is in love with somebody else, but does not wish to break up the marriage. Should he/she tell his/her partner or not?
4. When you were born, your godmother gave you a very valuable piece of jewellery. During a difficult period, your parents sold it to buy food. Your godmother asks about it. What should you say?
5. You find out, by accident, that your brother is adopted. He doesn't know. Should you tell him?
6. A teenager comes to realise that he/she is homosexual. Should he/she tell his/her parents?
7. A woman finds out that her sister's husband is having an affair. Should she tell her sister?

> **Learn/revise:** applicant; application; experience; interview; post; prison; qualification; receptionist; secretary; spot; truth; appear; apply; consider; deal with sbdy (dealt, dealt); lack; lie (lying); need; offer; regret; require; tell the truth (told, told); bilingual; nervous; silly; unable; unattractive; wrong; sufficiently; on the other hand.

59

C5 The voice of democracy

Reading and listening comprehension; Present Perfect and Simple Past tenses;
word stress; vocabulary study.

1 🔊 **Read the text of the news broadcast. Choose the correct tenses, and fill in the missing words and expressions from the box. Then listen to the recording and check your answers.**

according to	approximately	at least	due to	following	in spite of
which	with				

Free Fantasian Radio – the voice of democracy. It's ten o'clock, and here is Lucy Voronesk with the latest news.

Figures released today show that average earnings (1) *have gone up / went up* by 60% over the last twelve months. Official sources say that this is (2) .... the government's successful economic policies, which (3) *have led to / led to* more efficient management and greater productivity. Industrial output (4) *has risen / rose* by 43% during the last year, and exports (5) *have gone up / went up* by 52%. Inflation is down to (6) .... 3%.

(7) .... police figures, about 5,000 people (8) *have taken part / took part* in yesterday's anti-government demonstration. (9) .... police efforts to maintain order, (10) *there has been / there was* violence throughout the march. Stones and petrol bombs (11) *have been thrown / were thrown* at government buildings, and (12) .... 200 people (13) *have been hurt / were hurt* in fighting (14) .... (15) *has broken out / broke out* after speeches by opposition leaders in Wesk Square.

(16) *There has been / There was* flooding in the south of the country, (17) .... last week's heavy rains. Prompt action by local army units (18) *has limited / limited* the damage, and the few people affected (19) *have now been able / were now able* to return to their homes.

Dr Joseph Brodsk, Deputy Governor of Stranvegan from 1976 to 1981, (20) *has died / died* yesterday at his home in Banhooly. He was 78. The President (21) *has sent / sent* a message of sympathy to Mrs Brodsk.

News (22) *has just come in / just came in* of a plane crash at East Mork Airport. First reports say that two aircraft were involved, and that several people were killed, but no further details are available for the moment.

And now the weather forecast. It (23) *is / will be* warm, (24) .... continuous sunshine in all parts of the country. The outlook for the weekend is similar, with temperatures in the high thirties.

2 🔲 Practise pronouncing these words with the correct stress.

Stressed on the first syllable: average details exports figures forecast government management message outlook output sunshine sympathy temperature yesterday

Stressed on the second syllable: affected available democracy efficient industrial inflation involved official police released successful throughout

Main stress on the third syllable: demonstration economic opposition productivity

3 🔲 Copy the table and fill in the left-hand column with facts from the Free Fantasian Radio broadcast. Then listen to the recording. You will hear the ten o'clock news broadcast on another Fantasian Radio station – Democratic Fantasian Radio. Fill in the right-hand column in the table. What do you think is the main reason for the differences?

	FFR	DFR
Number of demonstrators:		
Was march violent?		
How many hurt?		
Average earnings up/down by:		
Industrial output up/down by:		
Exports up/down by:		
Inflation:		
Number of homeless due to flooding:		
Weather:		

4 Choose some words and expressions to learn from Exercise 1. Show your list to another student and explain the reasons for your choices.

5 Work in groups, and choose one of the following exercises.

A. Make up a news broadcast including three untrue reports. Read your broadcast to the class, and see if they can tell you which things were not true.

B. Make up two versions of a news report (as if from two different radio or TV stations). Give your reports to the class and see how many differences they can spot.

C. Discussion: How true are your radio and TV reports? Is it necessary for the media to tell lies in some circumstances? Have you any experience of official lying? Make notes of what is said in your discussion and report to the class.

D. Invent a news item, and then report it to the class by mime (acting without words). The other students must guess what you are reporting and put it into words.

Learn/revise: bomb; detail; democracy; demonstration; economic; exports; figure; forecast; government; management; message; opposition; outlook; output; plane crash; police; productivity; stone; sunshine; sympathy; temperature; violence; affect; break out (broke, broken); die (dying); hurt (hurt, hurt); lead to (led, led); release; rise (rose, risen); take part in (took, taken); throw (threw, thrown); available; average; efficient; industrial; involved; official; successful; according to; approximately; at least; due to; following; in spite of; throughout.

C6 Focus on systems

A choice of exercises: relative clauses without pronouns; reduced relative clauses; opposites; pronunciation and spelling ('silent *e*', doubling); hearing unstressed syllables.

GRAMMAR: RELATIVE CLAUSES WITHOUT PRONOUNS

1 We often leave out *that/which/who(m)* in sentences with relative clauses. Sometimes this makes them more difficult to understand. Can you make these sentences easier to read by putting in *that/which/who(m)*?

1. The eggs you're eating came from our farm.
2. That motorbike Jake built fell to pieces.
3. The letter the postman just brought isn't for us.
4. A man my brother met when he was travelling in Italy this summer turned out to be a famous film director.
5. The woman Pete's in love with doesn't know he exists.
6. Where does the wood that table's made of come from?
7. Because he forgot to write to the one person he really should have invited his father was furious.
8. When he met the soldier he wanted to buy the guns from the police were watching him.

It's not possible to leave out *who/that* in these two sentences. Why not?

9. The people who live next door never get up before ten o'clock.
10. I'm going to do something that will really surprise you.

2 Put these pairs of sentences together without using *that/which/who(m)*.

1. I've lost the book.
   I borrowed it from you.

2. The glasses aren't ready.
   You ordered them.

3. Those people couldn't come.
   We invited them to spend the weekend with us.

4. The phone number is 325-3547.
   You were asking about it.

5. A dictionary is a kind of book.
   People look up words in it.

3 Can you make complete sentences including these groups of words? (Don't separate them.)

the food I	the man the police
a thing people use	she bought didn't
a thing children	saw wasn't

GRAMMAR: REDUCED RELATIVE CLAUSES

4 Look at this way of using *-ing* forms and *-ed* forms.

I know the man **sitting** on the wall over there.
   (= ... the man who is sitting ...)
Food **kept** in a freezer will stay good for several months. (= Food that is kept ...)

Now change these sentences as shown in the examples.

Who is the woman who is standing at the bus stop?
Who is the woman standing at the bus stop?

The forms that were sent to the embassy last week never arrived.
The forms sent to the embassy last week never arrived.

1. A road that was opened last Friday has had to be closed again for repairs.
2. The number of new cars that were sold in this country fell by 25% in the first half of this year.
3. The men who are working on our house have been there for nearly three weeks.
4. Clothes that are made of artificial fibres often feel uncomfortable in hot weather.
5. Not many of the people who were invited turned up.
6. The money that is lying on the table is your change.

5 Change these sentences as shown in the example.

Nobody could read the words written on the paper.
Nobody could read the words that were written on the paper.

1. The address list published last month is already out of date.
2. A lot of things taught in school are useless.
3. Lewis said that the money offered was not nearly enough.
4. The people hurt in the accident are recovering in hospital.
5. More than 100 prisoners captured during the recent fighting in East Grange will be released today.
6. Three men accused of organising an attack on an Irish police station in which several officers were injured have been arrested.

6 Make three or more sensible sentences from the table.

A young civil servant	questioned after the attack	had escaped from a zoo.
The man	posted in Brighton in 1904	said he believed his son had made three visits to Buckingham Palace.
Three children	found in a London tax office	agreed with the government.
The father of the man	brought up in the country	has just been delivered.
Most of the people	found on Friday morning in the Queen's bedroom	told police that they had seen nothing.
Scientists have found that children	seen running away	often talk to themselves.
A letter	interviewed by newspaper reporters	is believed to be a member of a terrorist group.
A monkey	arrested after a man was shot in Oxford Street last night	used to work as a driving instructor.
People	chosen to lead the British team	may be charged with murder.
The woman	left alone for long periods	are on average taller than city children.

PRONUNCIATION AND SPELLING

7 'Silent *e*.' Look at the following pairs of words. What difference does the letter *e* make to the pronunciation of the vowel before it?

mad made   win wine   hop hope   cut cute

Now read these pairs of words. You can pronounce them correctly even if you don't know them.

sin sine   cap cape   lop lope   run rune
pip pipe   pan pane

8 Doubling. Look at these pairs of words. Why does the second word in each pair have a double letter?

big bigger   run runner   mad madder
hot hotter   sit sitting   begin beginning

How would you pronounce these words if they didn't have double letters?

dinner   happy   butter   summer   middle

How would you pronounce these words if they had double letters in the middle?

inviting   amusing   voted   hated   writer

Do you know why not all of these words have double letters?

forgetting   visiting   regretted   deposited
beginning   opening   preferring   offering

9 Listen to the recording. How many words do you hear in each sentence? (Contractions like *What's* count as two words.)

VOCABULARY: SIXTY OPPOSITES

10 Do you know the opposites of all these words?

agree   always   awake   beginning   buy
cheap   dark   dead   dirty   early   easy
empty   fast   female   find   first   generous
happy   heavy   high   honest   hot   indoors
intelligent   interesting   into   laugh   left
long   love   most   new   nice   north-east
optimistic   outside   pull   question   quiet
remember   rough   safe   shallow   sharp
shy   soft   stop   strong   take off   tall
thin   top   true   up   upstairs   warm
wet   win   wrong   young

Learn/revise: accident; artificial fibre; attack; bus stop; change (= money returned); civil servant; film director; freezer; information; murder; prisoner; repair; scientist; accuse; arrest; bring up (brought, brought); capture; exist; fall to pieces (fell, fallen); fight (fought, fought); hurt (hurt, hurt); injure; invite; keep (kept, kept); leave (left, left); offer; organise; question; receive; recover; release; shoot (shot, shot); teach (taught, taught); turn up; furious; uncomfortable; useless; on average; *vocabulary from Exercise 10.*

C7 People going hungry

Listening skills: listening for specific information;
reading skills: reading for gist; vocabulary;
discussion.

1 Work in groups of three or four to discuss these points and make a group report. Each person in the group should take responsibility for one or two points and make sure that everyone else in the group contributes a view.

1. How important do you think it is to give money to help people in need?
2. Name one or more charities that have asked you for money in the past year. Who do these charities benefit? Do you think it is worth giving money to them? Why (not)?
3. Do you ever worry about how the money you give to charity actually gets spent? What are some of the ways money given to Third World charities can be misused?
4. Can you think of any of the causes of poverty and hunger in the Third World? List as many as you can think of.

2 📼 Copy the grid and make sure you understand all the words and expressions. Then listen to Roger Elbourne from Oxfam and Alison Whyte from War on Want talking about their charities, and complete the grid, using *T* (true), *F* (false), and *?* (don't know).

	Oxfam	WoW
Founded during the Second World War		
Funds small-scale projects		
Funds long-term projects		
Has field officers overseas		
Works in almost every Third World country		
Concentrates on women ('poorest of the poor')		

3 Look at the words in the box. Use your dictionary to find out the meanings of the ones you don't know, and then divide them into two or three groups, based on their meanings.

capital (= money)	cattle	consumption
debt	economics	hunger
interest (= money)	international	lend
peanuts	repay	rise	surplus	world

4 📼 Look at the pictures and try to fill in the blanks in the captions – use some of the words from the box and any other words you need. Then listen to Roger Elbourne talking about international economics and world hunger, to check your answers.

1. 1970s: oil money flooded to Western ...., who .... money to Third World countries.

2. Later, interest rates .... Third World countries couldn't pay back the .... or the ....

3. West African farmers sold .... (their food) to the West.

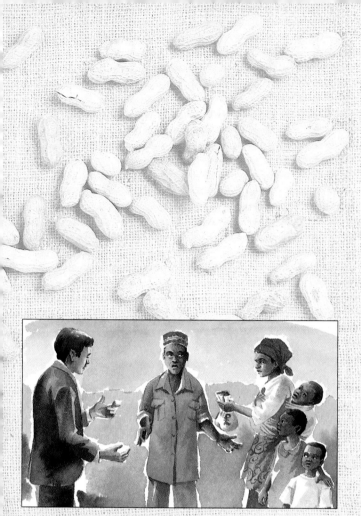

4. Money from food sales was used to .... the debt.

5. Western farmers fed the .... to their .... A .... of milk was produced.

6. The .... dried milk was sent to hungry West African children.

5 Do this exercise in groups of four to six. Imagine you are villagers in a small Third World village called Yar. Oxfam has agreed to fund projects in your village for up to 1,500 crowns in local currency each year for the next two years. Read the texts (with dictionaries) and decide how you will spend the first year's money.

Yar is a small agricultural village on the edge of the jungle, about twenty miles from a market town. The village is very poor; no one can read or write. You are a tribal people, with a chief for the village.

POSSIBLE PROJECTS
1. Yar needs clean water; many babies die because of dirty water. You can bring in Western volunteers and drill a well quickly for 300 crowns; the well will have to be serviced and repaired by outside people. Or you can do most of the work on the well yourselves, and learn to service and repair it; this will take longer and cost 500 crowns.
2. The chief's sister is a midwife and herbal medicine specialist. Her medicines are good (and free), and she is an important person in the village. But in some other villages, midwives have been on courses to learn about ways of keeping babies healthy; more babies in those villages live past the age of two, and more children are healthy. You could send the chief's sister on a course for 200 crowns, if you can persuade her to go.
3. There is a fruit that grows in the forest for a short time each year. It is delicious, and healthy. But you have no way to keep it. For 300 crowns some people could go on a two-week course to learn to bottle fruit juice and jam, for use in the village and sale in the market town. The cost of the course includes equipment for the village.
4. 400 crowns will buy new tools for farming. 500 crowns will send one of the men on a two-month course to learn to make farming tools from materials that can be found locally; he will come home with the tools he has made.
5. You want a school for the children. The government will send a teacher if you give the land and the labour to build a school and a teacher's house. The building work will take about three months. You do not want to bring a teacher in until there is a clean water supply; and you will have to make sure there is food for the teacher. Your share of the teacher's salary: 600 crowns a year.
6. All the village cattle (five) died in the last floods. Now only half as much land can be farmed as before. New cattle cost 100 crowns apiece.
7. A wagon that could be pulled by one of the cattle to carry things to market would cost 100 crowns to buy. If one of the men went on the tool-making course he would learn to make a wagon as well, and it would only cost 50 crowns for the materials he would need to make one.
8. Last year some of the seeds that you were saving to plant were lost in the floods. New seeds will cost 50 crowns.
9. The women want help organising a crèche and setting up a group to weave beautiful traditional cloth and sell it in the market town. An adviser can come and help the women organise a business for 100 crowns.

Learn/revise: capital; cattle; cause; charity; cloth; consumption; country; course; crèche; debt; economics; factory worker; farmer; flood; hunger; interest; jam; jungle; labour; market town; midwife; poverty; seed; surplus; Third World; tool; village; volunteer; wagon; well; world; break down (broke, broken); convince; go wrong (went, gone); lend (lent, lent); repay (repaid, repaid); service; set up (set, set); healthy; hungry; international; local; main; overseas; poor; small-scale; worth ...ing; regularly.

C8 A lot needs doing to it

Listening and note-taking; discussion; vocabulary (changes, houses).

1 Look at the pictures and say what needs doing to the outside of the house. Use the nouns and verbs in the box. Example:

'Some bricks need replacing.'

bricks	chimney	door	garage	garden	gate	hedge	path
roof	steps	TV aerial	window frames		window pane		clean up
cut	paint	rebuild	repair	replace	straighten		

2 🖭 Listen to the recording or ask the teacher about the inside of the house. Find out how many rooms there are on each floor, how they are arranged, and what size they are. Work in pairs; each student should draw a plan of one of the two floors.

3 🖭 Listen to the recording. You will hear somebody being shown round the house. Write the names of the different rooms on your plan.

4 When the owners of the house first moved in, they had a lot of things done. Can you remember any of them? Listen to the recording again, if necessary, and complete the sentences. Use the words in the box to help you.

build	ceiling	convert	cupboard
lower	make	put in	raise	redecorate
take down			

1. In the dining room, they had a new .... put in.
2. And they .... the dining room decorated.
3. They had the study doorway ....
4. In the main bedroom, they had ....
5. In the kitchen, ...
6. They had the downstairs store room ....
7. (staircase)
8. (living room)
9. (upstairs ceilings)
10. (upstairs bedroom)
11. (upstairs bathroom)

5 Work in groups. Your task is to convert the house into one of the following:

– a casino
– a hotel
– a clothes shop
– a health club and gymnasium
– a language school
– a residential hostel for six physically handicapped people (who will go out during the day to work) and their full-time caretaker.

Produce a detailed plan (with words and drawings) of the changes you will make, and report to the class. Use some of the new words and expressions from the lesson. The following may also be useful:

add	car park	change (into)	divide
emergency exit	entrance	fire escape
gents'/ladies' (toilet)	improve	increase
strengthen	turn (into)	widen

Learn/revise: brick; car park; ceiling; chimney; cupboard; door; emergency exit; entrance; fire escape; floor; garage; garden; gate; gents'/ladies' (toilet); hedge; inside; outside; path; roof; staircase; steps; TV aerial; window frame; window pane; add; arrange; build (built, built); change (into); clean up; convert; cut (cut, cut); divide; improve; increase; lower; need (+ ...ing); paint; put in (put, put); raise; rebuild (rebuilt, rebuilt); redecorate; repair; replace; show sbdy round (showed, shown); size; straighten; strengthen; take down (took, taken); turn into; widen; full-time; main; downstairs; upstairs.

Summary C

Present Perfect and Simple Past

Connection with the present:

Average earnings **have gone up** by 60% over the last twelve months.
The government's economic policies **have led to** more efficient management and greater productivity.

Reference to finished time:

About 5,000 people **took part** in yesterday's anti-government demonstration. Stones and petrol bombs **were thrown** at the police.

Future Progressive

> I will (I'll) be working/seeing/...
> you will (you'll) be working/seeing/...
> *etc.*
>
> will I be working/seeing/...?
> *etc.*
>
> I will not (won't) be working/seeing/...
> *etc.*

At eight o'clock tomorrow morning I'll **be brushing** my teeth.
At half past eight tomorrow morning I'll **be driving** to work.
What **will** you **be doing** this time tomorrow?

Future Perfect

> I will (I'll) have worked/seen/...
> you will (you'll) have worked/seen/...
> *etc.*
>
> will I have worked/seen/...?
> *etc.*
>
> I will not (won't) have worked/seen/...
> *etc.*

In a couple of years she **will have got married** and **settled** down.
By next summer I expect I'll **have passed** all my exams.
Ten years from now, **will** you **have forgotten** me?

need ...ing

The roof **needs repairing**. (= ... needs to be repaired)
The door **needs painting**.

have something done

They **had** the dining room **redecorated**.
They **had** a new staircase **put in**.

make and let + object + infinitive

It **makes me laugh**. (It makes me laughing.)
It **makes me want** to scream.
Do you **let small things upset** you? (... to upset you.)

make + object + adjective

It **makes me cross**.
It **made me sick**.

Relative clauses without object pronouns

(This structure is more common in informal speech and writing.)

The eggs you're eating came from our farm.
  (= The eggs **that** you're eating ...)
That motorbike Jake built fell to pieces.
  (= That motorbike **that** Jake built ...)

Subject relative pronouns can't be left out

The people **who** live next door never get up before ten o'clock.
  (The people live next door never get up ...)
I'm going to do something **that** will really surprise you.
  (I'm going to do something will really surprise you.)

Reduced relative clauses

I know the man **sitting on the wall** over there.
  (= ... the man **who is sitting** ...)
Who is the woman **standing at the bus stop**?
Food **kept in a freezer** will stay good for several months. (= Food **that is kept** ...)
The forms **sent to the embassy** never arrived.
Three men **accused of organising an attack on an Irish police station** in which several officers were injured have been arrested.

Making dates and appointments

Are you free this evening?
Are you doing anything this evening?
I thought we might …
unless you're too busy/tired.

I'm not sure.   Maybe, maybe not.
It depends.   I can't remember.

Just a minute.
Let me just look in my diary.

It looks as if I'm not free.
I'm not free after all.
I've just remembered.
No, I'm afraid I'm baby-sitting / washing my hair /
    going to the theatre / working / playing bridge /
    …ing.
I really ought to wash my hair / write letters / …
I'm away tomorrow.
I've got a terrible headache.

What/How about tomorrow / the day after
    tomorrow?

I'm really a bit busy at the moment / for the next few
    weeks.
You know how it is.

It's ages since I …   I haven't … for ages.

I'll give you a ring one of these days / some time /
    when things get easier.

That would be lovely.   I'd love to.

Where shall we meet?   What time?
What time were you thinking of?

I'll come round to your place.
I might be a bit late.

That's difficult.
Could we make it a bit later?

See you then.

Emphatic synonyms

angry – furious   nervous – terrified
pleased – delighted   unhappy – miserable
worried – frantic

'Was she **worried**?' 'She was **frantic**!'
'I suppose you were **angry**.' 'I was **furious**!'

Contradiction, softening and emphasis

'My brother's just told me he's getting married next
    week.' 'Are you pleased?'
(–)   'Well, no, actually, I'm not.'
(±)   'Quite pleased, but he could have told me
        earlier.'
(++) 'I'm absolutely delighted.'

Informal and formal expressions

INFORMAL	FORMAL
We have thought about	We have considered
We are sorry	We regret
We can't	We are unable to
job	post
good enough	up to the level we require
	up to the standard required
	sufficiently good
need	require
you don't seem to have	you appear to lack

Pronunciation and spelling: 'silent *e*'

mad made   win wine   hop hope   cut cute

Pronunciation and spelling: doubling

big bigger   run runner   mad madder
hot hotter   sit sitting   begin beginning

We don't double in unstressed syllables. Compare:

forgetting carpeting   regretted targeted
beginning opening   preferring offering

Irregular verbs in Lessons C1–C8

INFINITIVE	PAST	PAST PARTICIPLE
break	broke	broken
bring	brought	brought
build	built	built
cut	cut	cut
deal	dealt	dealt
fall	fell	fallen
feel	felt	felt
fight	fought	fought
hide	hid	hidden
hurt	hurt	hurt
keep	kept	kept
lead	led	led
leave	left	left
lend	lent	lent
meet	met	met
put	put	put
rebuild	rebuilt	rebuilt
repay	repaid	repaid
rise	rose	risen
see	saw	seen
set	set	set
shoot	shot	shot
show	showed	shown
take	took	taken
teach	taught	taught
tell	told	told
throw	threw	thrown

Vocabulary

Look through the 'Learn/revise' boxes at the end of
Lessons C1–C8.

Revision and fluency practice C

A choice of activities.

1 📼 In these sentences, some of the words are wrong. Listen to the recording and correct them.

1. 'Hello, Mary, I'm home,' said John, speaking rather fast.
2. 'Listen!' she said happily. 'A wonderful thing has happened!'
3. 'How's the car running?' 'Very well.'
4. 'Is your bath OK?' 'Just fine.'
5. 'Peter, how are you?' she said coldly.
6. Sally knocked at the door. 'Come in!' said a friendly voice.
7. It's a fine day. The sun's shining.
8. Little birds are singing.
9. Rupert walked quietly up the stairs.

2 General knowledge quiz. Work with two or three other students, and make up a general knowledge quiz of ten or more questions. When you are ready, give your quiz to the class. Examples of general knowledge questions:

Who wrote *Hamlet*?
Where is Belfast?
In what year did the first person walk on the moon?
What is the next word: 'Happy birthday to ...'?

3 Family move. Work in groups. Read the following paragraph; then the teacher will give you a card telling you who you are. Improvise a conversation for the situation.

The group is a family, their friends and neighbours. (Each student in the group should play the part of one of the people.) The family have lived in a house in the suburbs of a big town for the last fifteen years. Mother's firm has recently moved to the other side of town, and she now has a very long way to travel to work; this takes up a lot of her time, and is expensive. The family are discussing whether to move to a flat in the centre of town; friends and neighbours drop in while they are talking.

4 Selling. Choose one of the following products (or invent an unusual product) and try to sell it to the class (as if you had a stall in a market). You can talk for a maximum of three minutes. When all the salespeople have spoken, the class must decide which product they are going to buy.

edible CDs   perfumed books   musical mousetraps
electric eyebrow-brushes   bicycle-seat warmers
centrally-heated bikinis   portable lie-detectors
anti-yawning pills   automatic umbrellas
portable folding toilets   coloured tooth-varnish

5 'Balloon debate.' Imagine that a group of famous historical and modern characters are travelling by balloon. They are over the North Atlantic when a leak is discovered. The balloon can only reach land if it is lightened – all the characters except one must jump out. Choose one of the characters, and speak for three to five minutes to explain why you are the best person to stay in the balloon (and why the others should not). Possible characters:

Father Christmas   Queen Elizabeth
Columbus   Charlie Chaplin   Kiri te Kanawa
Picasso   Shakespeare   Eve   Napoleon
Mozart   Chairman Mao

6 'Who said what?' Two students give three-minute talks on similar subjects (their houses; their plans for the next three days; what they have in their pockets *etc.*). When they have finished, the class have to remember what each one said without confusing the two lots of information.

7 Party conversation. You are just arriving at a party. As you go in, the teacher will give you a card telling you what your job is. Get into conversation with the other people; find out about them and tell them about yourself.

8 Read the following text, and write two or more of the missing descriptions. What do you think – do dreams mean anything?

If you dream about...

...climbing
If you climb stairs, hills or mountains in your dreams, you're ambitious and don't let people get in your way. If you dream that you're falling, this can mean that you say too much to the wrong people at the wrong times. Think before you open your mouth.

...flying
You're fed up with your problems, and want to rise above them. If it's easy to fly, you'll get what you want. If not, you're doing something wrong – it's time for a different approach to the person or thing that is causing the trouble.

...dancing
Fast mad dancing – you'll be lucky in love. Slow dreamy dancing means you want love and peace. Dancing by yourself – what do you think?

...teeth falling out
If you lose teeth in your dreams, it means you are having trouble with personal relationships. If you spit teeth out, you haven't got any money. A filling in a tooth means you'll get some.

...travel
....
....

...being chased
....
....

...being naked in public
....
....

...fire
....
....

...water
....
....

...animals
....

---

9 📼 Listen to the recording. You will hear three songs: *The Riddle Song*, *Logger Lover* and *What did you learn in school today?* Copy the table and mark your reactions to each song (✔ = like; ✗ = dislike; ▬ = no opinion).

	Tune	Words	Singer
Riddle Song			
Logger Lover			
What did you learn?			

Compare your reactions with another student's. Examples:

'I like "Logger Lover" best.'
'I like the tune.'
'I think the words are silly.'
'I can't stand it.'
'I don't like the singer's voice.'

Choose one of the songs to listen to again. Study the words (they are on pages 118 and 119): use a dictionary or ask questions.

10 Read the poems and say what you think of them. Do you like any of them? Do you dislike any of them? Do you find any of them boring? Is there anything in them that you don't understand or don't agree with?

The star

Suddenly I pulled one arm free
from the arms that enclosed me
and stretched it out to touch a star:
yes, she was there, she hadn't changed colour,
the star was as deep as ever with blue spikes
and mine, only mine –
    the star was in her place
we sent each other a little smile
and both of us turned round
    each to our heaven

(from the Swedish of Solveig von Schoultz, translated by Anne Born)

When my ship comes in

At last it was on the horizon, a big three-islander, and it was coming in.
I waited on the sand with the sandflies pricking my ankles. I smiled. My ship.
Still it came, but as it came somehow it wasn't getting any bigger.
Perhaps it had stopped. No, I could see it clearer now, rigging and wash.
I could almost make out the captain, red in the face from sun and yelling.
I waited, and still it came, clearer, frothing at the bow, getting no bigger.
I had only to wait, so I waited, and my ship came in, shrinking and shrinking.
The tide washed it right to my feet. I picked it up. Shook the sea out.
Held it to my ear to hear the captain's hello. Listened hard. No hello. No captain.
Carefully I returned it to the sea and shoved it off and watched it leave.
Slow at first, and then full ahead, making a coot's wake, a swan's wake,
a ship's wake, and soon it was miles away, growing as it went.

(Richard Venner)

For women who wait at bus-stops

At the bus-stop at the world's end,
We wait for the bus that never comes.
Our patience is worn through, an old cardigan
Each one of us must wear and never can discard.
Some of us curse and some of us wait sullenly;
One couple gossip endlessly,
And one there is who stands apart,
Whispers to herself and laughs from time to time.

At the bus-stop at the world's end
Our children are dusty and tired;
They spill out untidily into the road,
Crying and making impossible demands of us:
There are no more sweets left,
We give them instead obscenities, threats and promises,
One woman rocks her baby and herself.
The one who stands alone has no children,
Whispers to herself and laughs from time to time.

At the bus-stop at the world's end
We wait, and have waited in our lives for many things,
So say the lines between our eyes.
We are tired of all this waiting for buses, babies, men,
But we cannot walk away for we are encumbered
With shopping bags that are heavy with other people's needs.
Though the one who stands alone carries only a purse,
Whispers to herself and laughs from time to time.

(Sue Hawkes)

Test C

LISTENING

1 📼 Listen to the recording and write down five things that the owners have had done. Example:

They've had the stairs completely rebuilt.

GRAMMAR

2 Rewrite the sentences using *make* or *let*.

1. I wanted to go on holiday with my boyfriend; my parents said 'No.' (Begin *My parents didn't let …*)
2. When I see a spider, I want to scream. (Begin *Spiders make …*)
3. The people I work with always know how I am feeling. (Begin *I always …*)
4. Whenever I'm with my sister Joanne, I laugh a lot. (Begin *My sister Joanne always …*)

3 Put the verbs into the correct tenses.

1. By the time you read this I (*lie*) on the beach.
2. When I see my sister again, she (*finish*) all her exams.
3. 'Did you find out what was wrong with your car?' 'Yes, the voltage regulator needs (*replace*).'
4. Industrial output (*rise*) by 16% since last May.
5. Unemployment (*fall*) by 2% last month alone.
6. Anita Lansdon (*die*) yesterday at her home, at the age of 93.
7. Motorists are urged to drive carefully – there (*be*) flooding in the north of the country.

LANGUAGE IN USE

4 Write one sentence or question for each situation.

1. You have been very worried that your sister will not pass her exams, as she has been having personal problems. You love her very much, and the exams are important to her. She has passed. Someone asks you, 'Are you pleased?'
2. Yesterday you waited in the rain for an hour for a friend who never came. It made you feel like killing him. You have just told another friend what happened. She says, 'Were you cross?'
3. You have not got a place on the badminton team, but you know that you will have a good chance of getting one next year. Someone asks you, 'Are you disappointed?'
4. Find out if a friend can go out with you this evening.
5. Tell a friend you can't go out with them this evening, but try and make them realise that you would like to go out with them sometime.

6. Tell a friend you can't go out with them this evening, and try to make them realise that you really don't want to go out with them at all.
7. You do want to go out with your friend, but the time suggested is too early. What do you say?
8. You have told someone that you can probably go out with them on Saturday, but you have just looked in your diary and found out that you have promised to spend the day with your grandmother.

VOCABULARY

5 Write opposites for these words.

1. agree	5. deep	9. rough
2. clean	6. full	10. sharp
3. dangerous	7. honest	11. strong
4. dark	8. quiet	12. warm

6 *Make, take, do, have* or *get*? Put each word into one or more columns, adding *a* if necessary. Two examples are done for you.

Words: bed, bus, changed, holiday, housework, medicine, nothing, phone call, plan, rest, something stupid, supper, train, work

MAKE	TAKE	DO	HAVE	GET
a bed	a bus			

7 Write words for these definitions.

1. mother or father
2. very, very angry
3. very, very unhappy
4. chairs, tables, sofas, desks, *etc.*
5. stop working at, for example, age 65
6. a small book to write appointments in
7. someone who has asked for a job
8. able to speak two languages well
9. a group of people marching in the street to try and change something
10. go up
11. killing someone deliberately
12. politically most important city (in a country)
13. person who helps a mother give birth to a baby

PRONUNCIATION

8 Where is the main stress in each word? The first word is done for you as an example.

affected   average   economic   efficient
figures   involved   management   output
productivity   released   temperature

9 Which vowels are pronounced /ə/? Example:

This is @ pen.

1. Where are your brothers?
2. When shall we leave?
3. I got a pound of bacon for breakfast.
4. I saw Maureen at the shop.

READING

10 Find the answers in the text.

1. Find two other words that mean the same as *oxen*.
2. Why haven't the poorer farmers got oxen?
3. Why do the poorer farmers plant their crops later?
4. Give two reasons why the oxen are weak.
5. What happens on *grazing lands*?
6. When the farmers pay back the price of the oxen, what will happen to the money they pay back?

ACTIONAID in ETHIOPIA
providing oxen for poor farmers

The Background

Ethiopia is one of the poorest countries in Africa. Outside the cities, minimal government services exist. Unlike some poor communities, the farmers in this area are dependent on cattle, and ActionAid sees livestock provision as an important part of improving food security.

The Problem

During the drought of 1984–86 farmers progressively exchanged their household assets and livestock for food. The area's stock of oxen was seriously depleted. Local ownership of oxen also changed – with the relatively richer farmers being able to increase their herds at the expense of the poorer farmers. The poorer farmers have to rent oxen at a cost equivalent to £15 per day, paid in labour or a share of the harvest. They also have to wait until the oxen owners have ploughed their own fields first. The oxen are worked exhaustively. Scarce and poor pasture weakens the animals. Late planting jeopardises the poorer farmers' potential yields.

The Solution

ActionAid Ethiopia intends to redress the imbalance by helping poorer farmers to build up their assets and improve production by increasing the area of cultivation and by making timely land preparation more possible. Before oxen are provided to a farmer, however, it is necessary to assess whether or not each beneficiary could sustain extra animals within the present availability of grazing lands and materials. This will be done by ActionAid Ethiopia's own agricultural workers.

Participating farmers will receive oxen on credit after they have identified the animals to be purchased and negotiated the price. ActionAid agricultural workers will provide veterinary and marketing advice. ActionAid Ethiopia will then cover the transportation and provide follow-up advice to ensure that the oxen are being used productively. Credit repayments are made to a revolving fund to be used to purchase further oxen. Sixty oxen will be bought and distributed within the first year.

Oxen ploughing a field

WRITING

11 Read the interviewer's notes on two job applicants. The post is that of driver for the managing director of a company (see picture). Choose one of the candidates, and then write *either* a letter offering the job to the successful candidate *or* a letter telling the unsuccessful candidate that you will not be offering him the job.

Applicant 1:   Colin Sanderson
November 16, 2.30
Clothes untidy
Has only had driving licence for a year
Friendly, charming, but talks too much
Not very strong - how will he lift the wheelchair?
No work experience

Applicant 2:   Liam Docherty
November 16, 4pm
Polite; quiet but self-confident
Tidily dressed
Has been driving for 7 years
Drove a taxi for one year
Clean driving licence
Seems very fit and strong
Good references from previous employers

SPEAKING

12 Work with another student. Imagine you have been given the building where your English classes take place, and a large sum of money to turn it into anything you want. Come to an agreement about what you want to use the building for, and discuss in detail some of the changes you will make.

D1 What do they look like?

Grammar and vocabulary for descriptions; listening skills: listening for gist; speaking and writing skills: descriptions.

1 📼 Listen to the song. (The words are on page 119.) Each verse describes one of the four people in the pictures. Which picture goes with which verse?

2 Here are some words, expressions and structures that can be used for describing people's appearance. Do you know all of them? Can you think of any important words that have been left out?

Hair: long, medium-length, short; straight, curly, wavy; blond(e), fair, dark, brown, black, red, grey, going grey, white, thinning; a beard, a moustache, bushy eyebrows
   He's (going) bald. He's got a bald patch.
Eyes: green, blue, brown, greenish-blue, grey
Nose: long, turned-up
Mouth: wide, generous; thin lips, full lips
Chin: pointed, firm, weak
Face: oval, round, long; high cheekbones; a scar
Forehead: high, low
Ears: big, small
Shoulders: broad, narrow
Build: thin, slender, slim, muscular, heavily-built, plump, overweight, fat
Height: tall, of medium height, short
Age: young, middle-aged, elderly, old; in his early thirties; in her mid-fifties; in their late forties
Expression: serious, cheerful, worried, friendly
General appearance: good-looking, pretty, beautiful, handsome, attractive, plain; well-dressed, casually dressed
   He looks old. She looks like a businesswoman.

Structures:
She has (she's got) blue eyes and brown hair.
a woman with blue eyes and brown hair
a blue-eyed, brown-haired woman

a man with a beard
a girl with glasses

a woman in a blue dress
a man in a grey jacket

3 A person with fair hair is *fair-haired*. Somebody who writes with his or her left hand is *left-handed*. What are the adjectives for these people?

1. a person with grey hair
2. a person with a thin face
3. somebody with broad shoulders
4. somebody with long legs
5. people who write with their right hands
6. a person with green eyes

Now say these in another way.

1. a brown-eyed man
   '*a man with brown eyes*'
2. a grey-haired old lady
   '*an old lady* ....'
3. a left-handed child
   '*a child who* ....'
4. a thin-faced person
   '*somebody who has* ....'
5. a dark-eyed woman
   '............'

4 Prepare and give a short description *either* of one of the people in the pictures *or* of somebody in the class. (Don't be rude!) See if other students can guess who it is.

5 Complete the text with words from the box.

I'm in my .... fifties. I'm very tall, and quite .... built, but I have rather .... shoulders. I'm a little overweight.
   I have .... medium-length .... hair, but I'm going ...., so there isn't a lot of it left. I have a grey .... and moustache. My eyes are ...., and I wear .... I've got a rather long face, with a .... chin, a big nose and big .... I have .... lips, and I usually have a .... expression; my face changes a lot when I .... I have a high forehead; I like to think that it looks intelligent.
   Clothes are not very important to me, and I'm usually very .... dressed.
   I don't think I'm very ...., but I'm not all that bad-looking either. I probably .... a bit younger than I am.

bald	beard	blue	casually	early
ears	fair	glasses	good-looking	
heavily	look	narrow	serious	smile
straight	strong	thin		

6 Write a description of yourself; don't put your name on it. When you are ready, give it to the teacher.

7 Listen to the descriptions as the teacher reads them out. Can you guess who wrote each one?

Learn/revise: appearance; bald; beard; businesswoman; chin; expression; eyebrow; forehead; height; lip; moustache; describe; attractive; beautiful; broad; cheerful; elderly; firm; friendly; generous; good-looking; handsome; low; middle-aged; narrow; overweight; oval; plain; pointed; pretty; round; serious; slim; straight; thin; weak; well-dressed; wide; worried.

D2 Focus on systems

A choice of exercises: structures with *I wish* and *if only*; polite and rude intonation; the vowels /eə/, /ɜː/ and /ɪə/; word families.

GRAMMAR: *I WISH; IF ONLY*

1 Can you write some more of the thoughts of the person who received this letter? Use *I wish ... had ...*

14 Railway Gardens
South Wick
Tuesday

My Darling,

What has happened? You don't answer the phone; you aren't at home when I call; you don't write. Is something wrong? Have I upset you in some way?

We only met five weeks ago, but I feel as if I had lived a whole new life since then. So many wonderful memories!

That party when I first saw you. I asked you to dance. You said yes! You are so beautiful, you could have danced with anybody, but you chose me! I couldn't believe my luck.

Then you came back to my place for coffee, and I showed you my stamp collection, and told you all about my plans, my hopes, my life. What an evening!

Other memories flood into my brain. The day we went on the river. The weekend when we went shooting with Joe and Daphne. The time we went swimming — I got into trouble, and you pulled me to safety with your beautiful strong arms.

And then last weekend. We stood on the edge of the cliffs, looking down. You threw a stone into the sea, and I kissed you. You laughed with pleasure, and I told you I loved you, and you were so happy you cried, and you couldn't say anything. What were you thinking?

Please write. I can't wait to hear from you.

I love you,

Alex

I wish we'd never met!

If only I'd stayed at home!

2 Here is a list of regrets. Practise saying the sentences. Then choose three regrets that you share, and add two or more of your own.

I wish I had been nicer to my parents when I was younger.
I wish my family had had more money when I was small.
I wish I had listened to my mother's advice.
I wish I had worked harder at school when I was younger.
I wish I had gone to a different school.
I wish I had stayed at school for longer.
I wish I had left school earlier.
I wish I had not started learning English.
If only I had saved more money when I was younger!
If only I had travelled more when I was younger!
If only I had taken a different job!
If only I had not got married!
If only I had been born more beautiful!
If only I had been born more intelligent!
If only I had looked after my teeth better!
If only I had never started smoking!
If only I had gone to bed earlier last night!

3 Look at the pictures. What do you suppose the people in them are thinking? See if other students have the same ideas as you.

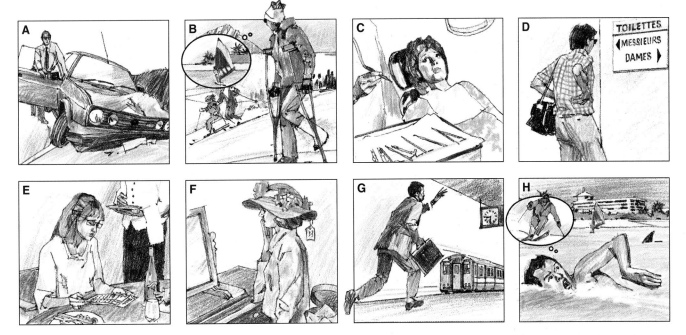

4 Here are some wishes for the present or future. Choose three that you share, and add one or more.

I wish it was cooler/warmer.
I wish it was the end of the lesson.
I wish I was at home.
I wish I could sing / play the guitar.
I wish I had more money/time.
If only I spoke better English!
If only I knew more people!
If only people were more honest!
If only the government would do something about unemployment!
If only somebody would write me a letter!

5 Write your most important wish on a piece of paper, but without your name. Give it to the teacher.

6 Work in groups. The teacher will read out all the class's wishes to you. Write them down and divide them into different kinds of wish (e.g. wishes for material things; wishes for changes in one's situation). Report to the class: how many kinds of wish have you found, and what is the commonest kind of wish? What did you feel was the most surprising wish?

PRONUNCIATION

7 📼 Which twelve of these words contain the sound /eə/ (as in *chair*)? How are the others pronounced? Can you think of any more words with /eə/?

air   care   dear   fair   hair   her   here
pear   pair   share   tear (*verb*)   their   there
they're   were   we're   where

8 📼 Do these sentences sound polite or rude? Listen, and mark them *P* or *R*. Then say them all politely.

1. Could you lend me a pen, please?
2. Have you got a light, please?
3. Can you tell me the time, please?
4. Could I look at your newspaper for a moment?
5. Could you send this to my address in Tokyo?
6. Can you show me some sweaters, please?

VOCABULARY: WORD FAMILIES

9 Do you know (or can you find out) twenty words or expressions in one of the following groups?

1. Things that you might find on a desk.
2. Things that you might find in a railway station.
3. Things that you might find in a kitchen.
4. Things that you can do to a piece of wood.
5. Things that you can do to communicate with somebody else.
5. Things that you enjoy.
6. Things that you dislike.

Learn/revise: advice (*uncountable*); brain; cliff; collection; edge; hope; luck; memory; plan; pleasure; safety; stamp; stone; thought; tooth (teeth); unemployment; wish (*noun and verb*); be born; choose (chose, chosen); cry; feel (felt, felt); flood; happen; kiss; laugh; look after; meet (met, met); pull; receive; save; shoot (shot, shot); throw (threw, thrown); upset (upset, upset); cool; honest; nice; strong; warm; whole; wonderful; in some way; I can't wait to ...; get into trouble; *vocabulary from Exercise 9*.

D3 I don't like playtime

Talking about education; the language of discussion; Present Perfect Progressive and Simple Past.

1 Can you think of at least ten different subjects or activities that you did at primary school? (Ask the teacher if you don't know the English names.) Which ones did you like, and which did you dislike?

2 📼 Listen to the recording. Do the children mention any things that are not on your list?

3 📼 Listen to the next part of the recording. What eight things do the children say they dislike?

4 📼 Now you are going to hear the children saying what they like about their teacher, Mrs Cabeldu. Can you guess what they will say? Listen and see if you were right.

Mrs Cabeldu by Anita Bryon, age 5½

5 Grammar. Simple Past or Present Perfect Progressive?

1. Paul is 14. Alice is 50. Which of them do you think probably said each of these sentences? Why?

   'I did English at school for three years.'
   'I've been doing maths at school for seven years.'
   'I've been doing chemistry for a year.'
   'I didn't do physics at school.'
   'I've been going to school for eight years.'
   'I went to school for eight years.'

2. Ask other students (or the teacher) two questions beginning *How long have you been studying ...?* (practise the pronunciation) and two questions beginning *How long did you study ...?*

6 Here are some expressions which are often used in discussions. Do you know what they all mean and how to pronounce them?

Definitely.
Certainly.
Of course.
Do you think …?
Yes, I do.
I certainly do.
I agree.
Yes, I think so.
I'm not sure.
It depends.

What do you mean by …?
I suppose so.
I don't know.
Perhaps.
I don't think so.
I don't agree.
Definitely not.
Certainly not.
Of course not.

7 Choose one or more of the following exercises.

A. Make a list of the subjects that you studied (or are studying) at school, with the ones you think are most useful at the top and the ones you think are least useful at the bottom. Use a dictionary or ask the teacher for help if necessary. Write *I* against the subjects you found (or find) interesting, and write *B* against the boring ones. Then work in small groups and discuss your lists. Which are the most and least popular school subjects?

B. Work in groups. Each group is a committee, which has to work out a plan for secondary education reform. Write a list of the changes that you would like to make. You may want to consider some of the following:

subjects
organisation and length of the school day
size of classes
teaching methods
examinations
teacher training
teacher-pupil relationships
the aims of secondary education

C. Say what you think about one or more of the following questions. Use a dictionary or ask for help if necessary.

1. Do schools do a good job of preparing people for life? Should education be more practical?
2. Should all children have to learn maths?
3. Should all children have to learn English?
4. Who should be paid most – the teachers of small children or the teachers of older children?
5. Which is more important – a good upbringing or a good education?

D. Prepare a lesson (on any subject of your choice) and give it to the class in English. After your lesson, get the class's reactions – what was good, and what could have been done differently?

> **Learn/revise:** aim; chemistry; committee; education; examination; maths; method; organisation; physics; plan; primary school; reform; relationship; secondary education; size; (school) subject; training; upbringing; mention; prepare; boring; popular; practical; sure; useful; least; most; definitely; certainly; of course; I suppose so; What do you mean by …?

D4 I knew everyone

Reading skills: scanning, reading for overall meaning, dictionary work; writing skills: expanding a text from notes; speaking skills: class survey.

1 Look at the questions and make sure you understand them. Then find the answers to the questions in the text. *Don't* read the whole text; only look for the answers to the questions.

1. True or false? When Mr Packard was a boy, his mother's sister lived in New York.
2. Is the countryside around Troy, Pennsylvania flat or hilly?
3. Does Mr Packard's sister have any sons?
4. How long ago did the Packards move to New Canaan?
5. Do the Packards know all their neighbours?
6. True or false? Half of US heads of families live more than 100 miles from where they were born.

PERSONAL ISOLATION

To the best of my knowledge, all my aunts, uncles and grandparents spent most of their lives within thirty miles of Troy, Pennsylvania. They were farmers, horse traders, merchants, mailmen. As a boy I believe I knew everyone living within four miles of our farm. And I guess Dad knew just about everyone in the county. He enjoyed talking. We met people as families at suppers on Saturday nights. We met at church festivities, at cattle auctions, at the milk station, at the icehouse pond, and at the contests on the steep road leading to Granville Summit on Sunday afternoons. The contest was to see who could drive his car the farthest up the hill in high gear.

Today a number of my relatives still live near Troy, but several of my cousins, my nieces, my brother and my sister are scattered in many states. The nearest relative to my home in New Canaan, Connecticut, is a niece who lives about a hundred and ten miles away. My two sons live in Wisconsin and Pennsylvania; my mother-in-law, until her recent death, lived much of the time in Florida.

When my wife Virginia and I moved to New Canaan twenty-four years ago it was a semi-rural town and I soon knew most of the people living within a mile of us. In recent years almost all the old neighbors have moved and many dozens of new houses have sprung up near us, many of them occupied by highly-mobile managerial and professional families. One house very close by, for example, has been occupied by four families in five years. Today I wouldn't even recognize half of the people living within five hundred yards of our house. Virginia and I feel increasingly isolated.

Personal isolation is becoming a major social fact of our time. A great many people are disturbed by the feeling that they are rootless or increasingly anonymous, that they are living in a continually changing environment where there is little sense of community. The phrase "home town" may well fade from our language in this century. Already half of all US heads of families live more than a hundred miles from where they were born – and one out of every five lives more than a thousand miles from his birthplace.

(abridged from *A Nation of Strangers* by Vance Packard)

2 Here are three summaries of the text. Which one do you feel is the most accurate?

Life used to be more fun when I was a child: I lived in a happy family and had lots of friends. Now there are fewer opportunities for enjoying the company of other people, because we are all becoming rootless and anonymous.

My family used to live close together, but now we are scattered. We used to know most of our neighbours, but this is no longer the case. People move around more now, and the old kind of close community is disappearing.

The population is growing and towns are getting bigger. People are more mobile, and they don't know each other so well as they used to. Personal isolation is a big problem nowadays.

3 Dictionary skills. Use your English-English dictionary, or turn to page 120. Look at the explanations of the three words which follow: each word is given several definitions. Decide which of the definitions is the best for the word as it is used in the text.

1. gear (last line of first paragraph)
2. spring (*have sprung*, middle of the third paragraph)
3. fade (middle of the last paragraph)

4 Read through the questionnaire. Look up any words you don't know, and make sure you can answer all the questions in English.

1. Where are you from?
2. Where were your parents from?
3. Where have you spent most of your life?
4. Are you in close contact with your immediate family (parents/brothers/sisters/children)?
5. Is your family the most important thing in your life?
6. How important to you is your 'extended family' (aunts/uncles/cousins *etc.*)?
7. How many of your relations live within 30 miles of your home?
8. Is your family very scattered, or do they mostly live close together?
9. How many of your relations do you know personally?
10. Have you seen more or less of your family in recent years?
11. Do you think big families or small families are better?
12. Do you think it is a good thing for parents to live with their married children?
13. Do you know a lot of your neighbours?
14. Do you recognise all the people who live within a hundred yards of your home?
15. Would you rather live in: an isolated house; a village; a small country town; a medium-sized town; a big city?
16. Who do you get on best with?
    – people you are related to
    – people you went to school/college with
    – people you work with
    – other people (who?)
17. What places do you feel most at home in?
    – the place you were born in
    – the place(s) you grew up in
    – the place you live in now
    – other places (where?)
18. Do you consider yourself a) rootless b) well-rooted c) something between the two?

5 Choose one of the questions from Exercise 4 and ask as many people as possible. When you have finished, report to the class on what you have found out.

6 Work in groups. First read the text. Then read the notes, which give points that can be added to the text. Decide where to add the points and how to make them into sentences or to join them to other sentences.

Childhood in an Indian Village

Going back as far as I can remember as a child in an Indian community, I had no sense of knowing about the other people around me except that we were all somehow equal. There was only one class.

You could see it in our games. We were involved in lots of activity (I was not like I am now; I was in pretty good shape at that time) and we were organized, but not in the sense that there were ways of finding out who had won and who had lost. We played ball like everyone else, but no one kept score. Even if we did formally compete in the games we played, no one was a winner though someone may have won. It was only the moment. If you beat someone by pulling a bow and arrow and shooting the arrow farther, it only meant that you shot the arrow farther at that moment. That's all it lasted. It didn't mean that you were better in any way whatsoever. Maybe it was just the way you let the bow go. These kinds of things are very important to me and that is why I am talking about them.

One of the very important things was the relationship we had with our families. We didn't always live at home. We lived wherever we happened to be at that particular time when it got dark.

People would feed you even if they didn't know who you were. We'd spend an evening, perhaps, with an old couple, and they would tell us stories. In the summer people would generally take us out and we would do a number of things which in some way would allow us to learn about life and what it was all about. In all the years I spent there, I don't remember anyone teaching us anything.

(Wilfrid Pelletier, in *This Book is About Schools*)

Notes
– most stories legends, told mostly in winter time
– helping children to learn by talking about some particular person, demonstrating what person did
– if 2/3 miles from home, that's where slept
– just meant arrow went farther
– nobody interested in getting on top of anybody else
– no competitive sports

Learn/revise: arrow; birthplace; city; class; death; dozen; environment; extended family; farm; immediate family; knowledge; neighbour (US neighbor); phrase; relative; score; stranger; summer; town; village; winter; yard; compete; get dark (got, got); grow up (grew, grown); keep score (kept, kept); occupy; recognise (US recognize); sleep (slept, slept); win (won, won); personal; recent; rootless; social; related to; scattered; a number of; continually; increasingly; generally; almost; even; within; everyone else.

D5 A beautiful place

Reading comprehension; vocabulary (describing places); grammar (Past Perfect); writing descriptions.

1 Read the text and look at the pictures. Which place do you think is described in each section?

Extracts from the report of **Zargon**, a space explorer, written in the year 2050

1 As I approached the planet, my thermoanalytic detectors told me that there was a great variety of plant life, but no animal life at all. In my three hundred years of space exploration, I had never before come across a world where there were no animals. It was so strange that I wondered whether something had happened – some war or natural disaster which had killed off all animal life on the planet …

2 I made my first landing on soft ground near a group of red rocks. As soon as I had tested the atmosphere, I stepped out and began to look round. In front of me there were large plants, on which grew a kind of fruit like none that I had ever seen before. On my left, not far away, the ground rose gently to some low hills. On my right and behind me the ground was level, stretching away into the distance. It was an impressive but monotonous landscape …

3 After I had rested and written my report I flew to another part of the planet. Detecting a high level of radioactivity, I did not land; but I flew over the area several times. It was a place of deep valleys with vertical walls; in them regular square or rectangular openings had been made, whose purpose I was not able to guess. There was little vegetation, but my instruments showed a good deal of metal. Not far away there was a great expanse of water containing various chemicals …

4 It was impossible to see very far, and movement was very difficult. I could tell that many different kinds of animals had lived here, and I collected some bones in the hope that our analysts would be able to find out what had killed them …

5 The temperature was very low, and the oxygen thin. There were few plants, and those I found were small. In front, the horizon was very close; behind, I could see for a long way. Far below, a stretch of water shone in the sun. It was a beautiful place, and I was sorry to leave. But my time had run out, and I had to return to Rozul …

(translation copyright Swan and Walter)

A

B

C

D

E

F

G

H

2 Grammar. Choose the right tense (Simple Past or Past Perfect).

1. When I was a child, I (*often dreamt / had often dreamt*) of being a space explorer.
2. When I was 25 I (*applied / had applied*) for a place at the space training academy.
3. I will never forget the day when the Principal (*told / had told*) me that I (*passed / had passed*) my final exams.
4. On my first mission, I (*went / had gone*) to visit a small planet in star system 18B.
5. The planet (*stopped / had stopped*) sending out radio signals some months before, and my orders were to find out what (*happened / had happened*).
6. It was early morning when I landed. As soon as I (*found / had found*) somewhere to leave the space-ship, I (*started / had started*) to explore the surrounding countryside.
7. There was no sign of animal life, and I (*wondered / had wondered*) what (*happened / had happened*) to the people.
8. I (*found / had found*) several kinds of plant that I (*never saw / had never seen*) before.
9. Not far from my landing place, I (*discovered / had discovered*) a small house.
10. It was in a very poor condition; obviously nobody (*lived / had lived*) there for years.
11. Suddenly I (*heard / had heard*) a footstep, and a woman (*appeared / had appeared*) from behind the house.
12. I asked her what (*happened / had happened*), but she (*just looked / had just looked*) at me with a strange smile.

3 Vocabulary: position and shape. As quickly as you can, write down:

1. something that is on your right
2. something that is on your left
3. something that is in front of you
4. something that is behind you
5. something that is in front of the building where you are now
6. something that is opposite the building where you are now
7. something that is a long way away
8. something that is not far away
9. something that is very close
10. something you can see that is level
11. something you can see that is not level
12. something you can see that is square
13. something you can see that is rectangular
14. something you can see that is round
15. something you can see that is oval
16. something you can see that is vertical
17. something you can see that is horizontal
18. something that is directly above your head
19. something that is high above you
20. something that is far below you

4 🎙 Pronunciation. Listen to the sentences. You will hear either a Present Perfect, a Past Perfect or a Simple Past verb (for example *I've heard*, *I'd heard* or *I heard*). Write down the verbs that you hear.

5 Do one or more of these exercises.

A. Work individually or with other students, as you prefer. Write a paragraph from a space explorer's report (like Exercise 1), about a well-known place. Show your paragraph to other students and see if they can guess where it is. Use some of the words and expressions from Exercise 3, and some of the structures in the box. Include some examples of the Past Perfect tense.

> in front (of me)   on my left/right
> behind (me)   high above   far below
> in(to) the distance   not far (away)
> a long way (away)   I could see
> There was/were   I had never …
> I wondered whether …   As soon as I had …

B. Work with three or four other students. Tell your group about a place that you like very much. Describe it in as much detail as possible, so that the others can really 'see' the place.

C. 🎙 Listen to the song. (The text is on page 120.)

> **Learn/revise:** area; atmosphere; distance; ground; hill; horizon; kind; opening; part; planet; rock; star; valley; variety; describe; rest; rise (rose, risen); shine (shone, shone); wonder; deep; high; horizontal; large; level; low; natural; oval; rectangular; round; soft; square; vertical; gently; above; away; behind; below; round (*adverb*); obviously; several; whether; in(to) the distance; not far away; a long way away.

D6 Focus on systems

A choice of exercises: identifying and non-identifying expressions; punctuation and intonation in relative clauses; *whose*; spellings of /ɜː/; common prefixes and suffixes.

GRAMMAR: IDENTIFYING EXPRESSIONS

1 Here are three ways of identifying people and things – of saying *which one(s)* you mean.

the girl *in the corner*
the girl *sitting in the corner*
the girl *who is sitting in the corner*

the man *in a red T-shirt / wearing a red T-shirt / who is wearing a red T-shirt*

the picture *over the door / hanging over the door / which hangs over the door*

Now express these ideas in the other two ways.

1. the woman in the front seat of the car
2. the girl in purple jeans
3. the man at the end of the platform
4. the car which is standing outside our house
5. the stairs which lead down to the cellar
6. the children who are playing in our garden
7. students living in London
8. a man staying in the Mexico City Hilton Hotel
9. the papers lying on the bed

2 Look at the picture. How could you identify the people marked A, B, C *etc.*? Example:

'E is the woman holding a camera.'

3 Choose three other people in the class. Say who you are thinking of without giving the people's names; see if the other students can decide who they are. Examples:

'I'm thinking of a girl who's wearing glasses.'
'I'm thinking of a person sitting at the front.'
'I'm thinking of a man in a red shirt.'

GRAMMAR: RELATIVE CLAUSES WITH *WHOSE*

4 Do you know how to join sentences with *whose*? Look at the examples.

Jake Thong is an artist. His pictures sell for thousands of pounds. → *Jake Thong is an artist **whose** pictures sell for thousands of pounds.*

Hungary is a country in central Europe. Its capital is divided into two parts. → *Hungary is a country in Central Europe **whose** capital is divided into two parts.*

Match the beginnings and ends.

An unsuccessful writer is	one whose victim stays alive.
An unsuccessful husband is	one whose lion eats him.
An unsuccessful murderer is	one whose books aren't read.
An unsuccessful lion tamer is	one whose food is uneatable.
An unsuccessful cook is	one whose wife leaves him.

Now can you complete these?

An unsuccessful builder is one whose ...
An unsuccessful doctor is one whose ...
An unsuccessful teacher is one whose ...
An unsuccessful parent is one whose ...
An unsuccessful gardener is one whose ...

PUNCTUATION AND PRONUNCIATION: IDENTIFYING AND NON-IDENTIFYING EXPRESSIONS

5 📼 Look at these pairs of sentences. Why do you think some sentences have commas (,,) while others don't? Practise saying the sentences.

A. The biggest city in Bavaria is Munich.
   Munich, in Bavaria, has a population of 1.25 million.
B. The village where I was born has changed a lot.
   North Barton, where I was born, has changed a lot.
C. A person who lives in Glasgow is called a Glaswegian.
   My sister, who lives in Glasgow, prefers Scotland to England.
D. Some people who come from Wales speak Welsh.
   The poet Dylan Thomas, who came from Wales, didn't speak Welsh.
E. The room which I'm sitting in at the moment isn't very well lighted.
   Our kitchen, which I'm sitting in at the moment, isn't very well lighted.

Which of these sentences should have commas? If you are not sure, listen to the recording. Practise saying the sentences.

1. Fantasia   which is a federal republic   has a basically democratic form of government.
2. San Fantastico   which is the capital of Fantasia   is also the largest city.
3. Fantasia has seventeen political parties   which are all very different.
4. The party   which has been in power for the last five years   is the Free Democratic Radical Conservative Party.
5. The party   which I support   is called the New Democratic Movement.
6. The New Democratic Movement   which I support   is led by Arnold Kronsk.
7. Our own Member of Parliament   who is on the left wing of her party   had a majority of 15,000 at the last election.
8. The party   which our MP belongs to   is called the New Radical Alliance.
9. The election   which is due to take place next month   will probably be won by the Progressive Democratic Party.
10. The people   who really run the country   are the Cabinet Ministers.
11. The politician   whom I admire most   is Ann Wesk, the leader of the opposition.
12. Ann Wesk   whom I greatly admire   is the daughter of a coal miner.

6 Look again at the sentences in Exercise 5. In which sentences do you think you could use *that* instead of *who* or *which*? Do you know why? In which sentences could you leave out *who/which/that*? Do you know why?

PRONUNCIATION: SPELLINGS OF /ɜː/

7 📼 In standard British English, the following words are all pronounced with the same vowel /ɜː/. Can you say them? And can you think of ten more words with the same vowel that are written with *er, ir, ur* or *wor*? Can you find any words written with *ear* that are pronounced with /ɜː/?

bird   certainly   first   hers   purpose   turn
word   world

VOCABULARY

8 Here are some common prefixes. Can you match them with their uses and meanings? Can you think of any other words with the same prefixes?

anti- (*anti-American, anticlockwise*)	too much
dis- (*disappear, dishonest*)	opposite to
mis- (*misunderstand, misspell*)	again, back
over- (*overeat, overwork*)	wrongly
re- (*rewrite, repay*)	against
un- (*unhappy, unable*)	too little
under- (*underpaid, undervalued*)	opposite to

Can you do the same with these suffixes?

-ance (*appearance, insurance*)	without
-en (*widen, strengthen*)	*makes noun from verb*
-er (*driver, waiter*)	
-ful (*beautiful, hopeful*)	rather
-ise (*computerise, modernise*)	*makes noun from verb*
-ish (*reddish, fattish*)	
-less (*hopeless, careless*)	*makes verb*
-ment (*government, advertisement*)	make more
	makes noun from verb
	with

Learn/revise: builder; camera; capital; cellar; city; election; husband; majority; Member of Parliament (MP); parent; party; picture; platform; population; republic; seat; stairs; village; belong (to); divide (into); hang (hung, hung); hold (held, held); lie (lying, lay, lain); run (= govern) (ran, run); support; take place (took, taken); wear (wore, worn); win (won, won); democratic; federal; political; purple; (un)successful; basically; in power; *words from Vocabulary section.*

D7 Boy meets girl

Listening and writing practice; discussion (talking about relationships); *had better*; *ought to* and other modal verbs.

1  Listen to the recording. It is taken from an old BBC comedy programme called 'Take it from here'. In this episode, Ron has a conversation with his father about shyness. Then Ron's father goes out, and Ron meets Eth for the first time. After listening, write 50–100 words summarising what happens.

2 Listen to the first few sentences of the recording again. Try to write down the exact words. Then look at the script on pages 120 and 121 and check your answer.

3 Listen again to the conversation between Ron and his father. Can you hear any non-standard pronunciations?

4 Listen to the whole of the recording, and match the modal verbs with the infinitives.

MODAL VERBS	INFINITIVES
can't	come
might	get
can	go
won't	think
had better	say
shall	see
could	sit

5 Listen again to the conversation between Ron and Eth. Then work in groups, and see how much you can remember of what they said. Write down what you remember and/or act it out. Then look at the script to check.

DO EITHER EXERCISE 6, EXERCISE 7 OR EXERCISE 8.

6 Prepare and act out a 'boy meets girl' scene.

7 Read the letter, which was sent to a British newspaper. Then write an answer to the letter, giving advice to the writer. Useful expressions:

Why don't you …?
Why not …?
What/How about …ing?
I/We think you should …
You really ought to …
You could/might …
If I were you, I would …
A good way to … is to …
The best way to … is to …
I/We think it's a mistake to …
Stop …ing and start …ing

> I have a terrible shyness problem. I don't remember the last time I had a real conversation with a girl. When I try to talk, my mouth goes dry and I just can't say anything.
>
> I am in my twenties, and other men my age seem to have no trouble talking to girls. Sometimes I wonder if I will ever manage it.
>
> Please tell me what I ought to do.

8 Work in groups of three or four. In each group, choose one of the following subjects. Prepare some more questions. When your questionnaire is ready, go round the class asking your questions. Note the answers. Then report to the class on what people think. Give your own opinions as well.

FRIENDSHIP
How important are your friends to you?

....

LOVE AND SEX
Do you think you can love more than one person at the same time?

....

MARRIAGE
Do you think marriage is a good thing?

....

PARENT-CHILD RELATIONSHIPS
Do you think most children communicate well with their parents?

....

RELATIONSHIPS IN WORK AND SOCIETY
Do you ever start conversations with strangers?

....

Learn/revise: cap; friendship; marriage; nut; phrase; relationship; society; shyness; stranger; stroll; get married; get over sth (got, got); happen (to); manage (to); meet (met, met); mention; ought (to); pull; turn out; wonder; (all) alone; dark-skinned; dry; scared (of); shy; had better (+ *infinitive without 'to'*); for the first time; next to; why don't you …?; why not …? (+ *infinitive without 'to'*); what/how about …ing?; if I were you, I would …; I hope you don't mind my …ing.

D8 Different kinds

Listening for specific information; classifying in English; describing things without naming them.

1 Do you know the names of some of these? Work in groups, and try to match as many of the words and pictures as possible.

backbone	bat	dinosaur	dog	eagle
frog	insects	shark	shell	skeleton
snake	tiger	trout	whale	

2 🎧 Listen to the talk and then complete the table.

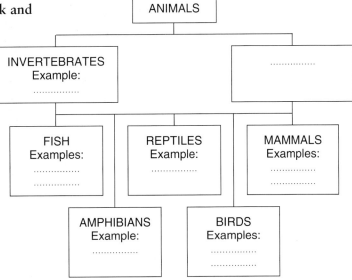

3 Complete the sentences with words and expressions from the box.

all	although	are related		be divided	
belong	different	except for		for example	
in many ways	kinds	main	most		only
or	others	several	typical		while

1. There are two .... of bank account: current and deposit.
2. Chinese looks like Japanese, but actually the two languages are very ....
3. Most Chinese words have one syllable, ... most Japanese words have two or more syllables.
4. British and American people are like each other ....
5. Some birds – .... robins – eat insects.
6. .... bats can fly, they are not birds.
7. Dogs can .... into two kinds: those that .... to wolves and those that are more like jackals.
8. Spaghetti is a .... Italian food.
9. Not .... people who live in the United States speak English.
10. February is the .... month that has only 28 days.
11. Cows .... to a group of mammals called herbivores, ... grass-eaters.
12. .... birds can fly.
13. There are .... different kinds of bicycles.
14. All European languages belong to the same family .... Finnish, Hungarian, Basque and one or two ....

4 Complete four or more of these sentences and put them together to make a text. (You can change the order of the sentences, and you can make other small changes if you like.)

1. There are .... kinds of ....
2. Most of them are ...., but some are ....
3. .... look like ...., but actually they are very different.
4. .... is a typical ....
5. .... belong to a group of .... called ....
6. The difference between .... and .... is that .... is/are ...., while .... is/are ....
7. .... is/are like .... in many ways.
8. .... is/are not at all like ....
9. All .... are ...., except for ....
10. Most .... can ....
11. .... is/are like ...., because ....
12. .... is/are like ...., although ....

5 Do one or both of these exercises.

A. Work in groups of four or five. You have just arrived in a spaceship from a distant world. You are studying the earth's civilisation, but you don't know much about it yet. The teacher will give you some everyday objects: try to decide what they are for.

B. Write the name of an everyday object on a piece of paper (or draw the object). Give the paper to another student. He/She has 30 seconds to describe the thing to the class *without using its name*, so that the class can decide what it is.

Learn/revise: backbone; bank account; current account; deposit account; bicycle; bird; civilisation; example; family; fish; group; insect; kind; object; skeleton; world; belong (to); decide; divide (into); draw (drew, drawn); fly (flew, flown); different; distant; European; everyday; main; related (to); typical; actually; only; all; most; several; although; while; except for; for example; in many ways.

Summary D

Simple Past and Present Perfect Progressive

Speaker is not at school any more:

'I **did** English at school for three years.'
'I **didn't do** physics at school.'
'I **went** to school for eight years.'

Speaker is still at school:

'I've **been doing** maths at school for seven years.'
'I've **been doing** chemistry for a year.'
'I've **been going** to school for eight years.'

Simple Past and Past Perfect

When I was a child, I **often dreamt** of being a space explorer.   (... I had often dreamt ...)
I will never forget the day when the Principal **told** me that I **had passed** my final exams.
On my first mission, I **went** to visit a small planet in star system 18B.
The planet **had stopped** sending out radio signals some months before.

I wish; if only

Talking about the present:

I wish it **was/were** cooler/warmer.
I wish I **could** sing.
I wish I **had** more money/time.
If only I **spoke** better English!
If only I **knew** more people!
If only people **were** more honest!

Talking about the future:

I wish the government **would do** something about unemployment.
If only somebody **would write** me a letter!

Talking about the past:

I wish I **had been** nicer to my parents when I was younger.
I wish I **had listened** to my mother's advice.
If only I **had taken** a different job!
If only I **had not got** married!

Relative clauses with *whose*

Jake Thong is an artist **whose** pictures sell for thousands of pounds.
An unsuccessful builder is one **whose** houses fall down.

Ways of identifying people and things

the girl **in the corner**
the girl **sitting in the corner**
the girl **who is sitting in the corner**

the man **in a red T-shirt**
the man **wearing a red T-shirt**
the man **who is wearing a red T-shirt**

the picture **over the door**
the picture **hanging over the door**
the picture **which hangs over the door**

Punctuation of identifying and non-identifying expressions

The biggest city in Bavaria is Munich.
Munich, in Bavaria, has a population of 1.25 million.

The village where I was born has changed a lot.
North Barton, where I was born, has changed a lot.

A person who lives in Glasgow is called a Glaswegian.
My sister, who lives in Glasgow, prefers Scotland to England.

The room which I'm sitting in at the moment isn't very well lighted.
Our kitchen, which I'm sitting in at the moment, isn't very well lighted.

Using *that* instead of *who(m)* or *which* in identifying clauses

The politician **whom/that** I admire most is Ann Wesk, the leader of the opposition.
   (BUT Ann Wesk, **whom** I greatly admire, is the leader of the opposition. NOT Ann Wesk, that I greatly admire, is ...)
The party **which/that** has been in power for the last five years is the Free Democratic Radical Conservative Party.
   (BUT NOT The Free Democratic ... Party, that has been in power ...)

Leaving out object relative pronouns in identifying clauses

The party I support is called the New Democratic Movement.   (= The party which/that I support ...)
   (BUT The New Democratic Movement, **which** I support, is led by Arnold Kronsk. NOT The New Democratic Movement, I support, ...)
The party our MP belongs to is called the New Radical Alliance.   (= The party which/that our MP belongs to ...)

had better

had better

You'd **better come** in.
Perhaps I'd **better dry** my clothes.

ought

ought

If you want to meet people, you **ought to join** a club.
You **ought to go** dancing.

Physical descriptions

She has (she's got) blue eyes and brown hair.
a woman **with** blue eyes and brown hair
a blue-ey**ed**, brown-hair**ed** woman

a man **with** a beard
a girl **with** glasses

a woman **in** a blue dress
a man **in** a grey jacket

Hair: long, medium-length, short; straight, curly,
  wavy; blond(e), fair, dark, brown, black, red, grey,
  going grey, white, thinning; a beard, a moustache,
  bushy eyebrows
  He's (going) bald. He's got a bald patch.
Eyes: green, blue, brown, greenish-blue, grey
Nose: long, turned-up
Mouth: wide, generous; thin lips, full lips
Chin: pointed, firm, weak
Face: oval, round, long; high cheekbones; a scar
Forehead: high, low
Ears: big, small
Shoulders: broad, narrow
Build: thin, slender, slim, muscular, heavily-built,
  plump, overweight, fat
Height: tall, of medium height, short
Age: young, middle-aged, elderly, old; in his early
  thirties; in her mid-fifties; in their late forties
Expression: serious, cheerful, worried, friendly
General: good-looking, pretty, beautiful, handsome,
  attractive, plain; well-dressed, casually dressed
  He looks old. She looks like a businesswoman.

Suggestions

Why don't you ...?
Why not ...?
What/How about ...ing?
I/We think you should ...
You really ought to ...
You could/might ...
If I were you, I would ...
A good way to ... is to ...
The best way to ... is to ...
I/We think it's a mistake to ...
Stop ...ing and start ...ing

Spellings of /ɜː/

hers   bird   turn   word

Discussion

Definitely.	What do you mean by ...?
Certainly.	I suppose so.
Of course.	I don't know.
Do you think ...?	Perhaps.
Yes, I do.	I don't think so.
I certainly do.	I don't agree.
I agree.	Definitely not.
Yes, I think so.	Certainly not.
I'm not sure.	Of course not.
It depends.	

Some common prefixes and suffixes

anti-	**anti**-American, **anti**clockwise
dis-	**dis**appear, **dis**honest
mis-	**mis**understand, **mis**spell
over-	**over**eat, **over**work
re-	**re**write, **re**pay
un-	**un**happy, **un**able
under-	**under**paid, **under**valued
-ance	appear**ance**, insur**ance**
-en	wid**en**, strength**en**
-er	driv**er**, wait**er**
-ful	beauti**ful**, hope**ful**
-ise	computer**ise**, modern**ise**
-ish	redd**ish**, fatt**ish**
-less	hope**less**, care**less**
-ment	govern**ment**, advertise**ment**

Irregular verbs in Lessons D1–D8

INFINITIVE	PAST	PAST PARTICIPLE
choose	chose	chosen
draw	drew	drawn
feel	felt	felt
fly	flew	flown
grow	grew	grown
hang	hung	hung
hold	held	held
keep	kept	kept
lie	lay	lain
meet	met	met
rise	rose	risen
run	run	run
shine	shone	shone
shoot	shot	shot
sleep	slept	slept
take	took	taken
throw	threw	thrown
upset	upset	upset
wear	wore	worn
win	won	won

Vocabulary

Look through the 'Learn/revise' boxes at the end of
Lessons D1–D8.

Revision and fluency practice D

A choice of activities.

1 📼 Listen to the story and write down what you can remember. You will need these names.

Pytheas   Marseilles   Gibraltar   Mediterranean   Atlantic

2 Fast reading practice. Choose one of the first two cars advertised below. Then look quickly at the rest of the advertisement, and find the cheapest car with all of these:

– a similar colour to yours
– the same number of doors as yours
– similar accessories to yours
– a much lower mileage than yours

EVAN STABETSI
GUARANTEED USED CARS
Not just as good as new – BETTER than new!

This month's bargains
★★★★★★★★★★★★★★★★★★★★★★★

FORD ESCORT 1600, 5 door, powder blue, radio-cassette, sunroof, 34,000 miles, price **£3,900**.

BMW 318i, 4 door, red, electric windows, fog lamps, radio-cassette, 14,000 miles, price **£9,375**.

Renault 11 TSE, 5 door, white, sunroof, radio-cassette, electric windows, only 17,000 miles, **£6,300**.

Mercedes-Benz 500SEL, 4 door, diamond blue metallic, electric sunroof, air conditioning, 28,000 miles, **£27,500**.

Volvo 340DL, 5 door, deep red, sunroof, radio-cassette, only 8,000 miles, **£10,000**.

Toyota Carina GL, 5 door, sky-blue, radio-cassette, sunroof, central locking, 34,000 miles, **£3,200**.

MG Maestro 1.6i, 4 door, cherry red, air conditioning, central locking, 5,500 miles, **£8,200**.

Saab 900 Turbo, 5 door, Admiral blue, electric sunroof, radio-cassette, only 1,500 miles, **£12,200**.

Toyota Corolla GL, 4 door, green metallic, fog lamps, electric windows, radio-cassette, 35,000 miles, **£5,400**.

Jaguar XJ6 3.4 automatic, 4 door, ruby red, stereo radio-cassette, electric sunroof, electric windows, fog lamps, only 4,000 miles, **£19,650**.

Volvo 740DL, 4 door, deep red, radio-cassette, fog lamps, sunroof, electric windows, 6,000 miles, **£10,500**.

Peugeot 505, 5 door, royal blue, sunroof, radio-cassette, 4,200 miles, **£8,850**.

Vauxhall Carlton 2.0CD1, 4 door, dark red, fog lamps, radio-cassette, 125,000 miles, **£1,200**.

Metro 1.3L, 5 door, light blue, fog lamps, 17,000 miles, **£5,400**.

3 📼 Copy the table. Then listen to the recording and fill in the missing details.

	UNITED MOTORS BANGER	MASSCAR BURNUP
number of doors	5	
engine capacity		
number of gears		
petrol consumption		
acceleration 0–60		
top speed		
number of seats		1
accessories		
number of colours		
price		

4 Reading report. Talk to the class about what you have been reading recently in English.

5 How good is your memory? Stand with some other students in two lines, facing each other. Observe the students in the other line for one minute. Then go away and (without looking at them) see if you can remember and write down what everybody was wearing. Work together with the other students in your line.

6 'Twenty questions.' One student thinks of something. The student doesn't tell the others what it is; he/she only tells them that it is 'animal', 'vegetable', 'mineral' or 'abstract'. (For example: a leather handbag is animal; a newspaper is vegetable; a glass is mineral and a surprise is abstract.) The other students must find out what the thing is by asking questions (maximum twenty); the only answers allowed are *Yes* and *No*. Useful questions:

Can you eat it?
Can you wear it?
Is it made of wood/metal/glass/…?
Is it useful?
Can you find it in a house/shop/car/…?
Is it liquid?
Is it solid?
Is it hard/soft/heavy/light?
Have you got one of these?
Is there one in this room/building/street/…?
Is it manufactured?
Is it bigger/smaller than a cat/chair/car/…?

7 Work in groups of six to eight. In each group, imagine that you are in a doctor's waiting room. The last patient went in about half an hour ago and hasn't come out again. A conversation starts up …

8 In groups, invent a political party and write a campaign speech for it. Choose one person to make the speech and help him or her practise it. Listen to the other groups' speeches; then vote for the party of your choice.

9 Interview. Prepare questions for an interview with an English-speaking stranger. You must find out as much as possible about him/her, including details of his/her childhood, education, family, work, interests, and social and political attitudes. Prepare 'follow-up questions' for some of your questions. Examples:

'Do you like music?' 'Yes, I do.' 'What kind?'
'What's your job?' 'I'm a builder.' 'Do you like it?'

When you have prepared your interview, arrange for one or more English-speaking people to visit your class. (Get your teacher to help if necessary.) Interview the person/people, and write a report on what you have found out.

10 Write a really unwelcome letter to another student (from the tax office, from a boy/girlfriend, or from anybody else you like). He/She will reply.

11 🖭 Listen to the song. The words are on page 121.

12 Look at the cartoons. Tell other students what you think about them. Find out which are the most and least popular cartoons. Useful expressions:

I don't see the joke.
What do you think of this one?
This one's really funny.
It isn't funny at all.
I think it's wonderful/stupid.
It makes / doesn't make me laugh.

"There are garden plants and there are house plants. Now get back to the garden."

"There are two sides to every argument, George, and I've presented them both."

"You know, I think you're right."

Test D

LISTENING

1 Annemarie is an Australian who has lived and worked in Europe and the Far East for over ten years. In the recording, she explains why she left Australia, and how she feels about it now. Read the questions; then listen to the recording twice and answer the questions.

1. Which of these reasons did she have for travelling to Europe?
   a. She wanted to escape from Australia.
   b. Her parents were from Europe, and she wanted to see the places they came from.
   c. She was in love with somebody in Europe.
   d. She was interested in European history and culture.
   e. She had relatives in Europe.
   f. She thought she could get a better job in Europe.
2. What is her attitude to Australia now?
   a. She hates Australia.
   b. She still likes it, and would like to go back there to live one day.
   c. She doesn't feel at home there any more.
   d. She feels equally at home in Europe and Australia.

PRONUNCIATION

2 Do these sentences sound polite or rude? Listen, and mark them *P* or *R*.

1. Could you sit here, please?
2. Can I borrow your pen for a moment, please?
3. Could you lend me your book, please?

3 Look at these words. In each list, are all the underlined letters (or groups of letters) pronounced the same, or is one different? Write *S* if they are the same, or write the word with the different sound.

1. st<u>air</u>s   c<u>are</u>less   b<u>ear</u>d   f<u>air</u>
2. w<u>ear</u>   p<u>air</u>   sc<u>are</u>d   th<u>eir</u>
3. th<u>eir</u>   th<u>ere</u>   th<u>ey're</u>   w<u>ere</u>
4. b<u>ir</u>thplace   env<u>ir</u>onment   f<u>ir</u>m   b<u>ir</u>d
5. c<u>er</u>tainly   th<u>ir</u>d   p<u>ur</u>ple   w<u>or</u>ld
6. <u>ear</u>ly   f<u>ur</u>niture   ins<u>ur</u>ance   t<u>ur</u>n

GRAMMAR

4 Put each verb into the correct form.

1. My grandfather (*study*) physics at secondary school for four years.
2. Anne (*do*) physics at school for two years now, and hopes to go on to do it at university.
3. By the time my mother (*be born*), all her older brothers and sisters (*leave*) home.
4. When I was younger, I (*think*) I would like to be a doctor.
5. I wish I (*have*) longer holidays.
6. If only someone (*have*) Karel's telephone number!
7. I wish my parents (*stop*) treating me like a baby.
8. I wish I (*not say*) that to Emma yesterday.

5 Put an appropriate relative pronoun (*who(m)*, *whose*, *that* or *which*) into each sentence.

1. Ann Winterston, ... I admire enormously, has been nominated for this year's Nobel prize.
2. Marie Vigée-Lebrun was a 16th-century artist .... portraits were world famous.
3. Our parish council, ... is elected by all the voters in the village, has not got much power over local affairs.

6 Only put in a relative pronoun (*who(m)*, *that* or *which*) if it is absolutely necessary; otherwise just put a dash (–).

1. Isn't that the woman .... Diane Krantz interviewed on the telly last night?
2. It's important to keep fit, but you should choose a sport .... you enjoy as well.
3. Ms Senarath, ... the president has appointed to head the commission, has served on several committees before.
4. The Vegetable Liberation Front, ... was founded last year, has bombed three food stores this month.

7 Put in commas (,,) if they are needed.

1. San Antonio in central Texas has a large Mexican-American population.
2. Farmers still sometimes find bombs in the fields where World War I took place.
3. My aunt's apple orchard where several rare birds come to nest in the spring is often visited by scientists.
4. We use the room between the living room and the dining room as a study.

VOCABULARY

8 Write words for these meanings.

1. make more modern
2. make wider
3. paid too little
4. rather red
5. someone who drives
6. spell wrongly
7. the opposite of *appear*
8. without care
9. eat too much
10. write again

9 Give an example of something that is:

1. deep   2. dry   3. high   4. level   5. oval
6. popular   7. soft   8. warm

10 Give an example of something that can:

1. be saved   2. be thrown   3. be won   4. be worn
5. fly   6. rise   7. shine   8. take place

11 Divide this list into three groups of words and expressions according to meaning.

beard   chin   education   examination
eyebrow   family   forehead   friendship
husband   lip   marriage   primary school
relationship   secondary   subject   training

READING

12 Read the text and do the tasks that follow.

Examine the types of questions teachers ask in classrooms, and you will find that most of them are what might technically be called 'convergent questions', but which might more simply be called 'Guess what I'm thinking'
5   questions. Here are a few that will sound familiar:
What is a noun?
What were the three causes of the American Civil War?
What is the principal river of Uruguay?
What is the real meaning of this poem?
10 How many sets of chromosomes do human beings have?
     So, what students mostly do in class is guess what the teacher wants them to say. Constantly, they must try to supply the Right Answer. It does not seem to matter if the subject is English or history or science; mostly, students *do*
15 the same thing. And since it is indisputably recognized that the ostensible 'content' of such courses is rarely remembered beyond the last quiz, it is safe to say that just about the *only* things students learn in classrooms are the things they learn by *what they do* in classrooms. What are
20 these things? Here are a few among many, none of which you will ever find officially listed among the aims of teachers:
     – Passive acceptance is a more desirable response to ideas than active criticism.
25 – Discovering knowledge is beyond the power of students and is, in any case, none of their business.
     – Recall is the highest form of intellectual achievement, and the collection of unrelated 'facts' is the goal of education.
     – There is always a single, unambiguous Right Answer to a
30 question.
     Watch a man – say, a politician – being interviewed on television, and you are observing a demonstration of what both he and his interrogators learned in school: all questions have answers, and it is a good thing to give an
35 answer even if there is none to give, even if you don't understand the question, even if you are ignorant of the facts required to answer. Have you ever heard a man being interviewed say, 'I don't have the faintest idea', or 'I don't know enough even to guess'? One does not 'blame' men,
40 especially if they are politicians, for providing instant answers to all questions. The public requires that they do, since the public has learned that instant answer giving is the most important sign of an educated man.

(from *Teaching as a subversive activity* by Neil Postman and Charles Weingartner)

1. Which of the following sentences would the authors of the text agree with?

1. Discovering knowledge is beyond the power of students.
2. In most classrooms the most important thing is the Right Answer.
3. It is better in school to be passive and accept what teachers tell you.
4. Most of the questions teachers ask mean 'Guess what I'm thinking'.
5. It is very important for the world that politicians should be ready to give instant answers to questions.
6. Politicians always give an answer, even when they know nothing about the subject, because of what they and their public learnt at school.
7. Students learn more from what they say in class than from what they do in class.
8. What teachers really teach is not what they say they are teaching; what they really teach is a way of acting and thinking.

2. Choose three of these words from the text and write what you think they mean.

aims (*line 21*)
recall (*line 27*)
ignorant (*line 36*)
faintest (*line 38*)
requires (*line 41*)

LANGUAGE IN USE; WRITING

13 Choose one of these tasks to do. Write at least 150 words.

1. Write a description for your teacher of a beautiful place where you would love to be. Try to make your teacher feel what it is like to be in that place.
2. Write a letter of advice to a teenage friend (decide if it is a boy or a girl) who wants to go out more and meet more people, but who is terribly shy.
3. Think of a person you know and describe the person's appearance as completely as possible, so that an artist could draw the person from your description.

SPEAKING

14 Work with another student. You must choose three everyday objects to describe to your partner *without saying the name of the object.* Your partner will do the same. If you can't guess immediately what your partner's object is, ask him/her questions that can be answered *Yes* or *No* until you can guess.

E1 They saw wonderful things

Grammar (tenses); vocabulary; reading and listening for gist and for detail; writing a story from several sources.

Work in groups. Your job is to write the story of Marco Polo's journey to China. You can get the information you need:

– from the map
– from the pictures
– from the tape-recording 📼
– from the grammar exercise
– from the teacher
  (if you ask the questions
  in correct English).

You don't need to include all the information in your story – just put in what you think is most important.

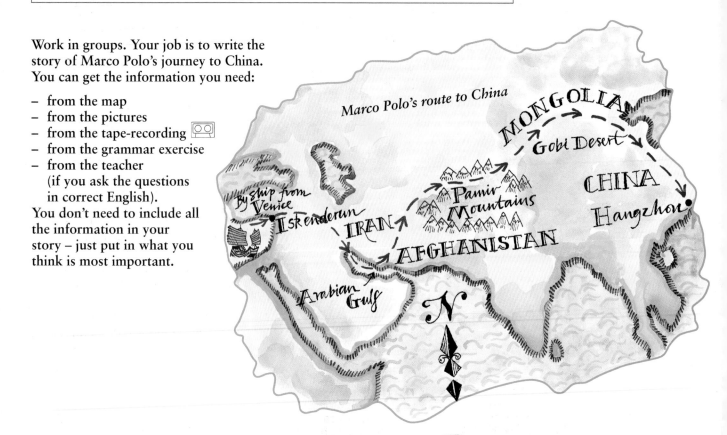

Marco Polo's route to China

MONGOLIA
Gobi Desert
CHINA
Hangzhou
Pamir Mountains
IRAN
AFGHANISTAN
By ship from Venice
Iskenderun
Arabian Gulf
N

They saw wonderful things unknown in Europe.

a kind of stone that would burn (coal)

a liquid that came out of the ground and could be used as fuel for lamps (petroleum)

a mineral like cloth that wouldn't burn (asbestos)

enormous nuts with juice inside (coconuts)

Marco was surprised to find that China was more civilised than Italy.

Cities like Hangzhou had good roads

public parks

canals with bridges that ships could go under

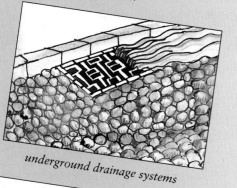

underground drainage systems

a police force   a fire brigade   a postal service

GRAMMAR EXERCISE

Put in the correct tense (Simple Past, Past Progressive or Past Perfect).

1. After the two brothers (*return*) from China, they (*plan*) a new journey.
2. While they (*travel*) to China, Marco (*keep*) a diary.
3. Marco (*become*) ill while they (*cross*) Afghanistan.
4. This (*delay*) them for a year.
5. After Marco (*recover*), they (*go*) on.
6. Several times they (*have*) to change their route to avoid wars and bandits.
7. In China, Marco (*become*) the emperor's friend and adviser.
8. While he (*work*) for the emperor, he (*travel*) all over the Far East on imperial business.
9. The Polo family (*stay*) in China for twenty years.
10. In 1292, when the emperor (*get*) old, they (*decide*) to return home.
11. When they (*arrive*) in Venice, they (*tell*) everyone about their experiences, and Marco (*publish*) his diary.
12. But people (*think*) they (*lie*). Nobody (*believe*) their fantastic stories about the strange countries they (*visit*) and the wonderful things they (*see*).

QUESTIONS

You can get this information from the teacher if you ask questions in correct English:

1. The names of Marco Polo's father and uncle.
2. Their reason for making the first trip to China.
3. Marco's age when he left Venice.
4. The length of the journey.
5. The date when they arrived in China.
6. The countries to which Marco Polo travelled when he was working for the emperor.

Learn/revise: adviser; age; Asia; business; city; cloth; coal; country; date; diary; experience; fuel; (the) ground; journey; juice; lamp; length; liquid; market; member; mineral; nut; reason; route; ship; stone; trip; war; arrive; avoid; become (became, become); burn (burnt, burnt); cross; decide; delay; get (for changes) (got, got); keep (kept, kept); lie (lying); plan; reach; record; recover; return; spend (spent, spent); stay; take (time) (took, taken); travel (travelled); visit; welcome; civilised; enormous; ill; official; wonderful; south-east; inside; fire brigade; police force; postal service; the Far East.

E2 Focus on systems

A choice of exercises: five difficult conjunctions; contrastive stress; *this/that/these/those, here/there, come/go.*

GRAMMAR: FIVE CONJUNCTIONS

1 *Although.* Look at the examples and then change the sentences in the same way.

Whales look like fish, but they are mammals.
'Although whales look like fish, they are mammals.'

Bats can fly, but they are not birds.
'Although bats can fly, they are not birds.'

1. She's a famous actress, but she's very shy.
2. I understand your feelings, but I don't agree with you.
3. It was very late, but we went out.
4. I like my work, but I prefer doing nothing.
5. Switzerland, Japan and Britain are all democracies, but their systems of government are very different.
6. It was raining, but we decided to go for a walk.

2 *Although* (continued). Complete one or more of the sentences.

1. Although I look ..., actually I'm ...
2. I don't know much about ..., although we study/studied it at school.
3. I'm not much good at ...ing, although I really like it.
4. Although I like this country, I don't think much of ...
5. Although I like languages, I find ... difficult.
6. Although ...
7. ..., although ...

3 *So that.* Look at the examples and complete the sentences.

*A Frenchman went on holiday to California. He bought a bus pass **so that** he could travel cheaply. He took all his luggage in a backpack, **so that** he could get around easily.*

1. He took a tent ...
2. He took a camera ...
3. He took plenty of money ...
4. He took an English dictionary ...
5. He took swimming trunks ...
6. He took a pack of cards ...
7. He took a pen and paper ...
8. He took ...

4 *In case.* Look at the examples, and then complete the sentences with *if* or *in case.*

*I'll stay at home **if** it rains.*
*I'm going out, but I'm taking my umbrella **in case** it rains. (= ... because it might rain.)*

*I hate going downstairs **if** I get thirsty in the night.*
*So I like to take a glass of water up to bed **in case** I get thirsty in the night. (= ... because I might get thirsty.)*

1. We have insurance .... the house catches fire.
2. A driver has to have insurance .... he/she is in an accident.
3. I'll give you a ring tomorrow .... I have time.
4. I'm taking some biscuits up to bed .... I feel hungry in the night.
5. .... Ann comes, let's take her out to dinner.
6. He always carries a dictionary .... he finds a word he doesn't know.
7. Let me know .... you need any help.
8. Close the windows before you go out .... it starts raining.
9. Some people believe that .... you break a mirror you'll have seven years' bad luck.
10. Test the bath water before you get in, ... it's too hot.

5 *Whether.* Look at the examples and then complete two or more of the sentences.

*I'm not sure **whether** I like this music or not.*
*I haven't decided **whether** I want to go to London or Scotland next weekend.*
*Can you tell me **whether** this is the right train for Belfast (or not)?*

1. I'm not sure whether I like ...
2. I'm not sure whether I ... or not.
3. I haven't decided whether I want to ...
4. Can you tell me whether ...?
5. I wonder whether ... will ... or not.

6 *Unless.* Look at the examples and then complete two or more of the sentences.

*He'll take the job **unless** the pay's too low.*
    *(= ... **if** the pay's **not** too low.)*
***Unless** I'm lucky, I'm going to fail my exams.*
    *(= If I'm **not** lucky, ...)*

1. I'll ... next weekend unless ...
2. Unless I get some more money soon, ...
3. ... unless I phone you.
4. Unless the government ..., people will ...
5. I won't marry you unless ...

PRONUNCIATION: CONTRASTIVE STRESS

7 📼 Look at the dialogue: six people are ordering dessert in a restaurant. Which words do you think are especially stressed? Check with the recording and practise the dialogue.

W: What would you like for dessert?
A: I'll have a lemon ice cream.
B: I'll have a strawberry ice cream.
C: And I'll have some strawberry tart.
D: I think I'll have apple pie and cream.
E: Apple pie without cream for me, please.
F: Apple tart, please.
W: Coffee to follow?
A: White coffee with sugar, please.
B: Black with sugar, please.
C: Black without sugar.
D: I'll have white without sugar, please.
E: Can I have tea without sugar, please?

Which words do you think are especially stressed in this text?

We speak two kinds of English in my family: I speak British English, but my wife speaks American English. We speak some other languages, too. I speak German and French, while my wife speaks Spanish and French. My sister speaks Spanish and Russian, and my elder brother speaks Russian and a little Chinese. My younger brother speaks quite good Chinese.

"They call me waiter, but you've been waiting for half an hour."

"Look! They overcook the turkey individually at your table."

VOCABULARY: *THIS* AND *THAT*, ETC.

8 Choose the right word.

THIS
THESE
HERE
COME

THAT
THOSE
THERE
GO

1. I'd like to *come/go* away for a holiday soon.
2. You must *come/go* and see us again soon.
3. Let's all *come/go* and see Harry this weekend.
4. I've found something very strange. *Come/Go* and have a look.
5. I'm afraid Mrs Barnes is busy just now. Could you *come/go* back tomorrow morning?
6. 'Newport 361428.' 'Hello, is Helen *here/there*?' 'I'm sorry. She's not *here/there* just now.'
7. 'Moreton 71438.' 'Hello, *this/that* is Judith. Is *this/that* Paul?'
8. 'Do you know Canada?' 'No, I've never been *here/there*.'
9. '*This/That* is a nice flat. And I like the furniture.'
10. 'I'm glad you like it. I can't remember – have you been *here/there* before?'
11. 'No, *this/that* is the first time.'
12. 'Have you seen *this/that*?' 'What?' 'In *this/that* morning's paper. Look!'
13. I'll never forget *this/that* morning, nearly twenty years ago, when I first saw Mrs Newton.
14. Listen to *this/that*. You'll enjoy it. It's a great piece of music.
15. Who's *this/that* over there?
16. Jane, I'd like you to meet Peter. Peter, *this/that* is my friend Jane.
17. 'How's your lunch?' 'OK, but I don't like *these/those* potatoes much.'
18. Who were *these/those* people you were with last night?
19. Do you remember *these/those* cheese pies we used to buy in Parikia?
20. 'How do you like *these/those* trousers?' 'They really suit you.'

Learn/revise: accident; backpack; bird; biscuit; camera; (black/white) coffee; cream; democracy; dessert; dictionary; feelings; fish; government; insurance; lemon; (bad) luck; luggage; mammal; mirror; pack of cards; pay (*noun*); strawberry; sugar; swimming trunks; system; tent; umbrella; break (broke, broken); carry; catch fire (caught, caught); decide; fail (an exam); get around (got, got); hate; test; wonder; famous; hungry; shy; thirsty; actually; cheaply; although; whether; so that; unless; in case; give sbdy a ring (gave, given); go for a walk.

E3 Looking forward

The language of prediction; *will/shall*; Future Perfect; present tenses referring to the future; reading skills: guessing unknown words; discussion.

1 📼 Read the texts without a dictionary and listen to the recording. Say what you think of the two poems and the song. Do you like or dislike any of them? Do you have any other reactions?

WHEN YOU ARE OLD

When you are old and grey and full of sleep,
And nodding by the fire, take down this book,
And slowly read, and dream of the soft look
Your eyes had once, and of their shadows deep;
How many loved your moments of glad grace,
And loved your beauty with love false or true,
But one man loved the pilgrim soul in you,
And loved the shadows of your changing face;
And bending down beside the glowing bars,
Murmur, a little sadly, how Love fled,
And paced upon the mountains overhead,
And hid his face amid a cloud of stars.

(W.B. Yeats)

When you are old and grey

Since I still appreciate you,
Let's find love while we may,
Because I know I'll hate you
When you are old and grey.
So say you love me here and now,
I'll make the most of that;
Say you love and trust me,
For I know you'll disgust me
When you're old and getting fat.

Your teeth will start to go, dear,
Your waist will start to spread.
In twenty years or so, dear,
I'll wish that you were dead.
I'll never love you then at all
The way I do today,
So please remember, when I leave in December,
I told you so in May.

(from a song by Tom Lehrer)

WARNING

When I am an old woman I shall wear purple
With a red hat which doesn't go, and doesn't suit me,
And I shall spend my pension on brandy and summer gloves
And satin sandals, and say we've no money for butter.
I shall sit down on the pavement when I'm tired
And gobble up samples in shops and press alarm bells
And run my stick along the public railings
And make up for the sobriety of my youth.
I shall go out in my slippers in the rain
And pick the flowers in other people's gardens
And learn to spit.

You can wear terrible shirts and grow more fat
And eat three pounds of sausages at a go
Or only bread and pickle for a week
And hoard pens and pencils and beermats and things in boxes.

But now we must have clothes that keep us dry
And pay the rent and not swear in the street
And set a good example for the children.
We must have friends to dinner and read the papers.

But maybe I ought to practise a little now?
So people who know me are not too shocked and surprised
When suddenly I am old and start to wear purple.

(Jenny Joseph)

100

2 Choose one of the texts and read it again, still without a dictionary. Write down all the words you don't know. Can you guess what any of them might mean? Underline the words you have guessed, and compare your guesses with another student who is reading the same poem. Then use a dictionary to check any words that you want to.

3 Write your own 'warning' or 'promise' about what you will do (and not do) when you're old. Use some or all of the following structures.

When I am old, I will …
I will …
I will not …
I will (not) be able to …
I will (not) have to …
I (don't) suppose I will …
I doubt if I will …
I am sure I will (not) …
I might …

(NOTE: Instead of *I will*, you can use *I'll* or *I shall* if you want to.)

4 Choose five of the following predictions, and say whether or not you agree with them. Add three more predictions of your own.

IN THE YEAR 3000
Everybody will speak the same language.
Books will no longer exist.
There will be no religion.
Most animals and birds will be extinct.
People will be taller and stronger.
People will live much longer than now.
Large parts of the world will be uninhabitable.
The world will be seriously overcrowded.
Families will be limited to one child.
There will be a world government.
There will be no such thing as money.
There will be no shops.
Private houses will not exist.
Private cars will not exist.
Nobody will work.

BY THE YEAR 3000
War will have come to an end.
The world's climate will have completely changed.
Political systems will have become more democratic.
We will have colonised other planets.
The problem of world hunger will have been solved.

Useful expressions and structures:
I don't think … will (have) …
I don't suppose … will (have) …
I'm sure/certain that … will (not) …

It's …	likely not very likely unlikely very probable quite probable possible	that … will …

5 Work in groups. Each group must choose one of the following subjects, and spend a quarter of an hour discussing it. Then a member of each group must tell the class what the group has decided.

What sort of life do old people have in your society? How could society make things better for old people?
What will the housing situation be like in 50 years' time?
What kind of games and sports will people play in 200 years?
How will shopping work in 50 years' time? Will people still use money? If not, what will they use instead?
What do you think education will be like 100 years from now?
What will … be like in 100 years? (Your choice of subject.)

"Then, one day, they'll ask themselves how those big, heavy stones got to the top of the giant pyramids."

shall and *will*	contracted negatives
I shall/will (I'll)	won't
you will (you'll)	shan't
he/she/it will (he'll *etc.*)	
we shall/will (we'll)	
they will (they'll)	

Learn/revise: alarm; beauty; bell; climate; education; game; glove; hunger; member; planet; problem; promise; religion; sandal; shadow; situation; slipper; society; stick; waist; warning; youth; exist; pick flowers; solve; spit (spat, spat); democratic; (un)likely; limited; overcrowded; private; public; uninhabitable; seriously; forward; instead; no longer; no such thing as; a quarter of an hour; in 50 years; in 50 years' time; 50 years from now; by the year 3000.

E4 Coincidences

Reading skills: reading for gist, reading for main ideas, guessing words from context; vocabulary choice; writing skills: writing and polishing a narrative.

1 In 1989 the *Observer* newspaper asked readers to send in their experiences of coincidences in their own lives. The next year they published some of the stories they received. Here are three of them. Read them without a dictionary. Which one is the most interesting?

1

A 'SMALL WORLD' encounter occurred in 1936 to **Peter Elstob**, novelist, historian and vice-president of PEN. Twenty years old at the time, he was window-gazing outside Lillywhite's Piccadilly sports shop when a middle-aged American who had been standing beside him asked him for some advice.

Would it be all right to send a tennis racket to the daughter of the family he had been staying with or would they consider it over the top? Elstob reassured him.

The American then went on to say he had been unable to find the address of a young man to whom friends in the United States had asked him to deliver a letter. The man was not in the telephone directory, and nobody he had asked had been able to help him.

'He showed me the letter; it was addressed to me. I can still remember the shock, the shiver, the wild suspicion that he must have known who I was. But that was impossible.'

It was not a significant coincidence, Elstob comments. All the writer wanted was his address, and he never met the American again. 'I have no explanation other than one in a million chances do come up one in a million times.'

2

FLYING out to the South of France to interview Graham Greene in the summer of 1988, **Graham Lord**, Literary Editor of the *Sunday Express*, found that Greene had booked him into a hotel in Antibes; but because a friend, Julian ("Jules") Lewis, had decided to come with him, they cancelled the booking in order to stay instead at Jules's favourite hotel, the Auberge du Colombier in Roquefort-les-Pins.

'At the hotel Jules and I were lying by the swimming pool when there was a telephone call from London for "Mr Lewis". It turned out to be another Mr Lewis who was also lying by the pool, and he turned out to be an old schoolfriend of Jules whom he had not seen for 30 years. They started reminiscing about their schooldays, and I was introduced to the other Mr Lewis's wife, another "Jules" Lewis (Juliet), whom I knew immediately was going to be very important in my life.

'It was love at first sight. Eight weeks later she left her husband, and I left my wife, and we have since lived together with astonishing happiness. For both of us it was like coming home.'

3

MRS MAY BADMAN has often had intuitive experiences, 'knowing when a good or bad thing is going to happen, or a person I know well is going to ring, write or visit'; but one episode sticks out in her mind.

'I often used the diesel train to town and for years had the habit of getting into the first carriage.

'One morning I was, as usual, at the end of the platform, but just as the train came in, I suddenly found myself running down the platform towards the end of the train. When the train stopped I was more than half-way down.

'When it arrived at St Pancras the train crashed into the buffers. In my carriage we were all thrown about but not seriously hurt. I was very shaken, and when I left the carriage and walked the length of the train, the further along I got toward the front the worse the situation of the passengers was, and near the front people were bleeding and crying. Five ambulances were called to take away the injured.'

2 **What are the main points? Do the tasks; you can look back at the stories.**

1. *First story:* here is a summary of the first story, with mistakes. Copy it, correcting the mistakes.

   Peter Elstob is an American who was approached by a stranger outside a sports shop. The man wanted advice on where to buy a tennis racket. Then the man showed Elstob a letter that had been received by some friends in America; the friends wanted him to find out who had written it. The letter was from Elstob.

2. *Second story:* put one or more words in each gap.

   Graham Lord travelled to ......1...... on business. He went with a ......2......, 'Jules' Lewis, and changed ......3...... to stay at Mr Lewis's ......4...... . An ......5...... of Jules Lewis, also called Lewis, was also staying at ......6...... . Graham Lord and the schoolfriend's ......7...... (whose nickname was ......8......) fell in ......9......, and they are still ......10...... .

3. *Third story:* finish the summary.

   Mrs May Badman often took the train ... One morning when the train came in she began ... When the train arrived ... The people in Mrs Badman's carriage ..., but ...

3 **Guessing words from context. Do the tasks for each story.**

1. *First story:* look back at the text, and match the words and expressions in the first column with their meanings in the second column. (There are too many meanings.)

   a. encounter
   b. over the top
   c. shiver
   d. suspicion

   1. accidental meeting
   2. idea about the cause of something
   3. nervous laughter at something that is not really funny
   4. shaking that happens when someone is afraid or shocked
   5. too cheap for the situation
   6. too expensive for the situation

2. *Second story:* find words or expressions in the second story that seem to mean:

   a. happened by chance to be
   b. surprising

3. *Third story:* what do you think these words and expressions mean in the story?

   sticks out, carriage, buffers, shaken

4. *All the stories:* write down a list of five words that you would like to look up in the dictionary. Show your list to a partner, and discuss your reasons for choosing the words you did. Look the words up after class.

4 Write at least 100 words about one of these subjects. When you finish, exchange stories with another student. Read the other student's story and ask two or more questions about what happened.

1. Write about a coincidence that has happened to you or someone you know.
2. Write about a big surprise in your life (good or bad).
3. Write about a memorable trip you have made (pleasant or unpleasant).

5 Look back at the stories from Exercise 1. Notice how the devices in the box are used. Discuss with your partner from Exercise 4 whether you can improve your story by using some of these devices.

> Past Progressive tense + *when* + Simple Past tense
> Past Perfect tense
> Dividing the story into paragraphs
> Direct speech (with ' ') and reported speech
> Relative clauses with *who, whom, that,* and with no pronoun
> Conjunctions like *and, but*

> **Learn/revise:** advice (*uncountable*); ambulance; booking; carriage; coincidence; encounter; habit (of); passenger; shiver; surprise; suspicion; telephone directory; approach; astonish; bleed (bled, bled); book; cancel (cancelled); crash; deliver; hurt (hurt, hurt); interview; occur (occurred); publish; turn out; favourite; injured; middle-aged; shaken; worse; further; seriously; as usual; love at first sight.

E5 I don't know much about art, …

Listening for gist; asking for and giving opinions about art; -er and -or words; passive questions with final prepositions; pronunciation of the letter r.

1 [cassette icon] Listen to the first part of the recording. The people are all talking about the same picture. Which one do you think it is?

Now listen to the second part. Which picture are they talking about?

2 Do you like any of the pictures? Which do you like best (or least)? What kind of pictures do you like?

The National Gallery London

3 Match words from the two columns.

statues   composer
plays   potter
films   writer
music   actor
books   sculptor
pottery   director
pictures   painter

Can you find words ending in *-er* for the following?

a person who drives
somebody who dances
a person who climbs
a person who builds houses
somebody who looks after a garden
somebody who plays football
a person who sings
somebody who runs
somebody who cleans

4 🔲 Pronunciation. The letter *r* comes in all of these sixteen words. In standard British English, *r* is only pronounced in six of the words. Which six?

picture   potter   pottery   painter   runs
hurry   first   part   far   real   try   word
fourteen   foreign   tired   modern

Pronounce these words and expressions.

ordered   wondered   answered   preferred
remembered   covered   mattered

painter has   painter takes   painter makes
painter leaves   painter covers
painter asks   painter empties
painter isn't   painter orders
painter understands

5 Work in groups. Write ten questions ending in *by* about books, films, music *etc.* Then test other students. Examples:

*Who was **The Third Man** directed by?*
*Who was **Tom Sawyer** written by?*
*Who was **Carmen** composed by?*

6 Work with three or four other students. Choose one of the questions below. You must make sure that all the other students in your group express their opinions on the question you have chosen.

1. What is your favourite painting, or photograph, or film, or television programme? What is it that makes you like it so much?
2. What do you think of national museums? Should their contents be sold and the money used to help old people, poor people, *etc.*?
3. If you were a painter or sculptor yourself, what sort of things would you like to paint/sculpt?
4. Do you think that the statues and other works of art that have been taken from places like Greece and Nigeria should be returned to them? Why (not)?
5. Would you rather live in a beautiful old building with no lift or central heating, or a dull-looking building with every modern convenience? Why?
6. Do you think all art makes a political statement? Why (not)?

but I know what I like

Learn/revise: actor; art; composer; contents; director; lift; museum; painter; painting; picture; play; potter; pottery; sculptor; snow; statement; statue; writer; clean; compose; direct; look after; paint; political; return; sculpt; bright (colours); dull-looking; favourite; modern; national; real; central heating; every modern convenience; television programme; work of art.

E6 Focus on systems

A choice of exercises: relative *what* and the difference between *what*, *which* and *that*; spelling and pronunciation: vowel differences; hearing unstressed syllables; how to say expressions with numbers.

GRAMMAR: RELATIVE *WHAT* AND *WHICH*

1 Rewrite the sentences using *what*. Examples:

The thing that I need is something to eat.
What I need is something to eat.

You mustn't believe **the things that** are in the newspapers.
You mustn't believe what is in the newspapers.

1. Did you get the things that you wanted for Christmas?
2. I'm sorry about the thing that I said to you last night.
3. That child will have to pay for the things that he broke.
4. Take the things that you want.
5. Language is the thing that makes people different from animals.
6. The thing that really annoys me about Jane is her selfishness.
7. The thing that I like about Pete is his sense of humour.

What I need is something to eat.

You mustn't believe what is in the newspapers.

2 Complete two or more of these.

What I need now is ...
What I like about ... is ...
What I love about ... is ...
What I dislike about ... is ...
What I hate about ... is ...

3 We use *that*, not *what*, in these three sentences. What makes them different from the sentences in Exercises 1 and 2?

1. I'll give you everything that you want.
   (... ~~everything what you want.~~)
2. You believe me – that's all that matters.
   (... ~~all what matters.~~)
3. Nothing that you say will make me change my mind. (~~Nothing what you say ...~~)

106

4 We use *which*, not *what*, in these two sentences. What makes them different from the sentences in Exercises 1 and 2?

1. He passed his exam, which surprised everybody. (~~... what surprised everybody.~~)
2. She cycles 50 miles every weekend, which is pretty good for a woman of 60. (~~... what is pretty good ...~~)

Connect the sentences with *which*. Examples:

He passed his exam. This surprised everybody.
*He passed his exam, **which** surprised everybody.*

She had to work very long hours. She hated it.
*She had to work very long hours, **which** she hated.*

1. It rained the whole weekend. This meant we couldn't go camping.
2. She got married very young. It worried her parents.
3. She never said 'Thank you' for her birthday present. This made me angry.
4. The room is very noisy. This makes it difficult to concentrate.
5. We have to wear suits in the office. I don't like this.
6. He wants to work in advertising. This doesn't seem a good idea to me.

5 Put in *what*, *that* or *which*.

1. Thanks – that's exactly .... I wanted!
2. The thing .... really upset me was the way she spoke to Philip.
3. He told her he loved her, ... wasn't true.
4. You can have everything .... is in the fridge.
5. .... I need is a large drink.
6. I was surprised by .... she did.
7. He said he wasn't hungry, ... is what usually happens when I cook him something nice.
8. I understood absolutely nothing .... he said.
9. .... you want and .... you're going to get are two different things.
10. It snowed a little at the weekend, ... caused complete disorganisation on the railways.

6 Fill in the gaps in the letter, and choose between *which*, *what* and *that*.

Darling Peter,
I'm sorry to have to tell you that Daddy has ...,
which/what means that we will all have to ...

I hope you got everything *what/that* you wanted for Christmas. Mum gave me a ..., *which/what* shows that she thinks I'm ... But still, it's just *what/that* I need when I go ...ing.

Annie ... a ... last week, *which/what* upset Mum so much that she ...

How is your ...? I didn't mean *what/that* I said about it – it's really very nice, in a strange sort of way, but it's a pity it ...
Love,
Geraldine

PRONUNCIATION: VOWELS; HEARING UNSTRESSED SYLLABLES

7 ▭ Which word in each group has a different vowel sound?

1. earth   world   wear   bird
2. game   waist   paid   said
3. glove   push   much   luck
4. youth   round   group   too
5. kind   build   fist   stick
6. caught   draw   all   most
7. seat   break   mean   week
8. weight   meant   break   main

8 ▭ How many words do you hear in each sentence? (Contractions like *don't* count as two words.)

VOCABULARY: NUMBERS, MEASUREMENT AND MONEY

9 Do you know how to say these expressions? Work in groups, and then check with the teacher.

100   121   1,436   1,000,000   1,000,000,000
$\frac{1}{2}$ $\frac{3}{4}$ $\frac{2}{3}$ $\frac{9}{10}$ 1.5   2.75
31 + 46   64 – 32   17 ¥ 81   100 ÷ 10
5%   30°C   90°F
£1.25 $2.40
40 km   70 kg   15 lb   25 m   60 ft
6 ft 3 in   4 gal   30 kph   75 mph
a 40 km journey   a £5 note   a 500 gm packet
the year 1964   the year 1400   May 14, 1728

10 See if you can read this aloud.

A man drives at 40 mph up to a 9,000 ft mountain pass. The distance from the bottom of the mountain to the pass is 7 miles. Having crossed the pass, the man averages 43 mph on the descent, which lasts 37.5 min and finishes at 2,000 ft. If the journey starts at 1,740 ft above sea level at 10 a.m., and the car's petrol consumption is 24 mpg, and the temperature drops 14°C during the climb, and if the man is 6 ft 3 in tall, 75 kg in weight and 51 years old, how much petrol is left in the tank at the end?

Learn/revise: hundred; thousand; million; billion; half; quarter; third; fraction; decimal; one point five (1.5); plus; minus; multiply; multiplied by; divide; divided by; per cent; degree; Celsius; Centigrade; Fahrenheit; pound; dollar; kilometre (US kilometer); kilo(gram); mile; foot; inch; gallon; kilometres/miles an hour / per hour; note; packet; average; temperature; distance; weight; tall.

You can say that again

Listening for gist; conversational expressions; grammar: tags, short answers, reply questions; pronunciation: /ɒ/, /ɔː/ and /əʊ/; speaking practice.

---

1 Listen to the conversation. Where exactly do you think it takes place?

LUCY: So I said, well, I said, if that's what you think, there's nothing much I can do about it, is there? I mean, you can't please everybody, can you?

MARY: No, dear, of course you can't. Well, frankly, I never expect anything from men. I mean, they're all the same, aren't they?

LUCY: You can say that again, Mary. Well, anyway, –

JOHN: Excuse me –

LUCY: – then he wanted to go and see one of his old girlfriends who lives in Birmingham – or rather, Wolverhampton.

JOHN: Excuse me, could I have a timetable for Manchester, please?

MARY: Did he really?

LUCY: So I said, you can go and see her if you like –

MARY: Yes.

JOHN: Hello!

LUCY: – but don't expect me to be here when you get back.

JOHN: Excuse me. You do work here, don't you?

MARY: Work here? Oh, yes, love. We do, yes. So what did he say to that?

JOHN: I'M SORRY TO INTERRUPT YOUR VERY IMPORTANT DISCUSSION, BUT COULD I HAVE A TIMETABLE, PLEASE, IF IT'S NOT TOO MUCH TROUBLE?

LUCY: Well, really! There's no need to shout, dear. We're not deaf. Here you are. Where was I? Oh, yes. So he said he was going to go anyway – at least, he didn't say he wasn't …

JOHN: No, a timetable for Manchester, not Birmingham. I want to go to Manchester, you see.

LUCY: I beg your pardon?

JOHN: Manchester, not Birmingham.

LUCY: Well, make up your mind, dear. Here you are. So then I went to stay with my sister for a week.

MARY: Did you? You said you might.

LUCY: And I met this boy.

MARY: You didn't!

LUCY: Yes, I did. A really nice guy. He's the manager of a music shop – at least, he's going to be next year.

JOHN: Excuse me. This is a timetable for Wolverhampton.

LUCY: Just a minute, dear.

ANNOUNCER: The next train to arrive at platform 3 will be the delayed 10.56 service for Manchester …

2 Here are some words and expressions from the conversation. Why are they used? Match each one with its meaning or purpose in the conversation.

WORDS AND EXPRESSIONS (1)
Well, anyway, ...
I mean
frankly
You can say that again.
Excuse me.
... if it's not too much trouble.

MEANINGS/PURPOSES (1)
'I want to interrupt politely.'
'I'm giving a reason for what I've said.'
'I strongly agree.'
'I want to get back to the main point ...'
'I'm going to give my opinion very directly.'
Sarcastic 'polite request', really meaning 'Why aren't you doing your job?'

WORDS AND EXPRESSIONS (2)
Well, really!
Here you are.
Where was I?
at least
or rather
I beg your pardon?
Just a minute.
... you see.

MEANINGS/PURPOSES (2)
'I can't remember what I was saying.'
'What did you say?'
'I'm giving you something.'
'I want to correct myself.'
'I don't want to pay attention to you yet.'
'I'm giving an explanation.'
'I think you're behaving badly.'
'What I said was more than the truth.'

---

3 Grammar. Complete the sentences.

1. There isn't a waiting-room here, ... there?
2. You don't want to travel on Sunday night, ... you?
3. These trains are really dirty, ... they?
4. 'I wasn't trying to travel without a ticket.' 'No, of course you ....'
5. 'You have fastened your safety belt, ... you?' 'Yes, I ....'
6. 'I'd love to go to India.' '.............. you really?'
7. 'I flew to Miami last week.' 'You ....!' 'Yes, I ....'
8. 'I'll be in Cardiff next month.' '.............. you? How long for?'
9. 'I'm trying to get a job as an air hostess.' '.............. you?' 'I certainly ....'
10. 'Excuse me. Can you help me with my luggage?' 'I'm sorry. I'm afraid I .... just at the moment.'
11. 'Don't forget your passport.' 'Don't worry. I ....'

4 🔲 Pronunciation revision. Some of these words are pronounced with the vowel /ɒ/ (like *not*); some are pronounced with /ɔː/ (like *north*); and some are pronounced with /əʊ/ (like *note*). Can you write the words in three lists according to their pronunciation? Can you add any more words to the lists?

all course don't go important job
long moment more no not or
platform record shop so sorry
strongly want wasn't what your

5 Look back at Exercise 1 and choose some words and expressions to learn. Show your list to another student, and explain the reasons for your choices.

6 Work in pairs or groups of three. Make up and practise a conversation in a station, in an airport, on a train or on a plane. Include two or more of the following: a delay, a pleasant surprise, an unpleasant surprise, a misunderstanding, an interesting meeting. Use some of the words and expressions from the lesson.

Learn/revise: air hostess; airport; discussion; girlfriend; guy; luggage; manager; meeting; misunderstanding; passport; plane; platform; safety belt; ticket; timetable; trouble; waiting-room; arrive (at); expect; fasten; fly (flew, flown); interrupt; make up your mind (made, made); meet (met, met); shout; stay (with sbdy); deaf; dirty; frankly; important; delayed; *the words and expressions from Exercise 2.*

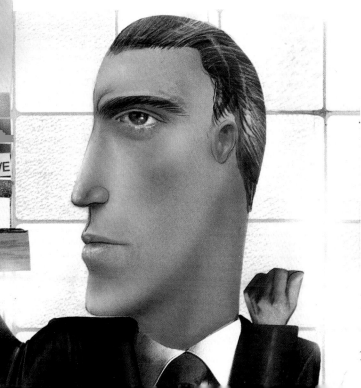

E8 Who invented writing?

Listening skills: note-taking; writing skills: summary; vocabulary.

1 Here are three different explanations of the origins of writing. Which one do you think is probably most correct?

1. According to archaeologists, the first writing was religious. 5,000 years ago, people in the Middle East invented signs for the names of their gods, and wrote them on clay tablets. Later, people started using writing for other purposes – for example, for keeping records and accounts.

2. Writing began 5,000 years ago in the Middle East with pictures on tablets made of baked clay. As time went by, more and more pictures were invented, until there was a picture for each word in the language.

3. About 10,000 years ago, people in the Middle East used small objects made of baked clay to keep records and accounts. Later, they made pictures of the objects on clay tablets, instead of using the objects themselves. Finally, this picture writing was used for other things besides accounting.

2 Copy the list of categories, and then put each of the words from the box into one of the categories (you can use your dictionary). Then underline the stressed syllables in the words of more than one syllable, and practise pronouncing all the words.

CATEGORIES:
Geography
What things can be made of
Research into ancient civilisations
Shapes of objects
Animals
Numbers

accounting	archaeologist	article	ball
cattle	check	Chinese	clay	cloth
cone	cylinder	disc	dog	excavate
flat	hollow	Iraq	journal	lamb
metal	Middle East	oil	pyramid
record	Roman	sheep	site	sphere
stone	theory	token	Western Asia
wood			

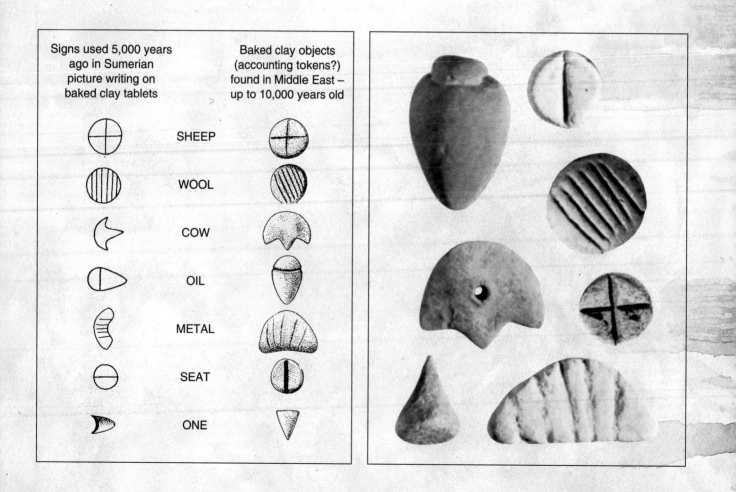

Signs used 5,000 years ago in Sumerian picture writing on baked clay tablets

Baked clay objects (accounting tokens?) found in Middle East – up to 10,000 years old

SHEEP
WOOL
COW
OIL
METAL
SEAT
ONE

3 Listen to the first half of a talk about the origins of writing. Write the numbers 1 to 17 on a piece of paper and then write down the words that go into the blanks in the notes.

Earliest writing by Sumerians (Middle East)
– Picture writing – 1,500 signs
– Written with ......1...... on ......2...... tablets → baked
Where from? Invented / developed?
– ......3...... knows, but ......4...... earlier writing found
Archaeologist D. Schmandt-Besserat has theory
– Writing perhaps from ......5...... and other ......6...... used for accounting
Many parts of world, people use ......7...... ......8...... for keeping records and accounts
– Examples: Romans, ...9......, today's shepherds in ......10......
In almost all ......11......, archaeologists have found objects made of ......12......
– Objects have many different ......13......
– Earliest ones ......14...... years old, seem to be tokens for ......15......
– Example: one shape for ......16......, used to check ......17...... and movements of animals.

Now work in small groups. Compare answers, and think of ways of shortening the notes. Example:

Earliest wrtg: Sumerians (MidEast)

4 Listen to the second half of the talk, and take notes.

5 Work in groups of three or four. Try to write a summary of the talk in 100–150 words. If you have the time, you can illustrate it.

Learn/revise: account; accounting; animal; article; Asia; ball; building; cattle; clay; cloth; dog; geography; god; Iraq; lamb; metal; Middle East; number; object; oil; origin; picture; purpose; record; research; shape; sheep; sign; stone; theory; wood; bake; check; invent; religious; Chinese; Roman; each; instead of.

Summary E

Simple Past and Past Progressive

While they **were travelling** to China, Marco Polo **kept** a diary.
In 1292, when the emperor **was getting** old, they **decided** to return home.

Simple Past and Past Perfect

After the two brothers **had returned** from China, they **planned** a new journey.
Nobody **believed** their stories about the strange countries they **had visited**.

shall and *will*

affirmatives	contracted negatives
I shall/will (I'll)	won't
you will (you'll)	shan't
he/she/it will (he'll *etc.*)	
we shall/will (we'll)	
they will (they'll)	

Talking about the future; probability

When I am old, I shall/will ...
I will not ...
I will (not) be able to ...
I will (not) have to ...
I'm sure/certain that ... will (not) ...
I (don't) suppose ... will ...
I (don't) think ... will ...
I doubt if I will ...
I am sure I will (not) ...
I might ...

It's	likely	that ... will ...
	not very likely	
	unlikely	
	very probable	
	quite probable	
	possible	

There will be ...

Future Perfect

By the year 3,000 war **will have come** to an end.
The world's climate **will have** completely **changed**.
Political systems **will have become** more democratic.
We **will have colonised** other planets.
The problem of world hunger **will have been solved**.

Tags, short answers and reply questions

You don't want to travel on Sunday, **do you?**
There isn't a seat free, **is there?**
You have got a ticket, **haven't you?**
These trains are dirty, **aren't they?**

'Don't forget your passport.' **'I won't.'**
'I wasn't travelling without a ticket.' 'Of course **you weren't.'**

'I'd love to go to America.' **'Would you?'**
'I'm trying to get a new job.' **'Are you?'** 'I certainly **am.'**

Irregular verbs in Lessons E1–E8

INFINITIVE	PAST	PAST PARTICIPLE
become	became	become
bleed	bled	bled
break	broke	broken
burn	burnt	burnt
catch	caught	caught
fly	flew	flown
hurt	hurt	hurt
keep	kept	kept
make	made	made
meet	met	met
spend	spent	spent
spit	spat	spat
take	took	taken

Relative *what*

What I need is something to eat.
(= **The thing that** I need is something to eat.)
You mustn't believe **what** is in the newspapers.
(= You mustn't believe **the things that** are in the newspapers.)

everything, all, nothing + that

I'll give you **everything (that)** you want.
(... everything what you want.)
You believe me – that's **all that** matters.
(... all what matters.)
Nothing (that) you say will make me change my mind. (Nothing what you say ...)

which referring back to a whole sentence

He passed his exam, **which** surprised everybody.
(... what surprised everybody.)
She cycles 50 miles every weekend, **which** is pretty good for a woman of 60.
(... what is pretty good ...)

Five conjunctions

Although whales look like fish, they are mammals.
Bats are not birds, **although** they can fly.

I'm not sure **whether** I like this music or not.
I haven't decided **whether** I want to go to London or
  Scotland next weekend.
Can you tell me **whether** this is the right train for
  Belfast (or not)?

I'm going out, but I'm taking my umbrella **in case** it
  rains. (= ... because it might rain.)
I like to take a glass of water up to bed **in case** I get
  thirsty in the night. (= ... because I might get
  thirsty.)

A Frenchman went on holiday to California. He
bought a bus pass **so that** he could travel cheaply. He
took all his luggage in a backpack, **so that** he could
get around easily.

He'll take the job **unless** the pay's too low.
  (= ... **if** the pay's **not** too low.)
Unless I'm lucky, I'm going to fail my exams.
  (= If I'm **not** lucky, ...)

---

come and go

You must **come** and see us again soon.
I've found something very strange. **Come** and have a
  look.

I'd like to **go** away for a holiday soon.
Let's all **go** and see Harry this weekend.

---

here and there

'Newport 361428.' 'Hello, is Helen **there**?' 'I'm
  sorry. She's not **here** just now.'

---

this and that

'Moreton 71438.' 'Hello, **this** is Judith. Is **that** Paul?'
This is a nice flat. And I like the furniture.
Listen to **this**. You'll enjoy it. It's a great piece of
  music.
I'll never forget **that** morning, nearly twenty years
  ago, when I first saw Mrs Newton.

Some conversational expressions and their uses

Getting back to the main point: Well, anyway
Giving a reason for what one has said: I mean
Giving one's opinion directly: frankly
Expressing strong agreement: You can say that again.
Interrupting politely: Excuse me.
Criticising somebody's behaviour: Well, really!
Giving something: Here you are.
Trying to remember what one was saying: Where
  was I?
Softening what one has said: at least
Correcting oneself: or rather
Asking for repetition: I beg your pardon?
Asking somebody to wait: Just a minute.
Giving an explanation: You see

Numbers, measurement and money

100	a/one hundred
121	a/one hundred and twenty-one
1,436	one thousand, four hundred and thirty-six
1,000,000	a/one million
1,000,000,000	a/one billion
$^1/_2$	a/one half
$^3/_4$	three quarters
$^2/_3$	two thirds
$^9/_{10}$	nine tenths
1.5	one point five
2.75	two point seven five
31 + 46	thirty-one plus forty-six
64 − 32	sixty-four minus thirty-two
17 ¥ 81	seventeen multiplied by eighty-one
100 ÷ 10	a hundred divided by ten
5%	five per cent
30°C	thirty degrees Celsius (Centigrade)
90°F	ninety degrees Fahrenheit
£1.25	one pound twenty-five (pence)
$2.40	two dollars forty / two dollars and forty cents
40 km	forty kilometres
70 kg	seventy kilos/kilograms
15 lb	fifteen pounds
25 m	twenty-five miles/metres/minutes
60 ft	sixty feet
6 ft 3 in	six feet/foot three inches
4 gal	four gallons
30 kph	thirty kilometres an/per hour
75 mph	seventy-five miles an/per hour
a 40 km journey	a forty-kilometre journey
a £5 note	a five-pound note
a 500 gm packet	a five-hundred-gram packet
(the year) 1964	nineteen sixty-four
(the year) 1400	fourteen hundred
May 14, 1728	May the fourteenth / the fourteenth of May, seventeen twenty-eight

---

Vocabulary

Look through the 'Learn/revise' boxes at the end of
Lessons E1–E8.

Revision and fluency practice **E**

> A choice of activities.

1 📼 Listen and follow the instructions.

2 📼 Read the text and then listen to the recording. There are some differences. See how many you can find.

Do you know how to make risotto? It's quite easy. First of all, you need some bacon, some garlic and an onion. Cut them up into small pieces, and then fry them very gently in butter for about three minutes.

I forgot to tell you. Before doing that, you should have warmed up some chicken stock. How much? Well, about a litre if you're cooking for four people. It should be nearly boiling.

When you've fried the garlic, bacon and onion for three minutes, add some rice. How much? I don't know. Enough. Fry it all gently for another minute.

Now pour on about a third of the hot stock, and turn up the heat a little under the frying pan. Stir from time to time. When the rice has absorbed the stock, add some more. Go on doing this until the rice won't absorb any more stock. This should take 15–20 minutes.

Now add the chicken. Sorry – didn't I tell you about the chicken? Yes, you need some roast chicken cut into small pieces. As much as you like.

Finally, add the mushrooms. So sorry – did I forget to tell you about the mushrooms? Ten minutes ago, you should have cut up some mushrooms and started frying them separately in butter.

Add salt, pepper and parmesan cheese. Start eating. It's delicious.

3 Half-dictation. The teacher will dictate the first half of some sentences; write what you hear, decide how to continue and write the rest.

4 The *yes/no* game. Work in groups. One person has to answer questions for one minute; the others ask him or her as many questions as possible. The person who answers must not say *yes* or *no*, or nod or shake his/her head.

5 Work in groups. Improvise (or prepare and act) a sketch for the following situation.

Mr or Mrs Allen is at home when somebody comes to the door trying to sell an encyclopaedia, a hoover, or something else. At exactly the same time, a neighbour calls to complain about the noise made by the children, and another neighbour calls to try to persuade Mr/Mrs Allen to start going to the local church. They all end up in the living room talking at the same time.

6 Are you a good detective? Read the following information, and then try to decide who was the thief. Write sentences about the others beginning 'X can't be the thief, because …'

Mr Cooper is a rich man who lives alone with a housekeeper, 30 minutes by car from the nearest town, Shiffley. His housekeeper is on holiday at the moment, staying with her sister in Wales. This morning a valuable old Chinese statue was stolen from Mr Cooper's study. It was there when he left to take the dog for a walk at 9.00, and it was gone when he returned at 9.15. The house was locked, and no windows were broken, so the thief must have had a key. The only people who have keys besides Mr Cooper and the housekeeper are his three nieces and his nephew. So the thief can only be Mary, Fiona (or her husband Gregory), Meryl (or her husband Christopher) or Jonathan. They all live and work in Shiffley. Here is what they said when questioned that evening.

Mary: I went to the greengrocer's first thing this morning: in fact, here's the parking ticket I got at five past nine. After that I went to Fiona's, at about half past, I imagine, and had a cup of tea with her. I left at about ten.

Fiona: I was home all morning. I had two visitors – Jonathan and then Mary. While Jonathan was there, Gregory phoned to say he was still at his mother's and wasn't coming home for lunch.

Gregory: I wasn't in Shiffley this morning. I went to visit my mother in Leeds the day before yesterday, and didn't get home until three o'clock this afternoon.

Meryl: I drove into the centre of Shiffley from home, and got to the office at about ten to nine. Christopher drove with me, as he always does, and I left him at the factory gate at about a quarter to nine. Jonathan got to the office a little late – about a quarter or twenty minutes past.

Christopher: Meryl and I drove in as usual this morning. I got to the factory at 8.47 – here's my ticket punched by the factory clock.

Jonathan: I walked to the office this morning. I stopped off at Fiona's at nine o'clock for a cup of tea, and to ask her about a tax problem. I stayed about ten minutes, and then I went to the office. Meryl was already there when I got there. Oh yes, while I was at Fiona's, Gregory phoned to say he wouldn't be home for lunch.

7 Prepare a short talk (not more than three minutes). In the talk, you have to explain to the class why they should believe in ghosts, visitors from space, werewolves, or something else of the same kind.

8 Work with some other students and prepare a modern version of a fairy story.

9 Questionnaire: are you a suitable person to have children? What sort of parent are you or would you be – strict, soft-hearted, or somewhere between the two? Answer the questions and check your score.

1. You have just been for a healthy five-mile run. Your pulse is somewhere over 200 and you wonder whether you are going to live. As you step out of the shower, your child walks into the bathroom, waves a paper in your face, and starts telling you all about the wonderful story he/she has just written about a rabbit with pink ears. As you stand there, dripping wet and searching for your glasses, what do you say? Something more like a, b or c?
   a. Lovely, dear. What's the rabbit's name?
   b. Super, darling. But could you just wait until I've dried myself and got dressed?
   c. If you and your bloody rabbit don't get out of the bathroom now you're both going down the toilet.
2. You have told your child, about seventeen times, to calm down and stop jumping on the living room furniture. Your child climbs up on to the window ledge and breaks a window. You tell the child that he/she will have to put two weeks' pocket money towards the cost of the repair, and you say that he/she can't go into the living room again for three days. Is this punishment:
   a. too strict?
   b. not strict enough?
   c. just right?
3. Your child is generally pretty well-behaved, but when his/her best friend Pat comes to play he/she turns into a wild beast. One day, they steal some lipstick and draw pictures all over the kitchen walls. Do you:
   a. say that Pat can never come again?
   b. try to explain to both of them why this is a bad thing to do?
   c. make them clean off the lipstick as well as they can.
4. What do you think about physical punishment?
   a. It's all right to smack a child occasionally for something very serious.
   b. Children need to be smacked when they're naughty – it's much better than telling them off.
   c. It's always wrong to smack a child.
5. Your child refuses to eat anything except crisps and ice cream. Do you:
   a. let him/her live on crisps and ice cream?
   b. make the child eat up everything that is on his/her plate at mealtimes?
   c. let the child have crisps and ice cream if he/she eats a certain amount of other food?
6. Your child is playing in the middle of the kitchen floor. When you say that you need to clean the floor, the child kicks and screams and refuses to move. Do you:
   a. forcibly move the child and his/her toys?
   b. explain to the child why it is important that you clean the floor now?
   c. put off cleaning the floor till later?
7. At weekends, your child watches an average of eight hours' TV a day. He/she is developing square eyes. Do you:
   a. have a discussion with the child, explaining why he/she should watch less TV?
   b. ration the child to three hours a day?
   c. let the child watch what he/she wants?
8. Your child's room looks like a rubbish dump that has been hit by a bomb. Do you:
   a. leave the child to tidy up the room when he/she feels like it?
   b. ask the child to tidy up the room?
   c. tell the child to tidy up the room?

(See score table and comments on page 121.)

10 The teacher will give you a card with the name of a present and a card with the name of an emotion. Act out what is on the cards so that the class can guess both the present and the emotion (for example, make it clear that you've been given a hat and you're delighted).

11 Here are three 'dictionary poems'. Can you see the reason for the name? Use your dictionary and see if you can make one.

Hullo
  hungry
    husband.

Be
  beautiful
    because
      bed.

Last
  late
    leaf.

12 🔘 Listen to the song. See how much you can understand. Then check on page 121.

Test E

LISTENING AND NOTE-TAKING

1 🔊 First make sure you understand the words in the box. You are going to hear a talk about the Shoshoni and their enemies the Minnetares. You will hear the talk twice. Make notes on it.

attack	berry	bison	capture	native
plains	root	seed	shelter	slave	tribe

GRAMMAR

2 Put the verbs into the correct tenses (Simple Past, Past Progressive or Past Perfect).

1. Just as the Shoshoni (*get*) up one morning, some Minnetares (*attack*) the camp.
2. The Minnetares (*attack*) Shoshoni camps before, but they (*never come*) this far west, so the Shoshonis (*be*) surprised.
3. When eleven-year-old Naya (*realise*) what (*happen*), she (*run*) to hide in some willow bushes.
4. After the noise (*die*) down, she thought she (*be*) safe; but a Minnetare dog (*run*) to the bush where she (*hide*) and (*bark*) loudly.
5. Naya and the other captives (*have*) to walk for weeks to the Minnetare village; while she (*walk*), Naya (*look*) round her and (*remember*) the path they (*take*).

3 Put an appropriate conjunction: *although*, *whether*, *in case*, *so that*, or *unless*.

1. Naya left the village after the Minnetares had gone to sleep, ... no one would look for her until morning.
2. She walked every day, never stopping before sunset .... she was ill, or the snow was too heavy.
3. When it began to snow heavily, she stopped and waited, ... she would not get lost.
4. Naya had secretly made an extra pair of moccasins to take on the journey, ... the ones she was wearing wore out.
5. All the time she was walking back to her people, Naya didn't know .... her parents and brothers were alive or dead.
6. .... she was only eleven years old, Naya managed to walk 1,800 km across plains and mountains to find her people.

4 Put in *that*, *which*, *what*, or *nothing* (–). In some cases *that* and (–) may both be possible.

1. After a while the Minnetares thought Naya was happy, ... made it easier for her to escape.
2. Getting back home was all .... mattered.

3. Naya didn't know .... had happened to her family.
4. .... Naya missed most about her Shosoni band was listening to stories around the fire.
5. Nothing .... Naya said could convince her friend Sacajawea to try and escape with her.
6. One day while escaping Naya found a freshly killed bison, ... was a great piece of luck.

LANGUAGE IN USE

5 Match each expression in group A with its conversational meaning or purpose in group B. Be careful: there are some extra items in group B.

A
1. Excuse me.
2. Here you are.
3. Just a minute, please.
4. Well, anyway …
5. Where was I?
6. You can say that again.

B
a. I can't remember what I was saying.
b. I don't want to pay attention to you yet.
c. I strongly agree.
d. I want to correct myself.
e. I want to get back to the main point.
f. I want to interrupt politely.
g. I'm giving a reason for what I've said.
h. I'm giving you something.

VOCABULARY

6 Match each word or expression in column A with a word or expression in column B.

A	B
catch	a walk
fire	belt
go for	brigade
instead	cent
make up	coffee
per	fire
pick	flowers
police	force
postal	of
safety	room
swimming	service
waiting	trunks
white	your mind

7 Write opposites for these words. The first one is done for you as an example.

1. book (*verb*) ..*Cancel*..
2. clean
3. get ill
4. on time
5. plus
6. private

116

8 Choose the correct word in each sentence.

1. Are *these/those* my glasses you're sitting on?
2. *There's/Here's* Rose over on the other side of the street.
3. I hope that my sister will *come/go* to visit me.
4. I'd like to *come/go* to New Zealand some day.

PRONUNCIATION

9 Which words are especially stressed? Example:

'Don't you speak French and German?' *'No, French and Russian.'*

1. 'Have you ever been to America before?' 'Not to North America.'
2. 'I'll have a steak and chips, please.' 'And I'll have a steak and salad.'
3. 'Hasn't Kate got five brothers?' 'No, five sisters.'

10 Look at these words. In each list, are all the underlined letters (or groups of letters) pronounced the same, or is one different? Write *S* if they are the same, or write the word with the different sound.

1. b<u>ir</u>d   <u>ear</u>th   res<u>ear</u>ch   d<u>ear</u>
2. <u>a</u>ge   s<u>ai</u>d   w<u>ai</u>t   w<u>eigh</u>t
3. interr<u>u</u>pt   l<u>u</u>ggage   n<u>u</u>t   rec<u>o</u>ver
4. b<u>ur</u>n   <u>ear</u>th   g<u>ir</u>lfriend   j<u>our</u>ney
5. c<u>ou</u>ntry   gr<u>ou</u>nd   sh<u>ou</u>t   s<u>ou</u>th
6. b<u>a</u>ll   h<u>a</u>lf   t<u>a</u>ll   w<u>a</u>lk

READING

11 Read the text quickly, for general meaning. Then choose the *five* most important facts of the story from the list and put them in the correct order.

JOHN BURKE is a free-lance writer, concentrating mainly on historical and topographical subjects but also producing light fiction. In the early 1970s he collaborated with his wife on three 'Victorian Gothic' novels; and for the third of them, having decided on a Fenland setting, they went to spend a week in Wisbech in order to get the 'feel' of the region.

'I had realised that a character would have to be made more substantial than at first envisaged. At that time I did not know Wisbech other than from passing round it; but having read somewhere that it had once been a thriving port, I invented a local merchant whose interests expanded until he could afford to have a couple of coasting vessels built for him, and built up contacts with Holland and Germany. He bought himself a house on the outskirts of the town, became Lord Lieutenant of the County, and ultimately Lord Mayor of London.

'On the day of our arrival we had planned to saunter round the town talking and simply soaking up the atmosphere. It began to snow heavily, and we sought refuge in the little local museum. I was on one side of the room when my wife called me across: "Look at this – here he is!"

'What she had discovered in a large glass case was the character I had invented. Every detail was correct, even down to the relevant dates, with only one exception: he did not become Lord Mayor of London – merely High Sheriff!'

(from *The Observer*)

a. Burke usually wrote about history and topography.
b. Mrs Burke found information about a real person who corresponded in nearly every detail to the character that her husband had invented.
c. John Burke and his wife were writing a novel which took place in the Wisbech region.
d. Mr Burke had invented a character for the novel, a local merchant who became very successful.
e. On the first day of the Burke's visit to Wisbech, it began to snow, so they went to the museum.
f. The character bought a house in Wisbech.
g. They went to Wisbech.

12 Guessing words from context. Look back at the text in Exercise 11 and find words that correspond to these meanings.

First paragraph:
1. not serious
Second paragraph:
2. important in the story
3. busy and successful
4. boat or ship
5. part furthest from the centre
Third paragraph:
6. walk in a relaxed way
7. a place to keep dry

WRITING

13 Do one of these tasks (150 words or more).

1. Write what you can remember about Marco Polo's journey to China.
2. Write about a famous historical figure from your own country or another country.
3. Write the story of a film you have seen, or a book you have read.
4. Write about a coincidence that has happened to you or someone else you know (it is all right if you have already written about this in Lesson E4).

SPEAKING

14 Work with another student. Each of you must talk about one of the subjects listed below. Speak for about two minutes while your partner listens carefully. Then the partner will ask three or more questions to get further information.

1. Who is your favourite singer / film director / artist / writer / actor / sportsperson? Why do you like this person better than the other people in his/her field?
2. Describe the most beautiful place you have ever been to; say what you liked about it and why.
3. Say what you think life will be like for the children in your family twenty years from now, and how it will be different from your own childhood.

117

Additional material

Revision and fluency practice A, Exercise 8

WHAT SHALL I SAY?

What shall I say
when our neighbours
want us to come to tea?
They don't know you're not with me.
What shall I say?

What shall I say
when the phone rings
and someone asks for you?
They don't know I ask for you too.
What shall I say?

How can I hide the tears inside?
How can I face the crowd?
I can make lips of mine be still,
But my heart sighs too loud.

I could explain that
you're gone for only a week to shop.
But after the week is up
what shall I say?

(words and music by Peter Tinturin)

Lesson B7, Exercise 4

The Lonely One (*continued*)

Lavinia ran across the bridge.

Oh God, God, please please let me get up the hill! Now up the path, now between the hills, oh God, it's dark, and everything so far away. If I screamed now it wouldn't help; I can't scream anyway. Here's the top of the path, here's the street, oh, God, please let me be safe, if I get home safe I'll never go out alone; I was a fool, let me admit it, I was a fool, I didn't know what terror was, but if you let me get home from this I'll never go without Helen or Francine again! Here's the street. Across the street!

She crossed the street and rushed up the sidewalk.

Oh God, the porch! My house! Oh God, please give me time to get inside and lock the door and I'll be safe!

And there – silly thing to notice – why did she notice, instantly, no time, no time – but there it was anyway, flashing by – there on the porch rail, the half-filled glass of lemonade she had abandoned a long time, a year, half an evening ago! The lemonade glass sitting calmly, imperturbably there on the rail …
and …

She heard her clumsy feet on the porch and listened and felt her hands scrabbling and ripping at the lock with the key. She heard her heart. She heard her inner voice screaming.

The key fit.

Unlock the door, quick, quick!

The door opened.

Now, inside. Slam it!

She slammed the door.

'Now lock it, bar it, lock it!' she gasped wretchedly.

'Lock it, tight, *tight*!'

The door was locked and bolted tight.

Behind her in the living room, someone cleared his throat.

(from *Dandelion Wine* by Ray Bradbury)

Revision and fluency practice B, Exercise 8

FIDDLING ACROSS THE USA

I left my home when I was ten.
Haven't seen my folks since then.
They sent me home from school one day,
So I took my fiddle and I ran away.

I had no money but I had some luck.
Got a ride in a pickup truck.
Driver bought me some rice and beans,
And took me all the way down to New Orleans.

Well, I've been to the East Coast, been to the West Coast,
Down on the border with Mexico.
Played my fiddle in the wind and rain
And storms and deserts and ice and snow. (twice)

Well, I've travelled round on boats and trains,
Buses, bikes, cars and planes.
Played in restaurants, clubs and bars,
Played in the street to the passing cars.

I learned how to fiddle as I went along.
Guess I know a thousand songs.
One of these days I'll settle down,
But for now I'll just keep moving around.

Well, I've been to the East Coast, …

(Jonathan Dykes and Robert Campbell)

Revision and fluency practice C, Exercise 9

THE RIDDLE SONG

I gave my love a cherry, it had no stone
I gave my love a chicken without a bone
I told my love a story, it had no end
I gave my love a baby with no crying.

How can there be a cherry without a stone?
How can there be a chicken without a bone?
How can there be a story that has no end?
How can there be a baby with no crying?

Well a cherry when it's blooming, it has no stone
A chicken when it's pipping, it has no bone
The story of I love you, it has no end
A baby when it's sleeping has no crying.

(Traditional)

LOGGER LOVER

As I walked out one evening
'Twas in a small café
A forty-year-old waitress
To me these words did say:

I see that you are a logger
And not just a common bum
For nobody but a logger
Stirs his coffee with his thumb.

My lover, he was a logger
There's none like him today
If you poured whisky upon it
He would eat a bale of hay.

My lover came to see me
'Twas on one winter's day
He held me in his fond embrace
And broke three vertebrae.

He kissed me when he left me
So hard he broke my jaw
And I could not speak to tell him
He'd forgot his mackinaw.

Well, the weather tried to freeze him
It did its level best
At one hundred degrees below zero
Well, he buttoned up his vest.

It froze clear through to China,
It froze to the stars above
At one thousand degrees below zero
It froze my logger love.

And so I lost my lover
To this café I did come
And here I wait till someone
Stirs his coffee with his thumb.

(Traditional)

WHAT DID YOU LEARN IN SCHOOL TODAY?

What did you learn in school today,
Dear little boy of mine?
What did you learn in school today,
Dear little boy of mine?
I learned that Washington never told a lie,
I learned that soldiers seldom die,
I learned that everybody's free
That's what the teacher said to me,
And that's what I learned in school today,
That's what I learned in school.

What did you learn in school today,
Dear little boy of mine?
What did you learn in school today,
Dear little boy of mine?
I learned that policemen are my friends,
I learned that justice never ends,
I learned that murderers die for their crimes,
Even if we make a mistake sometimes,
And that's what I learned in school today,
That's what I learned in school.

What did you learn in school today,
Dear little boy of mine?
What did you learn in school today,
Dear little boy of mine?
I learned our government must be strong,
It's always right and never wrong,
Our leaders are the finest men,
And we elect them again and again,
And that's what I learned in school today,
That's what I learned in school.

(Tom Paxton)

Lesson D1, Exercise 1

GOLD DIGGER

He was the kind of guy that made you check your
   purse,
Pulled his hat down low as he kicked the dirt.
His teeth were shiny and his eyes were cold,
Shot left to right as he dug for gold.
His tie was tight and his cuffs were clean.
He was the sharpest guy that I'd ever seen.

Gold digger – he was a gold digger – digging it up.
   (twice)

She was the kind of girl that turned every eye,
Strutting like a cat (be)cause her heels were high.
Her jewellery rattled as she sat at the bar,
Waiting for a man with a big fast car.
Her skin was tanned from the southern sun.
She was digging for gold so you'd better run.

Gold digger – she was a gold digger – digging it up.
   (twice)

He was the kind of guy that made you cross the
   street.
A scar on his face, he had two big feet.
His suit hung loose, he was big, he was mean,
A gun in his pocket and a blade in his sleeve.
Looking for action – a time and a place.
You'd better watch out, don't get in his way.

Gold digger – he was a gold digger – digging it up.
   (twice)

She was the kind of lady made you straighten your
   tie,
Dressed in black with a cool clear eye.
Her diamond rings they were so discreet,
With short black hair that was combed so neat.
In her bag is a telephone
To see how stocks and shares have grown.

Gold digger – she was a gold digger – digging it up.
   (twice)

(Steve Hall)

Lesson D4, Exercise 3

gear /gɪə(r)/ *n* **1** [U] a set of things collected together, esp. when used for a particular purpose: *climbing gear* **2** [C] an apparatus or part of a machine which has a special use in controlling a vehicle: *the landing gear of an aircraft* | *steering gear* **3** [C;U] any of several arrangements, esp. of toothed wheels in a machine, which allows power to be passed from one part to another so as to control the power, speed, or direction of movement: *"The car isn't moving!" "That's because you're not* **in gear."** **4** [U] *sl esp. BrE* clothes

spring /sprɪŋ/ *v* **sprang** /spræŋ/, **sprung** /sprʌŋ/ **1** to move quickly as if by jumping: BOUND: *He sprang to his feet / sprang to the door / sprang over the wall* **2** [esp. UP] to come into being or action quickly or from nothing; arise: *A wind suddenly sprang up.* | *Towns had sprung up in what was a dry desert.* | *I turned the key and the engine sprang into life.* **3** [esp. *from*] to be a product or result: *What unhappiness can spring from the love of money!* **4** [esp. *from*] to come out (as if) in a spring of water; ISSUE: *Tears sprang from her eyes.* **5** to crack or split: *The heavy weight sprang one of the beams.* **6** to open or close (as if) by the force of a spring: *The box sprang open when I touched the button.*

fade /feɪd/ *v* (AWAY) **1** to (cause to) lose strength, colour, freshness, etc.: *Cut flowers soon fade.* | *The sun has faded the material.* **2** to disappear or die gradually: *The shapes faded (away) into the night.* | *The custom is fading.*

(adapted from the *Longman Dictionary of Contemporary English*)

Lesson D5, Exercise 5C

I WILL TAKE YOU THERE

I lie awake at night and I go sailing,
When the worry of the day won't let me be.
I dream of a place where the sky is crystal blue,
And the sand reaches miles into the sea.
From my head down to my toes the sun it warms me,
And the pine spreads a sweetness in the air.
Should I sleep in the shade with a cool lemonade,
Or go running through the waves without a care?

I go sailing, yes I'm sailing; from the four walls of my room on a rainy afternoon.
I go sailing, yes I'm sailing; if you dream awhile then I will take you there.

I lie awake at night and I go skiing,
When the worry of the day won't let me go.
I dream of a place where the sky is cold and clear.
I go flying like an eagle down the slope.
I can hear the sound of laughter in the mountains.
I can hear the rush of wood upon the snow.
Should I sit by the fire, or take a cable ride?
I can watch the tiny people down below.

I go sailing, yes I'm sailing; ...

I lie awake at night and I go flying,
When the worry of the day won't let me be.
I dream of a place where the earth is small and round,
And the stars reach as far as you can see.
I can float above the world and it's so peaceful.
I'm a long long way from home and I don't care.
A million miles away from the heat of the day.
A million miles but I can take you there.

Let's go sailing, we'll go sailing; from the four walls of our room on a rainy afternoon.
We'll go sailing, let's go sailing; if you dream awhile then I will take you there.

(Steve Hall)

Lesson D7, Exercises 1–5

'Ron, are you scared of girls?'
'Yes, Dad. When I meet a girl I never know what to do. I just pull me cap down over me face and hope she'll go away.'
'Oh, Ron.'
'I can't think of anything to say.'
'Oh, Ron, knowing what to say is the easiest part. There's – there's hundreds of acceptable phrases. Er – "Excuse me, but do you come here often?" '
'I live here, Dad.'
'Ron – I – I know where you live. I mean, you might say, for example, "Can I get you a still lemon?" or "I find the company in here rather boring. Let's take a stroll in the shrubbery." You get it, Ron?'
'No, Dad.'
'Well, try and remember. It's important that you get over this shyness, Ron. I don't like it. How do you expect to get married and have children if you won't go near a girl?'
'I'll think of something.'

'Good evening. Are you the gentleman in the cinema to whom I sat next?'
'It's a girl! Go away! I'm all alone!'
'But it – it's about your cap.'
'My cap?'
'You left your cap under the seat when you went. I saw your address inside, so I, well, I took the liberty of bringing it round.'
'Oh.'
'I do hope you were up.'
'Up what?'
'I haven't got you out of bed, I mean.'
'No. Did you say I was the one who was sitting next to you?'
'Yes.'
'Then you must be the one who was sitting next to me.'
'Well, yes, that's right.'
'You'd better come in.'
'Oh? Come in? Well, I am rather soaked. Perhaps I'd better just dry off a bit. Thank you.'
'The parlour's through here.'
'Shall I sit on the sofa?'
'If you like.'

'Thank you.'
'Excuse me, but do you come here often?'
'Come where?'
'I don't know. Dad didn't tell me what's next.'
'You know, I hope you don't mind my saying this, but in the pictures I could only see your profile. I, I thought you were much darker skinned.'
'I'd been eating a choc ice.'
'You eat a lot in the pictures, don't you? I could hear.'
'Only mixed nuts and a choc ice and my chewing gum and an apple during the adverts.'
'I like eating in the pictures too.'
'Do you? What's your favourite flavour of the month?'
'Nealopitan.'
'Ne– That's mine too.'
'Is it?'
'Yeah.'
'Well, isn't that strange? Oh – there's me, just happening to find your cap, and then it turns out we both like Nealopitan ice cream. Sends a shiver up your spine, doesn't it?'
'If you have enough of it.'
'By the way, I don't believe I mentioned it – my name's Eth.'
'Eth.'
'How about yours?'
'No, mine isn't.'

(from the BBC programme Take it from here.
Script by Frank Muir and Denis Norden.
Dad acted by Jimmy Edwards,
Ron by Dick Bentley and Eth by June Whitfield.)

Revision and fluency practice D, Exercise 11

TAKE THIS HAMMER

Take this hammer, carry it to the captain
Take this hammer, carry it to the captain
Take this hammer, and carry it to the captain
You tell him I'm gone, you tell him I'm gone.

If he asks you, was I running *(three times)*
You tell him I was flying, tell him I was flying.

If he asks you, was I laughing *(three times)*
Tell him I was crying, tell him I was crying.

I don't want no cornbread or tomatoes *(three times)*
They hurts my pride, they hurts my pride.

I'm gonna bust right, bust right past that shooter
    (three times)
I'm going home, I'm going home.

Take this hammer, and carry it to the captain
Take this hammer, and carry it to the captain
Take this hammer, and carry it to the captain
You tell him I'm gone, you tell him I'm gone.
    (twice)

(American prison work song)

Revision and fluency practice E, Exercise 9

Are you fit to be a parent?

1. a–3 b–2 c–1
2. a–3 b–2 c–1
3. a–1 b–2 c–3
4. a–2 b–1 c–3
5. a–3 b–1 c–2
6. a–1 b–2 c–3
7. a–2 b–1 c–3
8. a–3 b–2 c–1

TOTAL 8–13: You are (or would be) a pretty strict parent. Don't forget that children need patience, understanding and love as well as firmness.
TOTAL 14–19: You (would) try to be neither too strict nor too easy-going. This can be very good if children know what to expect; but it is no good being strict about something one day and soft about it the next.
TOTAL 20–24: You tend towards soft-heartedness. Be careful: children need some limits, so they can define themselves as people and set their own limits later on. The children will know that you love them if you set the limits in a firm but loving way.

Revision and fluency practice E, Exercise 12

TRYING TO LOVE TWO WOMEN

Trying to love two women
Is like a ball and chain
Trying to love two women
Is like a ball and chain
Sometimes the pleasure
Ain't worth the strain
It's a long old grind
And it tires your mind

Trying to hold two women
Is tearing me apart
Trying to hold two women
Is tearing me apart
One's got my money
And the other's got my heart
It's a long old grind
And it tires your mind

When you try to please two women
You can't please yourself
When you try to please two women
You can't please yourself
Your best is only half good
A man can't stock two shelves
It's a long old grind,
And it tires your mind

(first verse twice)

(Sonny Throckmorton)

Vocabulary index

Irregular verbs: Verbs marked with an asterisk(*) are irregular. There is a complete list of the irregular verbs in *The New Cambridge English Course* at the back of the book.

Stress: In longer single words, only the main stress is normally shown (e.g. *appendicitis* /əpendɪˈsaɪtəs/). This is also usually the case with fixed two-word expressions like *bank account* /ˈbæŋk əkaʊnt/. However, some words and expressions have variable stress; in these cases two stresses are shown (e.g. *inside* /ɪnˈsaɪd/; *bad-tempered* /ˈbæd ˈtempəd/; *lie down* /ˈlaɪ ˈdaʊn/).

a bit /ə ˈbɪt/	C1	always /ˈɔːlweɪz/	C6	author /ˈɔːθə(r)/	B7
a day off /ə ˈdeɪ ˈɒf/	A8	amaze /əˈmeɪz/	A4	available /əˈveɪləbl/	C5
a long way away /ə ˈlɒŋ ˈweɪ əˈweɪ/	D5	amazement /əˈmeɪzmənt/	A7	average /ˈævrɪdʒ/	C5, E6
a number of /ə ˈnʌmbər əv/	D4	ambitious /æmˈbɪʃəs/	B5	average: on average /ɒn ˈævrɪdʒ/	C6
a quarter of an hour		ambulance /ˈæmbjələns/	E4	avoid /əˈvɔɪd/	A4, E1
/ə ˈkwɔːtər əv ən ˈaʊə(r)/	E3	America /əˈmerɪkə/	A2	awake /əˈweɪk/	C6
a whole lot of ... /ə ˈhəʊl ˈlɒt əv/	C3	American /əˈmerɪkən/,		away (= in another place) /əˈweɪ/	A4, C3
ability /əˈbɪləti/	B5	an American, the Americans	A2	away (= further distant, at a distance)	
above /əˈbʌv/	D5	amused /əˈmjuːzd/	C1	/əˈweɪ/	A4, D5
absolutely /ˈæbsəˈluːtli/	C1	-ance /əns/	D6	away: a long way away	
accent /ˈæksənt/	B1	angry /ˈæŋgri/	A7, C1	/ə ˈlɒŋ ˈweɪ əˈweɪ/	D5
accept /əkˈsept/	B1, C3	animal /ˈænɪml/	E8	away: I'm away tomorrow	
accident /ˈæksɪdənt/	A2, C6, E2	anniversary: wedding anniversary		/aɪm əˈweɪ təˈmɒrəʊ/	C3
according to /əˈkɔːdɪŋ tə/	A4, B1, C5	/ˈwedɪŋ ænɪˈvɜːsəri/	C2	away: not far away /ˈnɒt ˈfaːr əˈweɪ/	D5
account /əˈkaʊnt/	D8, E8	anti- /ˈænti/	D6	baby-sit /ˈbeɪbi sɪt/	C3
account: bank/current/deposit account		antiques /ænˈtiːks/	A1	baby-sitting /ˈbeɪbi ˈsɪtɪŋ/	A1, C3
/ˈbæŋk, ˈkʌrənt, dɪˈpɒzɪt əˈkaʊnt/	D8	anyway: Well, anyway, ...		back (*noun*) /bæk/	A6
accounting /əˈkaʊntɪŋ/	E8	/ˈwel ˈeniweɪ/	E7	backbone /ˈbækbəʊn/	D8
accuse (sbdy of sth) /əˈkjuːz/	B4, C6	apologise /əˈpɒlədʒaɪz/	B1	backpack /ˈbækpæk/	E2
across (*preposition*) /əˈkrɒs/	A3	appear /əˈpɪə(r)/	C4	bad luck /ˈbæd ˈlʌk/	E2
actor /ˈæktə(r)/	E5	appearance /əˈpɪərəns/	D1	bad-tempered /ˈbæd ˈtempəd/	B6
actually /ˈæktʃəli/	A6, C1, D8, E2	apple /ˈæpl/	B8	bake /beɪk/	E8
add /æd/	C8	applicant /ˈæplɪkənt/	C4	bald /bɔːld/	D1
adjective /ˈædʒɪktɪv/	B1	application /æplɪˈkeɪʃn/	C4	ball /bɔːl/	E8
advice (*uncountable*) /ədˈvaɪs/	D2, E4	apply /əˈplaɪ/	C4	bank /bæŋk/	B3
adviser /ədˈvaɪzə(r)/	E1	approach (*verb*) /əˈprəʊtʃ/	E4	bank account /ˈbæŋk əˈkaʊnt/	D8
aerial: TV aerial /ˈtiː ˈviː ˈeərɪəl/	C8	approximately /əˈprɒksɪmətli/	B3, C5	banker /ˈbæŋkə(r)/	B3
aeroplane /ˈeərəpleɪn/	A5	Are you doing anything this evening?	C3	bark (*verb*) /baːk/	B7
affect /əˈfekt/	C5	Are you free this evening?	C3	basically /ˈbeɪsɪkli/	D6
affectionate /əˈfekʃənət/	B6	area /ˈeərɪə/	D5	bath: have* a bath /ˈhæv ə ˈbaːθ/	C2
afford: can('t) afford		armed /aːmd/	A8	beard /bɪəd/	D1
/kən, ˈkaːnt əˈfɔːd/	B3	around /əˈraʊnd/	B7	beat* /biːt/	A7
afraid /əˈfreɪd/	B7, C1	around: get* around /ˈget əˈraʊnd/	E2	beautiful /ˈbjuːtɪfl/	D1
afraid: I'm afraid ... /aɪm əˈfreɪd/	A5, C3	arrange /əˈreɪndʒ/	C8	beauty /ˈbjuːti/	E3
after: look after /ˈlʊk ˈaːftə(r)/	D2, E5	arrest (*verb*) /əˈrest/	A7, B4, C6	be* born /bi ˈbɔːn/	D2
after all: I'm not free after all		arrive /əˈraɪv/	A4, E1, E7	become* /bɪˈkʌm/	A4, E1
/ˈaːftər ˈɔːl/	C3	arrive at /əˈraɪv ət/	E7	bed: make* a bed /ˈmeɪk ə ˈbed/	C2
against /əˈgenst/	B7	arrow /ˈærəʊ/	D4	beginning /bɪˈgɪnɪŋ/	A6, C6
age /eɪdʒ/	E1	art /aːt/	A1, E5	behind /bɪˈhaɪnd/	D5
age: middle-aged /ˈmɪdl ˈeɪdʒd/	E4	art: work of art /ˈwɜːk əv ˈaːt/	E5	Belgian /ˈbeldʒən/,	
ages: for ages /fər ˈeɪdʒɪz/	C3	article /ˈaːtɪkl/	E8	a Belgian, the Belgians	A2
ages: it's ages since ...		artificial fibre /ˈaːtɪˈfɪʃl ˈfaɪbə(r)/	C6	Belgium /ˈbeldʒəm/	A2
/ɪts ˈeɪdʒɪz ˈsɪns/	C3	artistic /aːˈtɪstɪk/	B5	bell /bel/	E3
aggressive /əˈgresɪv/	B6	as usual /əz ˈjuːʒuːl/	E4	belong (to) /bɪˈlɒŋ (tə)/	D6, D8
agree /əˈgriː/	C6	ashamed /əˈʃeɪmd/	B8	below /bɪˈləʊ/	D5
ahead: Go* straight ahead for ...		Asia /ˈeɪʃə/	E1, E8	belt: safety belt /ˈseɪfti ˈbelt/	E7
yards/metres		astonish /əˈstɒnɪʃ/	E4	bend (*noun*) /bend/	A3
/ˈstreɪt əˈhed ... ˈjaːdz/ˈmiːtəz/	A3	at least /ət ˈliːst/	C5, E7	beside /bɪˈsaɪd/	A5
aim (*noun*) /eɪm/	D3	at the top/bottom/side, *etc.*		better: had better /həd ˈbetə(r)/	D7
air hostess /ˈeə ˈhəʊstes/	E7	/ət.ðə ˈtɒp, ˈbɒtm, ˈsaɪd/	A6	bicycle /ˈbaɪsɪkl/	D8
airport /ˈeəpɔːt/	E7	Atlantic coast /ətˈlæntɪk ˈkəʊst/	A2	bilingual /ˈbaɪˈlɪŋgwəl/	C4
alarm /əˈlaːm/	A8, E3	atmosphere /ˈætməsfɪə(r)/	D5	bill /bɪl/	A7
all /ɔːl/	D8	attack (*noun*) /əˈtæk/	C6	billion /ˈbɪljən/	E6
all alone /ˈɔːl əˈləʊn/	D7	attack (*verb*) /əˈtæk/	A7	bird /bɜːd/	D8, E2
almost /ˈɔːlməʊst/	D4	attractive /əˈtræktɪv/	D1	bird-watching /ˈbɜːd ˈwɒtʃɪŋ/	A1
alone /əˈləʊn/	A2, D7	audience /ˈɔːdɪəns/	A5	birthplace /ˈbɜːθpleɪs/	D4
along (*preposition*) /əˈlɒŋ/	A3	Australia /ɒˈstreɪljə/	A2	biscuit /ˈbɪskɪt/	E2
already /ˈɔːlˈredi/	A5	Australian /ɒˈstreɪljən/,		bit: a bit /ə ˈbɪt/	C1, C3
although /ˈɔːlˈðəʊ/	A7, D8, E2	an Australian, the Australians	A2	bit: Could we make it a bit later?	C3

bit: I might be a bit late /C3

bite* /baɪt/ B4

black coffee /ˈblæk ˈkɒfi/ E2

bleed* /bliːd/ E4

boat /bəʊt/ A4

bomb /bɒm/ C5

book (verb) /bʊk/ E4

booking /ˈbʊkɪŋ/ E4

boring /ˈbɔːrɪŋ/ D3

born: be* born /bi ˈbɔːn/ D2

bottom /ˈbɒtm/ A6

bottom: at the bottom /ət ðə ˈbɒtm/ A6

bracket /ˈbrækɪt/ A5

brain /breɪn/ D2

break* /breɪk/ E2

break* down /ˈbreɪk ˈdaʊn/ A7, C7

break* into /ˈbreɪk ˈɪntə/ B4

break* out /ˈbreɪk ˈaʊt/ C5

breakfast: make* breakfast /ˈmeɪk ˈbrekfəst/ C2

brick /brɪk/ C8

bridge /brɪdʒ/ B7

bridge: playing bridge /ˈpleɪŋ ˈbrɪdʒ/ C3

brigade: fire brigade /ˈfaɪə brɪˈɡeɪd/ E1

bright (colours) /braɪt/ E5

bring* up /ˈbrɪŋ ˈʌp/ C6

broad /brɔːd/ D1

build* /bɪld/ C8

build* up /ˈbɪld ˈʌp/ C1

builder /ˈbɪldə(r)/ A7, C2, D6

building /ˈbɪldɪŋ/ B2, E8

bullet /ˈbʊlɪt/ A7

burn* /bɜːn/ E1

burn* down /ˈbɜːn ˈdaʊn/ B2

bury /ˈberi/ B2

bus stop /ˈbʌs ˈstɒp/ C6

bus: take* a bus /ˈteɪk ə ˈbʌs/ C2

business /ˈbɪznɪs/ A4, E1

business: on business /ɒn ˈbɪznɪs/ A2

businesswoman /ˈbɪznɪswʊmən/ D1

busy /ˈbɪzi/ B2, C3

busy: I'm really a bit busy at the
   moment C3

busy: The/His/Her line's busy A3

busy: unless you're too busy C3

buy* /baɪ/ C6

by the year 3000 /baɪ ðə ˈjɪə/ E3

call: I'll call again in a minute /kɔːl/ A3

call: I'll call you back A3

call: make* a phone call C2

calm /kɑːm/ B6, C1

camel /ˈkæml/ A5

camera /ˈkæmrə/ D6, E2

can('t) afford /kən, ˈkɑːnt əˈfɔːd/ B3

Can/Could I speak to …?
   /kæn, kʊd aɪ ˈspiːk tə/ A3

Can/Will you hold? (on telephone)
   /kæn, wɪl ju ˈhəʊld/ A3

cancel (cancelled) /ˈkænsl/ E4

canoe /kəˈnuː/ A7

cap /kæp/ D7

capital /ˈkæpɪtl/ C7, D6

capture /ˈkæptʃə(r)/ C6

car park /ˈkɑː ˈpɑːk/ C8

cards: pack of cards /ˈpæk əv ˈkɑːdz/ E2

careful /ˈkeəfl/ B3

carefully /ˈkeəfli/ B2

carriage /ˈkærɪdʒ/ E4

carry /ˈkæri/ E2

case: in case /ɪn ˈkeɪs/ E2

cash (noun) /kæʃ/ B3

catch* fire /ˈkætʃ ˈfaɪə(r)/ E2

cattle /ˈkætl/ C7, E8

cause (noun) /kɔːz/ C7

ceiling /ˈsiːlɪŋ/ C8

cellar /ˈselə(r)/ D6

Celsius /ˈselsɪəs/ E6

central heating /ˈsentrəl ˈhiːtɪŋ/ E5

certain /ˈsɜːtn/ B4

certainly /ˈsɜːtnli/ D3

chance /tʃɑːns/ B5

change (= money returned) /tʃeɪndʒ/ C6

change (verb) /tʃeɪndʒ/ C2

change (into) /ˈtʃeɪndʒ (ˈɪntə)/ C8

change the subject
   /ˈtʃeɪndʒ ðə ˈsʌbdʒɪkt/ B1

changed: get* changed
   /ˈget ˈtʃeɪndʒd/ C2

charge (sbdy with sth) /tʃɑːdʒ/ B4

charity /ˈtʃærəti/ C7

chat (noun and verb) /tʃæt/ B4

cheap /tʃiːp/ C6

cheaply /ˈtʃiːpli/ E2

check /tʃek/ B7, E8

cheerful /ˈtʃɪəfl/ B6, D1

chemistry /ˈkemɪstri/ D3

cheque /tʃek/ B3

chimney /ˈtʃɪmni/ C8

chin /tʃɪn/ D1

China /ˈtʃaɪnə/ A2

Chinese /ˈtʃaɪniːz/ A2, E8

Chinese: the Chinese /ðə ˈtʃaɪniːz/ A2

choice /tʃɔɪs/ B4

choose* /tʃuːz/ D2

circle /ˈsɜːkl/ A6

city /ˈsɪti/ A7, D4, D6, E1

civil servant /ˈsɪvl ˈsɜːvənt/ C6

civilisation /ˈsɪvəlaɪˈzeɪʃn/ D8

civilised /ˈsɪvəlaɪzd/ E1

class /klɑːs/ D4

classical music /ˈklæsɪkl ˈmjuːzɪk/ A1

clay /kleɪ/ E8

clean (verb) /kliːn/ E5

clean up /ˈkliːn ˈʌp/ C8

cliff /klɪf/ D2

climate /ˈklaɪmət/ E3

cloth /klɒθ/ C7, E1, E8

coal /kəʊl/ E1

coast /kəʊst/ A4

coast: Atlantic coast
   /ətˈlæntɪk ˈkəʊst/ A2

coast: Pacific coast /pəˈsɪfɪk ˈkəʊst/ A2

coast: sea coast /ˈsiː ˈkəʊst/ A2

coffee /ˈkɒfi/ E2

coffee: black coffee /ˈblæk ˈkɒfi/ E2

coffee: have* coffee /ˈhæv ˈkɒfi/ C2

coffee: make* coffee /ˈmeɪk ˈkɒfi/ C2

coffee: white coffee /ˈwaɪt ˈkɒfi/ E2

coincidence /kəʊˈɪnsɪdəns/ E4

cold (personality) /kəʊld/ B6

collect /kəˈlekt/ A1

collection /kəˈlekʃn/ D2

Come* on /ˈkʌm ˈɒn/ B3

committee /kəˈmɪti/ D3

compare /kəmˈpeə(r)/ B7

compete /kəmˈpiːt/ D4

complete (verb) /kəmˈpliːt/ A6

compose /kəmˈpəʊz/ E5

composer /kəmˈpəʊzə(r)/ E5

computer: home computer
   /ˈhəʊm kəmˈpjuːtə(r)/ A1

concrete (noun) /ˈkɒnkriːt/ B2

condition: in … condition
   /ɪn … kənˈdɪʃn/ B3

conditions: working conditions
   /ˈwɜːkɪŋ kənˈdɪʃnz/ B5

confused /kənˈfjuːzd/ B8

connect: (I'm) trying to connect you
   /kəˈnekt/ A3

consider /kənˈsɪdə(r)/ C4

considerably /kənˈsɪdrəbli/ B4

consonant /ˈkɒnsənənt/ B1

consumption /kənˈsʌmpʃən/ C7

contents /ˈkɒntents/ E5

continually /kənˈtɪnjəli/ D4

continue /kənˈtɪnjuː/ C3

control /kənˈtrəʊl/ A4

convenience: every modern convenience
   /ˈevri ˈmɒdən kənˈviːnɪəns/ E5

convert /kənˈvɜːt/ C8

convince /kənˈvɪns/ C7

cool /kuːl/ D2

corner /ˈkɔːnə(r)/ A6

correctly /kəˈrektli/ B1

Could we make it a bit later? C3

country (= nation) /ˈkʌntri/ C7, E1

countryside /ˈkʌntrisaɪd/ A1

course /kɔːs/ C7

court: in court (of law) /ɪn ˈkɔːt/ B4

court: tennis court /ˈtenɪs ˈkɔːt/ C2

cover (verb) /ˈkʌvə(r)/ B2

crash (verb) /kræʃ/ E4

crash: plane crash /ˈpleɪn ˈkræʃ/ C5

cream /kriːm/ E2

crèche /kreʃ/ C7

crew /kruː/ B8

crime /kraɪm/ B4

cross (adjective) /krɒs/ C1

cross (noun) /krɒs/ A6

cross (verb) /krɒs/ B7, E1

cry (verb) /kraɪ/ C1, D2

culture /ˈkʌltʃə(r)/ B1

cupboard /ˈkʌbəd/ C8

currency /ˈkʌrənsi/ B3

current (adjective) /ˈkʌrənt/ B3

current account /ˈkʌrənt əˈkaʊnt/ D8

customer /ˈkʌstəmə(r)/ A5

cut* /kʌt/ B2, C8

cut* off (e.g. water supplies) /ˈkʌt ˈɒf/ B2

cut* off: We were/got cut off
   (on telephone) A3

cyclist /ˈsaɪklɪst/ A2

daily /ˈdeɪli/ B3

damage /ˈdæmɪdʒ/ B2

Dane: a Dane /ə ˈdeɪn/, the Danes A2

Danish /ˈdeɪnɪʃ/ A2

dark /dɑːk/ C6

dark: get* dark /ˈget ˈdɑːk/ D4

dark-skinned /ˈdɑːk ˈskɪnd/ D7

date /deɪt/ E1

date: up to date /ˈʌp tə ˈdeɪt/ B8

dead /ded/ C6

deaf /def/ E7

deal* with sbdy /diːl/ C4

death /deθ/ D4

debt /det/ C7

decide /dɪˈsaɪd/ D8, E1, E2

decimal /ˈdesɪml/ E6

decision /dɪˈsɪʒn/ C2

decision: make* a decision C2

deep /diːp/ D5

definitely /ˈdefənətli/ D3

degree (= temperature) /dɪˈɡriː/ E6

delay (verb) /dɪˈleɪ/ A4, E1

delayed /dɪˈleɪd/ E7

delighted /dɪˈlaɪtɪd/ C1

France /frɑ:ns/ A2
frankly /'fræŋkli/ E7
frantic /'fræntɪk/ C1
free (= not busy) /fri:/ C3
free: Are you free this evening? C3
free: it looks as if I'm not free C3
freezer /'fri:zə(r)/ C6
French /frentʃ/, the French A2
Frenchman/woman
/'frentʃmən, wumən/ A2
friend of mine /'frend əv 'maɪn/ B3
friendly /'frendli/ B6, D1
friendship /'frendʃɪp/ D7
frighten /'fraɪtn/ B4
front /frʌnt/ A6
front: in front of /ɪn 'frʌnt əv/ A3
frost /frɒst/ B8
fuel /'fjʊəl/ E1
-ful /fl/ D6
full /fʊl/ B8
full-time /'fʊl 'taɪm/ C8
furious /'fjʊərɪəs/ C1, C6
furniture (uncountable) /'fɜ:nɪtʃə(r)/ C2
further /'fɜ:ðə(r)/ A4, E4
gallon /'gælən/ E6
game /geɪm/ E3
garage /'gærɑ:ʒ, 'gærɪdʒ/ C8
garden /'gɑ:dn/ C8
gardening /'gɑ:dnɪŋ/ A1
gas /gæs/ B2
gate /geɪt/ C8
generally /'dʒenrəli/ D4
generous /'dʒenərəs/ B3, B6, C6, D1
gently /'dʒentli/ D5
gents' (= toilet) /dʒents/ C8
geography /dʒi'ɒgrəfi/ E8
get* (for changes) /get/ E1
get* around /'get ə'raʊnd/ E2
get* changed /'get tʃeɪndʒd/ C2
get* dark /'get dɑ:k/ D4
get* dressed /'get 'drest/ C2
get* into trouble /'get ɪntə 'trʌbl/ D2
get* lost /'get lɒst/ C2
get* married /'get 'mærɪd/ D7
get* on (with sbdy) /'get ɒn/ B4
get* over sth /'get 'əʊvə(r)/ D7
get* stuck /'get 'stʌk/ A7
girlfriend /'gɜ:lfrend/ E7
give* sbdy a ring /'gɪv ... ə 'rɪŋ/ C3, E2
glad /glæd/ C1
glove /glʌv/ E3
glue (verb) /glu:/ B2
Go* straight ahead for ... yards/metres
/'streɪt ə'hed fər ... 'jɑ:dz, 'mi:təz/ A3
go* for a walk /'gəʊ fər ə 'wɔ:k/ E2
go* out /'gəʊ 'aʊt/ C3
go* wrong /'gəʊ 'rɒŋ/ C7
god /gɒd/ E8
God: My God! /'maɪ 'gɒd/ B7
gold /gəʊld/ A1
good at ... /'gʊd ət/ B5
Good heavens /'gʊd 'hevənz/ A5
good-looking /'gʊd 'lʊkɪŋ/ D1
government /'gʌvəmənt/ C5, E2
grab /græb/ A7
grammar /'græmə(r)/ B1
groceries /'grəʊsəriz/ B3
ground: the ground /ðə graʊnd/ D5, E1
group /gru:p/ D8
grow* up /'grəʊ 'ʌp/ D4
guard (noun) /gɑ:d/ A7
gun /gʌn/ B8

guy /gaɪ/ E7
habit (of) /'hæbɪt (əv)/ E4
had better (+ infinitive without 'to')
/həd 'betə(r)/ D7
half /hɑ:f/ E6
hand: on the other hand
/ɒn ði: 'ʌðə 'hænd/ C4
handsome /'hænsəm/ D1
hang* /hæŋ/ D6
happen /'hæpn/ D2
happen (to) /'hæpn (tə)/ D7
happy /'hæpi/ C1, C6
hate /heɪt/ E2
have* a bath /'hæv ə 'bɑ:θ/ C2
have* a holiday /'hæv ə 'hɒlədi/ C2
have* coffee /'hæv 'kɒfi/ C2
have* a rest /'hæv ə 'rest/ C2
have* supper /'hæv 'sʌpə(r)/ C2
have* tea /'hæv 'ti:/ C2
headache /'hedeɪk/ C3
headache: I've got a terrible headache
/'terəbl 'hedeɪk/ C3
healthy /'helθi/ A2, C7
heart /hɑ:t/ B8
heating: central heating
/'sentrəl 'hi:tɪŋ/ E5
heavens: Good heavens
/'gʊd 'hevənz/ A5
heavy /'hevi/ C6
hedge /hedʒ/ C8
height /haɪt/ D1
Here you are /'hɪə ju: 'ɑ:/ E7
hide* /haɪd/ C1
high /haɪ/ C6, D5
hill /hɪl/ D5
hold* /həʊld/ D6
hold*: Can/Will you hold? (on telephone) A3
hole /həʊl/ A7
holiday: have* a holiday
/'hæv ə 'hɒlədi/ C2
home computer /'həʊm kəm'pju:tə(r)/ A1
honest /'ɒnɪst/ B6, C6, D2
hope /həʊp/ D2
hope: I hope you don't mind my ...ing
/aɪ 'həʊp/ D7
horizon /hə'raɪzn/ D5
horizontal /'hɒrɪ'zɒntl/ D5
hostess: air hostess /'eə 'həʊ'stes/ E7
hot /hɒt/ C6
household /'haʊshəʊld/ B3
housework: do* housework
/'du: 'haʊswɜ:k/ C2
How about tomorrow / the day after
tomorrow? C3
however /haʊ'evə(r)/ A7
humour: sense of humour
/'sens əv 'hju:mə(r)/ B5
hundred /'hʌndrəd/ E6
hunger /'hʌŋgə(r)/ C7, E3
hungry /'hʌŋgri/ C7, E2
hurry: in a hurry /ɪn ə 'hʌri/ B3
hurt* /hɜ:t/ A8, C5, C6, E4
husband /'hʌzbənd/ D6
I beg your pardon?
/aɪ 'beg jɔ: 'pɑ:dn/ E7
I can't remember
/aɪ 'kɑ:nt rɪ'membə(r)/ C3
I can't wait to ... /aɪ 'kɑ:nt 'weɪt tə/ D2
I hope you don't mind my ...ing
/aɪ 'həʊp/ D7
I mean* /aɪ 'mi:n/ E7

I might be a bit late
/aɪ 'maɪt bi: ə 'bɪt 'leɪt/ C3
I really ought to wash my hair ...
/aɪ 'rɪəli 'ɔ:t tə/ C3
I suppose so /aɪ sə'pəʊz 'səʊ/ D3
I thought we might ...
/aɪ 'θɔ:t wi 'maɪt/ C3
I'd love to /aɪd 'lʌv 'tu:/ C3
I'd prefer ... /aɪd prɪ'fɜ:(r)/ B3
I'll come* round to your place C3
I'll give you a ring one of these days /
some time / when things get easier C3
I'll put you through (on telephone)
/aɪl 'pʊt ju: 'θru:/ A3
I'll ring/call again in a minute
/ɪn ə 'mɪnɪt/ A3
I'll ring/call you back A3
I'll see if I can transfer you
(on telephone) /trɑ:ns'fɜ: 'ju:/ A3
I'll tell you what /aɪl 'tel ju: 'wɒt/ B3
I'm afraid (= I'm sorry to tell you)
/aɪm ə'freɪd/ A5, C3
I'm away tomorrow C3
I'm not free after all C3
I'm not sure /aɪm 'nɒt 'ʃɔ:(r)/ C3
I'm really a bit busy at the moment /
for the next few weeks C3
I'm trying to connect you /kə'nekt/ A3
I've got a terrible headache
/'terəbl 'hedeɪk/ C3
I've got no idea /'nəʊ aɪ'dɪə/ B3
I've just remembered
/aɪv 'dʒʌst rɪ'membəd/ C3
I've/You've got the wrong
number/extension /ɪk'stenʃn/ A3
idea: I've got no idea /'nəʊ aɪ'dɪə/ B3
... if it's not too much trouble /'trʌbl/ E7
if I were you, I would ...
/ɪf 'aɪ wə 'ju:, aɪ wʊd/ D7
if you don't mind /ɪf ju: 'dəʊnt 'maɪnd/ B3
ill /ɪl/ E1
imitate /'ɪmɪteɪt/ B1
immediate family /ɪ'mi:dɪət 'fæməli/ D4
important /ɪm'pɔ:tənt/ E7
improve /ɪm'pru:v/ C8
in 50 years /ɪn 'fɪfti 'jɪəz/ E3
in 50 years' time /ɪn 'fɪfti 'jɪəz 'taɪm/ E3
in a hurry /ɪn ə 'hʌri/ B3
in case /ɪn 'keɪs/ E2
in court (of law) /ɪn 'kɔ:t/ B4
in fact /ɪn 'fækt/ A6
in front of /ɪn 'frʌnt əv/ A3
in many ways /ɪn 'meni 'weɪz/ D8
in power /ɪn 'paʊə(r)/ D6
in some way /ɪn 'sʌm 'weɪ/ D2
in spite of /ɪn 'spaɪt əv/ C5
in the middle /ɪn ðə 'mɪdl/ A6
in your opinion /ɪn 'jɔ:r ə'pɪnjən/ B1
in ... condition /ɪn ... kən'dɪʃn/ B3
in(to) the distance /ɪn(tə) ðə 'dɪstəns/ D5
inch /ɪntʃ/ E6
increase (verb) /ɪŋ'kri:s/ C8
increasingly /ɪŋ'kri:sɪŋli/ D4
indeed /ɪn'di:d/ A1
indoors /ɪn'dɔ:z/ B5, C6
industrial /ɪn'dʌstrɪəl/ C5
inflation /ɪn'fleɪʃn/ B3
informal /ɪn'fɔ:ml/ B1
information (uncountable)
/'ɪnfə'meɪʃn/ C6
informed: well informed
/'wel ɪn'fɔ:md/ B3

injure /'ɪndʒə(r)/ C6
injured /'ɪndʒəd/ E4
insect /'ɪnsekt/ D8
insert /ɪn'sɜːt/ B2
inside /'ɪn'saɪd/ C1, C8, E1
insist /ɪn'sɪst/ B4
instead /ɪn'sted/ B4, E3
instead of /ɪn'sted əv/ E8
insurance /ɪn'ʃɔːrəns/ E2
intelligent /ɪn'telɪdʒənt/ C6
interest (= money) /'ɪntrəst/ C7
interesting /'ɪntrəstɪŋ/ C6
international /'ɪntə'næʃənl/ C7
interrupt /'ɪntə'rʌpt/ E7
interview (noun) /'ɪntəvjuː/ A1, C4
interview (verb) /'ɪntəvjuː/ B4, E4
into /'ɪntə, 'ɪntuː/ C6
invent /ɪn'vent/ B8, E8
invite /ɪn'vaɪt/ B1, C6
involved /ɪn'vɒlvd/ C5
Iraq /ɪ'rɑːk/ E8
Ireland /'aɪələnd/ A2
Irish /'aɪrɪʃ/, the Irish A2
Irishman/woman /'aɪrɪʃmən, wumən/ A2
-ise /aɪz/ D6
-ish /ɪʃ/ D6
Israel /'ɪzreɪl/ A2
Israeli /ɪz'reɪli/, an Israeli, the Israelis A2
It depends /ɪt dɪ'pendz/ C3
It looks as if I'm not free
    /ɪt 'luks əz 'ɪf/ C3
It's a bad line (on telephone)
    /'bæd 'laɪn/ A3
It's ages since ... /ɪts 'eɪdʒɪz 'sɪns/ C3
It's on your right/left A3
It's ringing for you /ɪts 'rɪŋɪŋ fə juː/ A3
Italian /ɪ'tæljən/,
    an Italian, the Italians A2
Italy /'ɪtəli/ A2
jam (= food) /dʒæm/ C7
jam (verb) /dʒæm/ A7
Japan /dʒə'pæn/ A2
Japanese /'dʒæpə'niːz/, the Japanese A2
jazz /dʒæz/ A1
job /dʒɒb/ B5
job: part-time job /'pɑːt 'taɪm 'dʒɒb/ B5
journey /'dʒɜːni/ A4, E1
juice /dʒuːs/ E1
jungle /'dʒʌŋgl/ C7
just (= only) /dʒʌst/ A5
Just a minute /'dʒʌst ə 'mɪnɪt/ C3, E7
keep* /kiːp/ C6, E1
keep* ...ing /'kiːp ...ɪŋ/ C3
keep* score /'kiːp 'skɔː(r)/ D4
Kenya /'kenjə/ A2
Kenyan /'kenjən/,
    a Kenyan, the Kenyans A2
kill /kɪl/ A5
kilo(gram) /'kiːləu ('kɪləgræm)/ E6
kilometre (US kilometer)
    /'kɪləmiːtə(r), kɪ'lɒmɪtə(r)/ E6
kilometres/miles an hour / per hour
    /'kɪləmiːtəz, 'maɪlz ən 'auə(r),
    'pər 'auə(r)/ E6
kind (adjective) /kaɪnd/ B6
kind (noun) /kaɪnd/ D5, D8
kiss (verb) /kɪs/ D2
kitchen /'kɪtʃɪn/ B2
knowledge /'nɒlɪdʒ/ D4
knowledge: working knowledge
    /'wɜːkɪŋ 'nɒlɪdʒ/ B1
labour /'leɪbə(r)/ C7

lack (verb) /læk/ C4
ladies' (= toilet) /'leɪdiz/ C8
lamb /læm/ E8
lamp /læmp/ E1
land (verb) /lænd/ A4
land: on land /ɒn 'lænd/ A4
large /lɑːdʒ/ D5
last (verb) /lɑːst/ B4
last: my last word /maɪ 'lɑːst 'wɜːd/ B3
laugh (verb) /lɑːf/ C1, C6, D2
launderette /lɔːn'dret/ B8
lead* to /'liːd tə/ C5
lean* /liːn/ B7
learn* /lɜːn/ A7, B1
least /liːst/ A2, D3
least: at least /ət 'liːst/ C5, E7
leave* (= stay away from,
    do nothing with) /liːv/ B2, C6
left /left/ C6
left: It's on your right/left A3
left: on the left A6
left: Take* the first/second/etc. on
    the right/left A3
lemon /'lemən/ E2
lend* /lend/ C7
length /leŋθ/ B2, E1
Let* me just look in my diary
    /'daɪəri/ C3
letter: write* letters /'raɪt 'letəz/ C3
level /'levl/ D5
library /'laɪbrəri/ B2
lie (lying) (= not tell the truth)
    /laɪ ('laɪɪŋ)/ C4, E1
lie* /laɪ/ D6
-less /ləs/ D6
lift (noun) /lɪft/ E5
lights: traffic lights /'træfɪk 'laɪts/ A3
likely /'laɪkli/ E3
limited /'lɪmɪtɪd/ E3
line (double yellow) /laɪn/ A5
line: It's a bad line (on telephone) A3
line: railway line /'reɪlweɪ 'laɪn/ B8
line: The/His/Her line's engaged/busy
    /ɪŋ'geɪdʒd, 'bɪzi/ A3
lip /lɪp/ D1
liquid /'lɪkwɪd/ E1
list /lɪst/ A1
load (noun) /ləud/ A8
local /'ləukl/ C7
locked /lɒkt/ B8
logical /'lɒdʒɪkl/ B5
lonely /'ləunli/ B7, C1
long /lɒŋ/ C6
long: a long way away
    /ə 'lɒŋ 'weɪ ə'weɪ/ D5
look after /'luk 'ɑːftə(r)/ D2, E5
loss /lɒs/ B2
lost: get* lost /'get 'lɒst/ C2
lot: a whole lot of ... /ə 'həul 'lɒt əv/ C3
love (verb) /lʌv/ C6
love at first sight /'fɜːst 'saɪt/ E4
lovely: That would be lovely /'lʌvli/ C3
low /ləu/ D1, D5
lower (verb) /'ləuə(r)/ C8
luck /lʌk/ D2, E2
luggage (uncountable) /'lʌgɪdʒ/ E2, E7
machine /mə'ʃiːn/ B2
machine: washing machine
    /'wɒʃɪŋ mə'ʃiːn/ B8
main /meɪn/ C7, C8, D8
majority /mə'dʒɒrəti/ D6
make* a bed /'meɪk ə 'bed/ C2

make* a decision /dɪ'sɪʒn/ C2
make* a mistake /mɪ'steɪk/ C2
make* a phone call /'fəun 'kɔːl/ C2
make* a plan /'plæn/ C2
make* breakfast/supper
    /'brekfəst, 'sʌpə(r)/ C2
make* coffee /'kɒfi/ C2
make* soup /suːp/ C2
make* sure /ʃɔː(r)/ A5
make* up your mind
    /'meɪk ʌp jɔː 'maɪnd/ E7
make*: Could we make it a bit
    later? C3
mammal /'mæml/ E2
manage (to) /'mænɪdʒ (tə)/ D7
management /'mænɪdʒmənt/ C5
manager /'mænɪdʒə(r)/ B4, E7
map /mæp/ B7
market /'mɑːkɪt/ A4, E1
market: stock market /'stɒk 'mɑːkɪt/ A8
market town /'mɑːkɪt 'taun/ C7
marriage /'mærɪdʒ/ B8, D7
married: get* married /'get 'mærɪd/ D7
maths /mæθs/ D3
maybe /'meɪbi/ B7
Maybe, maybe not /'meɪbi 'nɒt/ C3
meal /miːl/ C3
mean (adjective) /miːn/ B3, B6
mean* /miːn/ A2
mean*: I mean /aɪ 'miːn/ E7
mean*: What do you mean by ...? D3
meaning /'miːnɪŋ/ B1
medicine: take* medicine
    /'teɪk 'medsən/ C2
meet* /miːt/ A2, B2, C3, D2, D7, E7
meet*: where shall we meet
    /'weə ʃəl wi 'miːt/ C3
meeting /'miːtɪŋ/ E7
melt /melt/ C2
member /'membə(r)/ E1, E3
Member of Parliament (MP)
    /'membər əv 'pɑːlɪmənt ('em 'piː)/ D6
memory /'meməri/ B5, D2
mend /mend/ B8
-ment /mənt/ D6
mention /'menʃən/ D3, D7
message /'mesɪdʒ/ C5
metal /'metl/ E8
method /'meθəd/ D3
midday /'mɪd'deɪ/ A4
middle: in the middle /ɪn ðə 'mɪdl/ A6
middle-aged /'mɪdl 'eɪdʒd/ D1, E4
Middle East: the Middle East
    /ðə 'mɪdl 'iːst/ A2, E8
midnight /'mɪdnaɪt/ B4
midwife /'mɪdwaɪf/ C7
might: I thought we might ... /maɪt/ C3
mile /maɪl/ E6
million /'mɪljən/ E6
mind: I hope you don't mind
    my ...ing /maɪnd/ D7
mind: if you don't mind /maɪnd/ B3
mind: make* up your mind
    /'meɪk ʌp jɔː 'maɪnd/ E7
mine: friend of mine /'frend əv 'maɪn/ B3
mineral /'mɪnrəl/ E1
minus /'maɪnəs/ E6
minute: Just a minute
    /'dʒʌst ə 'mɪnɪt/ C3, E7
minute: One minute /'wʌn 'mɪnɪt/ A3
mirror /'mɪrə(r)/ E2
mis- /mɪs/ D6

126

miserable /ˈmɪzrəbl/ — C1

miss: You can't miss it /jʊ ˈkɑːnt ˈmɪs ɪt/ — A3

mistake /mɪˈsteɪk/ — B1, C2

mistake: make* a mistake — C2

misunderstanding /ˈmɪsʌndəˈstændɪŋ/ — E7

modern /ˈmɒdən/ — E5

modern: every modern convenience /ˈevri ˈmɒdən kənˈviːnɪəns/ — E5

moment: at the moment /ət ðə ˈməʊmənt/ — C3

moment: One moment /ˈwʌn ˈməʊmənt/ — A3

month /mʌnθ/ — A4, C2

moody /ˈmuːdi/ — B6

most /məʊst/ — A2, C6, D3, D8

motorist /ˈməʊtərɪst/ — A5

moustache /məˈstɑːʃ/ — D1

move (verb) /muːv/ — A7

movement /ˈmuːvmənt/ — B7

MP /ˈem ˈpiː/ — D6

multiplied by /ˈmʌltɪplaɪd baɪ/ — E6

multiply /ˈmʌltɪplaɪ/ — E6

murder /ˈmɜːdə(r)/ — C6

museum /mjuːˈzɪəm/ — B5, E5

music: classical music /ˈklæsɪkl ˈmjuːzɪk/ — A1

music: pop music /ˈpɒp ˈmjuːzɪk/ — A1

My God! /ˈmaɪ ˈgɒd/ — B7

my last word /maɪ ˈlɑːst ˈwɜːd/ — B3

my own /maɪ ˈəʊn/ — B5

narrow /ˈnærəʊ/ — D1

national /ˈnæʃnl/ — E5

natural /ˈnætʃrəl/ — D5

nature /ˈneɪtʃə(r)/ — C2

nearby /ˈnɪəˈbaɪ/ — A8

need (verb) /niːd/ — C4, C8

need (+ ...ing) /niːd/ — C8

neighbour (US neighbor) /ˈneɪbə(r)/ — D4

neither /ˈnaɪðə(r)/ — A1

nervous /ˈnɜːvəs/ — C1, C4

nervy /ˈnɜːvi/ — B6

new /njuː/ — C6

next: next few weeks /ˈnekst ˈfjuː ˈwiːks/ — C3

next to /ˈnekst tə/ — D7

nice /naɪs/ — C6, D2

no longer /ˈnəʊ ˈlɒŋgə(r)/ — E3

no such thing as /ˈnəʊ ˈsʌtʃ ˈθɪŋ əz/ — E3

No, I'm afraid I'm ...ing — C3

noise /nɔɪz/ — B5

nor /nɔː(r)/ — A1

north /nɔːθ/ — A4

north-east /ˈnɔːθ ˈiːst/ — C6

not far away /ˈnɒt ˈfɑːr əˈweɪ/ — D5

not ... yet /ˈnɒt ... ˈjet/ — C3

note (= money) /nəʊt/ — E6

nothing: do* nothing /ˈduː ˈnʌθɪŋ/ — C2

notice (verb) /ˈnəʊtɪs/ — A5

noun /naʊn/ — B1

number /ˈnʌmbə(r)/ — E8

number: a number of /ə ˈnʌmbər əv/ — D4

number: I've/You've got the wrong number — A3

nut /nʌt/ — D7, E1

object (noun) /ˈɒbdʒɪkt/ — D8, E8

obviously /ˈɒbvɪəsli/ — D5

occupy /ˈɒkjʊpaɪ/ — D4

occur (occurred) /əˈkɜː(r)/ — E4

of course /əv ˈkɔːs/ — D3

off: a day off /ə ˈdeɪ ˈɒf/ — A8

off: take* the day off — A8

offer (verb) /ˈɒfə(r)/ — B1, C4, C6

office /ˈɒfɪs/ — A2, C3

official /əˈfɪʃl/ — C5, E1

Oh, very well /ˈəʊ ˈveri ˈwel/ — B3

oil /ɔɪl/ — E8

on a visit /ɒn ə ˈvɪzɪt/ — B4

on average /ɒn ˈævrɪdʒ/ — C6

on business /ɒn ˈbɪznɪs/ — A2

on his way (to) /ɒn hɪz ˈweɪ (tə)/ — A7

on land /ɒn ˈlænd/ — A4

on the other hand /ɒn ðiː ˈʌðə ˈhænd/ — C4

on the right/left /ɒn ðə ˈraɪt, ˈleft/ — A6

on top of /ɒn ˈtɒp əv/ — B2

on your own /ɒn jɔːr ˈəʊn/ — B5

One minute/moment /ˈwʌn ˈmɪnɪt, ˈməʊmənt/ — A3

one of these days /ˈwʌn əv ˈðiːz ˈdeɪz/ — C3

one point five (1.5) /ˈwʌn ˈpɔɪnt ˈfaɪv/ — E6

one's own /ˈwʌnz ˈəʊn/ — A7

only /ˈəʊnli/ — D8

opening /ˈəʊpnɪŋ/ — D5

opera /ˈɒprə/ — A1

opinion /əˈpɪnjən/ — B4

opinion: in your opinion /ɪn ˈjɔːr əˈpɪnjən/ — B1

opposite (preposition) /ˈɒpəzɪt/ — A3

opposition /ˈɒpəˈzɪʃn/ — C5

optimistic /ˈɒptɪˈmɪstɪk/ — B6, C6

or rather /ɔː ˈrɑːðə(r)/ — E7

organisation /ˈɔːgənaɪˈzeɪʃn/ — A2, C2, D3

organise /ˈɔːgənaɪz/ — A2, B5, C6

origin /ˈɒrɪdʒɪn/ — E8

ought (to) /ˈɔːt (tə)/ — C3, D7

outdoors /aʊtˈdɔːz/ — B5

outlook /ˈaʊtlʊk/ — C5

output /ˈaʊtpʊt/ — C5

outside /ˈaʊtˈsaɪd/ — C6, C8

oval /ˈəʊvl/ — D1, D5

over (= finished) /ˈəʊvə(r)/ — B7

over- /ˈəʊvə(r)/ — D6

over: get* over sth /ˈget ˈəʊvə(r)/ — D7

overcrowded /ˈəʊvəˈkraʊdɪd/ — E3

overseas /ˈəʊvəˈsiːz/ — C7

overweight /ˈəʊvəˈweɪt/ — D1

own: (my) own /(maɪ) əʊn/ — A7, B5

own: on your own /ɒn jɔːr ˈəʊn/ — B5

Pacific coast /pəˈsɪfɪk ˈkəʊst/ — A2

pack of cards /ˈpæk əv ˈkɑːdz/ — E2

packet /ˈpækɪt/ — E6

paint (verb) /peɪnt/ — C8, E5

painter /ˈpeɪntə(r)/ — E5

painting /ˈpeɪntɪŋ/ — E5

pair /ˈpeə(r)/ — A5

pane: window pane /ˈwɪndəʊ ˈpeɪn/ — C8

pardon: I beg your pardon? /aɪ ˈbeg jɔː ˈpɑːdn/ — E7

parent /ˈpeərənt/ — C1, D6

park (verb) /pɑːk/ — A5

park: car park /ˈkɑː ˈpɑːk/ — C8

Parliament: Member of Parliament (MP) /ˈmembər əv ˈpɑːlɪmənt (ˈem ˈpiː)/ — D6

part /pɑːt/ — D5

part: take* part in /ˈteɪk ˈpɑːt ɪn/ — C5

part-time (job) /ˈpɑːt ˈtaɪm (ˈdʒɒb)/ — B5

party (political) /ˈpɑːti/ — D6

pass an examination /ˈpɑːs ən ɪgˈzæmɪˈneɪʃn/ — C2

passenger /ˈpæsɪndʒə(r)/ — E4

passport /ˈpɑːspɔːt/ — A3

past (preposition) /pɑːst/ — A3

path /pɑːθ/ — C8

patient (adjective) /ˈpeɪʃənt/ — B5

pay (noun) /peɪ/ — E2

pencil /ˈpensl/ — B2

per cent /pə ˈsent/ — E6

perfect /ˈpɜːfɪkt/ — B8

perfectly /ˈpɜːfɪktli/ — B1

personal /ˈpɜːsənl/ — D4

personality /ˈpɜːsəˈnæləti/ — B5

pessimistic /ˈpesɪˈmɪstɪk/ — B6

phone call: make* a phone call /ˈfəʊn ˈkɔːl/ — C2

photo: take* a photo /ˈfəʊtəʊ/ — C2

phrase /freɪz/ — D4, D7

physics /ˈfɪzɪks/ — D3

pick flowers /ˈpɪk ˈflaʊəz/ — E3

pick up /ˈpɪk ˈʌp/ — A7

picture /ˈpɪktʃə(r)/ — D6, E5, E8

pieces: fall* to pieces /ˈfɔːl tə ˈpiːsɪz/ — C6

plain /pleɪn/ — D1

plan (noun) /plæn/ — D2, D3

plan (verb) /plæn/ — A4, E1

plan: make* a plan — C2

plane /pleɪn/ — E7

plane crash /ˈpleɪn ˈkræʃ/ — C5

planet /ˈplænɪt/ — B2, D5, E3

platform /ˈplætfɔːm/ — D6, E7

play (noun) /pleɪ/ — E5

pleased /pliːzd/ — C1

pleasure /ˈpleʒə(r)/ — C2, D2

plus /plʌs/ — E6

point (sharp end) /pɔɪnt/ — A6

point: one point five (1.5) /ˈwʌn ˈpɔɪnt ˈfaɪv/ — E6

pointed /ˈpɔɪntɪd/ — D1

police /pəˈliːs/ — C5

police force /pəˈliːs ˈfɔːs/ — E1

polish /ˈpɒlɪʃ/ — B2

polite /pəˈlaɪt/ — B6

political /pəˈlɪtɪkl/ — A5, D6, E5

poor /ˈpɔː(r)/ — C7

pop music /ˈpɒp ˈmjuːzɪk/ — A1

popular /ˈpɒpjələ(r)/ — B4, D3

population /ˈpɒpjəˈleɪʃn/ — D6

post /pəʊst/ — C4

post office /ˈpəʊst ˈɒfɪs/ — A8

postal service /ˈpəʊstl ˈsɜːvɪs/ — E1

potter /ˈpɒtə(r)/ — E5

pottery /ˈpɒtəri/ — E5

pound (£) /paʊnd/ — B3, E6

poverty /ˈpɒvəti/ — C7

power: in power /ɪn ˈpaʊə(r)/ — D6

practical /ˈpræktɪkl/ — B5, B6, D3

prefer (preferred) /prɪˈfɜː(r)/ — B8

prefer: I'd prefer ... /aɪd prɪˈfɜː(r)/ — B3

prepare /prɪˈpeə(r)/ — B2, D3

present (noun) /ˈprezənt/ — B8

pretty /ˈprɪti/ — D1

previous /ˈpriːvɪəs/ — A8, B4

primary school /ˈpraɪməri ˈskuːl/ — D3

prison /ˈprɪzn/ — C4

prisoner /ˈprɪznə(r)/ — C6

private /ˈpraɪvɪt/ — A5, E3

problem /ˈprɒbləm/ — B4, E3

productivity /ˈprɒdʌkˈtɪvəti/ — C5

programme (radio) /ˈprəʊgræm/ — B4

programme: television programme /ˈtelɪˈvɪʒn ˈprəʊgræm/ — E5

promise (noun) /ˈprɒmɪs/ — E3

promise (verb) /ˈprɒmɪs/ — B7

promotion /prəˈməʊʃn/ — B5

pronounce /prəˈnaʊns/ — A1

pronunciation /prəˈnʌnsiˈeɪʃn/ — B1

proud /praʊd/ — C1

public /ˈpʌblɪk/ — B2, E3
publish /ˈpʌblɪʃ/ — E4
pull /pʊl/ — A7, B8, C6, D2, D7
punish /ˈpʌnɪʃ/ — A7
purple /ˈpɜːpl/ — D6
purpose /ˈpɜːpəs/ — E8
purse (US; GB = handbag) /pɜːs/ — B7
push /pʊʃ/ — A7
put* in /ˈpʊt ˈɪn/ — C8
qualification /ˌkwɒlɪfɪˈkeɪʃn/ — C4
quarter /ˈkwɔːtə(r)/ — E6
quarter: a quarter of an hour
/ə ˈkwɔːtər əv ən ˈaʊə(r)/ — E3
question (noun and verb) /ˈkwestʃən/ — C6
quiet /ˈkwaɪət/ — C6
quite /kwaɪt/ — A6, C1
rage /reɪdʒ/ — A7
raid (noun) /reɪd/ — A8
railway line /ˈreɪlweɪ ˈlaɪn/ — B8
raise /reɪz/ — C8
rate: exchange rate /ɪkˈstʃeɪndʒ ˈreɪt/ — B3
rather (adverb) /ˈrɑːðə(r)/ — A6
rather: or rather /ɔː ˈrɑːðə(r)/ — E7
rather: would you rather …?
/wʊd ju ˈrɑːðə(r)/ — B5
re- /rɪ, riː/ — D6
reach /riːtʃ/ — A4, E1
real /ˈriːl/ — E5
reason /ˈriːzn/ — E1
reasonably /ˈriːznəbli/ — B3
rebuild* /ˌriːˈbɪld/ — C8
receive /rɪˈsiːv/ — C6, D2
recent /ˈriːsənt/ — D4
receptionist /rɪˈsepʃənɪst/ — C4
recession /rɪˈseʃn/ — A8
reckless /ˈrekləs/ — B3
recognise (US recognize) /ˈrekəgnaɪz/ — D4
record (= written statement) /ˈrekɔːd/ — E8
record (verb) /rɪˈkɔːd/ — E1
recording /rɪˈkɔːdɪŋ/ — A1
recover /rɪˈkʌvə(r)/ — C6, E1
recovery /rɪˈkʌvəri/ — A8
rectangular /rekˈtæŋgjʊlə(r)/ — D5
redecorate /ˌriːˈdekəreɪt/ — C8
reform (noun) /rɪˈfɔːm/ — D3
refuse (verb) /rɪˈfjuːz/ — C3
regret (verb) /rɪˈgret/ — C4
regularly /ˈregjələli/ — C7
related (to) /rɪˈleɪtɪd (tə)/ — D4, D8
relationship /rɪˈleɪʃənʃɪp/ — D3, D7
relative (noun) /ˈrelətɪv/ — D4
relaxed /rɪˈlækst/ — C1
release /rɪˈliːs/ — C5, C6
religion /rɪˈlɪdʒən/ — E3
religious /rɪˈlɪdʒəs/ — E8
remember /rɪˈmembə(r)/ — C6
remember: I can't remember
/aɪ ˈkɑːnt rɪˈmembə(r)/ — C3
remember: I've just remembered
/aɪv ˈdʒʌst rɪˈmembəd/ — C3
removal /rɪˈmuːvl/ — A7
remove /rɪˈmuːv/ — B2
reorganisation /ˌriːˌɔːgənaɪˈzeɪʃn/ — C3
repair (noun) /rɪˈpeə(r)/ — C6
repair (verb) /rɪˈpeə(r)/ — C8
repay* /ˌriːˈpeɪ/ — C7
replace /rɪˈpleɪs/ — C8
report (noun) /rɪˈpɔːt/ — B4
report (verb) /rɪˈpɔːt/ — A4
republic /rɪˈpʌblɪk/ — D6
require /rɪˈkwaɪə(r)/ — C4
research /rɪˈsɜːtʃ/ — E8

reserved /rɪˈzɜːvd/ — B6
responsibility /rɪˌspɒnsəˈbɪləti/ — A2, B5
rest: have* a rest /ˈhæv ə ˈrest/ — C2
rest (verb) /rest/ — D5
retire /rɪˈtaɪə(r)/ — C2
return (verb) /rɪˈtɜːn/ — A7, E1, E5
right: It's on your right/left — A3
right: on the right — A6
right: Take* the first/second/etc.
on the right/left — A3
ring: give* sbdy a ring
/ˈgɪv … ə ˈrɪŋ/ — C3, E2
ring: I'll give you a ring one of
these days — C3
ring*: I'll ring again in a minute — A3
ring*: I'll ring you back — A3
ring*: It's ringing for you — A3
rise (noun) /raɪz/ — C3
rise* /raɪz/ — A8, B1, C5, D5
road accident /ˈrəʊd ˈæksɪdənt/ — A2
rock /rɒk/ — D5
Roman /ˈrəʊmən/ — E8
roof /ruːf/ — C8
room: waiting-room /ˈweɪtɪŋ ˈruːm/ — E7
rootless /ˈruːtləs/ — D4
rough /rʌf/ — A4, C6
roughly /ˈrʌfli/ — A4
round (adjective) /raʊnd/ — D1, D5
round (adverb) /raʊnd/ — D5
round (preposition) /raʊnd/ — A4
round: I'll come round to your place
/aɪl ˈkʌm ˈraʊnd tə ˈjɔː ˈpleɪs/ — C3
round: show* sbdy round
/ˈʃəʊ ˈraʊnd/ — C8
roundabout /ˈraʊndəbaʊt/ — A3
route /ruːt/ — A4, E1
rude /ruːd/ — B6
ruin (noun) /ˈruːɪn/ — B2
run* (= govern) /rʌn/ — D6
run* out of /ˈrʌn ˈaʊt əv/ — A4
Russian /ˈrʌʃn/ — A1
sad /sæd/ — B8
safe /seɪf/ — C6
safety /ˈseɪfti/ — D2
safety belt /ˈseɪfti ˈbelt/ — E7
sail /seɪl/ — A4
salary /ˈsæləri/ — B5
sandal /ˈsændl/ — E3
satisfied /ˈsætɪsfaɪd/ — A7
save /seɪv/ — D2
say, … /seɪ/ — C3
scale: small-scale /ˈsmɔːl ˈskeɪl/ — C7
scared (of) /ˈskeəd (əv)/ — D7
scattered /ˈskætəd/ — D4
scientist /ˈsaɪəntɪst/ — C6
score (noun) /skɔː(r)/ — D4
Scot: a Scot /ə ˈskɒt/, the Scots — A2
Scotch (adjective) /skɒtʃ/ — A2
Scotland /ˈskɒtlənd/ — A2
Scottish /ˈskɒtɪʃ/ — A2
scream (verb) /skriːm/ — C1
sculpt /skʌlpt/ — E5
sculptor /ˈskʌlptə(r)/ — E5
sea coast /ˈsiː ˈkəʊst/ — A2
seat /siːt/ — D6
secondary education
/ˈsekəndri edʒuːˈkeɪʃn/ — D3
secret (noun and adjective) /ˈsiːkrɪt/ — A5
secretary /ˈsekrətri/ — C4
See* you /ˈsiː juː/ — C3
See* you then /ˈsiː juː ˈðen/ — C3
see* red /ˈsiː ˈred/ — C1

see*: … you see /ju ˈsiː/ — E7
seed /siːd/ — C7
self-confident /ˈself ˈkɒnfɪdənt/ — B6
send* /send/ — B2
sense of humour /ˈsens əv ˈhjuːmə(r)/ — B5
sensitive /ˈsensətɪv/ — B6
separate (adjective) /ˈseprət/ — B2
serious /ˈsɪərɪəs/ — B6, D1
seriously /ˈsɪərɪəsli/ — A8, E3, E4
servant: civil servant /ˈsɪvl ˈsɜːvənt/ — C6
service (verb) /ˈsɜːvɪs/ — C7
service: postal service
/ˈpəʊstl ˈsɜːvɪs/ — E1
set* off /ˈset ˈɒf/ — A4
set* up /ˈset ˈʌp/ — C7
settle down /ˈsetl ˈdaʊn/ — C2
several /ˈsevrəl/ — D5, D8
shade (of a colour) /ʃeɪd/ — A5
shadow /ˈʃædəʊ/ — E3
shaken (emotionally) /ˈʃeɪkn/ — E4
shallow /ˈʃæləʊ/ — C6
shape (noun) /ʃeɪp/ — E8
shape (verb) /ʃeɪp/ — B2
share (verb) /ˈʃeə(r)/ — B8
sharp /ʃɑːp/ — C6
sheep /ʃiːp/ — E8
shine* /ʃaɪn/ — D5
ship (noun) /ʃɪp/ — A4, E1
shiver (noun) /ˈʃɪvə(r)/ — E4
shoot* /ʃuːt/ — A1, A7, C6, D2
short of time /ˈʃɔːt əv ˈtaɪm/ — C3
shout (verb) /ʃaʊt/ — E7
show* sbdy round /ˈʃəʊ ˈraʊnd/ — C8
shy /ʃaɪ/ — B6, C6, D7, E2
shyness /ˈʃaɪnɪs/ — D7
sick /sɪk/ — C1
side /saɪd/ — A6
side: at the side /ət ðə ˈsaɪd/ — A6
sight: love at first sight
/ˈlʌv ət ˈfɜːst ˈsaɪt/ — E4
sign (in sign language) /saɪn/ — A1
sign (picture writing) /saɪn/ — E8
silly /ˈsɪli/ — C4
similar to /ˈsɪmələ tə/ — A6
single /ˈsɪŋgl/ — B7
situation /ˌsɪtʃuˈeɪʃn/ — E3
size /saɪz/ — C8, D3
size: take* size (9) shoes
/ˈteɪk ˈsaɪz (ˈnaɪn) ˈʃuːz/ — C2
skeleton /ˈskelɪtn/ — D8
skill /skɪl/ — B5
skin: dark-skinned /ˈdɑːk ˈskɪnd/ — D7
sleep* /sliːp/ — D4
slim (adjective) /slɪm/ — A8, D1
slim (verb) /slɪm/ — A8
slipper /ˈslɪpə(r)/ — E3
small-scale /ˈsmɔːl ˈskeɪl/ — C7
smash /smæʃ/ — A7
smile (verb) /smaɪl/ — C1
smoke (verb) /sməʊk/ — B2
snow (noun) /snəʊ/ — A7, E5
so /səʊ/ — A1
so that /ˈsəʊ ðət/ — E2
sober /ˈsəʊbə(r)/ — A7
sociable /ˈsəʊʃəbl/ — B6
social /ˈsəʊʃl/ — D4
society /səˈsaɪəti/ — D7, E3
sock /sɒk/ — B8
soft /sɒft/ — C6, D5
soldier /ˈsəʊldʒə(r)/ — A2
solve /sɒlv/ — E3
some time /ˈsʌm ˈtaɪm/ — C3

something: do* something stupid /'du: 'sʌmθɪŋ 'stju:pɪd/ — C2
somewhere /'sʌmweə(r)/ — C3
soup: make* soup /'meɪk 'su:p/ — C2
south /saʊθ/ — A4
south-east /'saʊθ 'i:st/ — E1
south-west /'saʊθ 'west/ — A4
space /speɪs/ — B8
Spain /speɪn/ — A2
Spaniard /'spænjəd/ — A2
Spanish /'spænɪʃ/, the Spanish — A2
speak: Can/Could I speak to ...? /'spi:k tə/ — A3
Speaking (on telephone) /'spi:kɪŋ/ — A3
spell* /spel/ — A1
spelling /'spelɪŋ/ — B1
spend* /spend/ — A7, B3, B7, E1
spend* time ...ing /'spend 'taɪm ...ɪŋ/ — B5
spit* /spɪt/ — E3
spite: in spite of /ɪn 'spaɪt əv/ — C5
split* the difference /'splɪt ðə 'dɪfrəns/ — B3
sport /spɔ:t/ — A1
spot (noun) /spɒt/ — C4
square /skweə(r)/ — A6, D5
staircase /'steəkeɪs/ — C8
stairs /steəz/ — D6
stamp /stæmp/ — A1, D2
star /stɑ:(r)/ — D5
statement /'steɪtmənt/ — E5
statue /'stætʃu:/ — E5
stay (verb) /steɪ/ — A7, E1
stay (with sbdy) /steɪ/ — E7
steadily /'stedəli/ — A4
steal* /sti:l/ — B4
steps /steps/ — C8
stick (noun) /stɪk/ — E3
still /stɪl/ — A7
stock market /'stɒk 'mɑ:kɪt/ — A8
stone (= piece of rock) /stəʊn/ — C5, D2, E1, E8
stone (= measure of weight) /stəʊn/ — A8
stop (verb) /stɒp/ — C6
stop: bus stop /'bʌs 'stɒp/ — C6
straight /streɪt/ — A3, D1
straight: Go* straight ahead for ... yards/metres /'streɪt ə'hed ... 'jɑ:dz, 'mi:təz/ — A3
straighten /'streɪtn/ — C8
stranger /'streɪndʒə(r)/ — B7, D4, D7
strawberry /'strɔ:bəri/ — E2
strengthen /'streŋθən/ — C8
stress (= pronunciation) /stres/ — B1
strike* /straɪk/ — A8
stroll (noun) /strəʊl/ — D7
strong /strɒŋ/ — C6, D2
strongly /'strɒŋli/ — C1
stuff (verb) /stʌf/ — A5
style /staɪl/ — B1
subject: (school) subject /('sku:l) 'sʌbdʒɪkt/ — D3
subject: change the subject /'tʃeɪndʒ ðə 'sʌbdʒɪkt/ — B1
successful /sək'sesfl/ — C5, D6
such: no such thing as /'nəʊ 'sʌtʃ 'θɪŋ əz/ — E3
sufficiently /sə'fɪʃəntli/ — C4
sugar /'ʃʊgə(r)/ — E2
suit (verb) /su:t/ — A5
summer /'sʌmə(r)/ — D4
sunshine /'sʌnʃaɪn/ — C5
supper: have* supper /'sʌpə(r)/ — C2
supper: make* supper — C2

supplies /sə'plaɪz/ — A4
supply (noun) /sə'plaɪ/ — B2
support (verb) /sə'pɔ:t/ — D6
suppose: I suppose so /aɪ sə'pəʊz 'səʊ/ — D3
sure /ʃɔ:(r)/ — C3, D3
surplus /'sɜ:pləs/ — C7
surprise (noun) /sə'praɪz/ — E4
surprised /sə'praɪzd/ — C1
surround /sə'raʊnd/ — A8
suspicion /sə'spɪʃn/ — E4
swimming trunks /'swɪmɪŋ 'trʌnks/ — E2
Swiss /swɪs/, the Swiss — A2
Switzerland /'swɪtsələnd/ — A2
sympathy /'sɪmpəθi/ — C5
system /'sɪstəm/ — E2
T-junction /'ti: 'dʒʌŋkʃən/ — A3
Take* the first/second/etc. on the right/left — A3
take* a bus /bʌs/ — C2
take* a photo /'fəʊtəʊ/ — C2
take* a train /'treɪn/ — C2
take* down /'teɪk 'daʊn/ — C8
take* medicine /'medsən/ — C2
take* off (plane, clothes) /'teɪk 'ɒf/ — C6
take* part in /'teɪk 'pɑ:t ɪn/ — C5
take* place /'teɪk 'pleɪs/ — D6
take* size (9) shoes /'teɪk 'saɪz ('naɪn) 'ʃu:z/ — C2
take* the day off — A8
take* (time) — E1
tall /tɔ:l/ — C6, E6
target /'tɑ:gɪt/ — A8
tea: have* tea /'hæv 'ti:/ — C2
teach* /ti:tʃ/ — C6
tear* /'teə(r)/ — A5
telephone directory /'telɪfəʊn dɪ'rektri/ — E4
television programme /'telɪ'vɪʒn 'prəʊgræm/ — E5
tell*: I'll tell you what /tel/ — B3
tell*: to tell you the truth /'tru:θ/ — B3
tell* the truth — C4
temper: bad-tempered /'bæd 'tempəd/ — B6
temperature /'temprɪtʃə(r)/ — A8, C5, E6
tennis court /'tenɪs 'kɔ:t/ — C2
tent /tent/ — A5, E2
terrible /'terəbl/ — C3
terrible: I've got a terrible headache /'hedeɪk/ — C3
terrified /'terɪfaɪd/ — C1
terrify /'terɪfaɪ/ — B7
test (verb) /test/ — E2
That would be lovely /'ðæt wʊd bi 'lʌvli/ — C3
That's difficult /'ðæts 'dɪfɪkʊlt/ — C3
the (first) time /taɪm/ — A5
the day after tomorrow /tə'mɒrəʊ/ — C3
theatre: going to the theatre /'θɪətə(r)/ — C3
theft /θeft/ — B4
theory /'θɪəri/ — E8
these days /'ði:z 'deɪz/ — C3
thin /θɪn/ — C6, D1
third /θɜ:d/ — E6
Third World /'θɜ:d 'wɜ:ld/ — C7
thirsty /'θɜ:sti/ — E2
This is ... (on telephone) /'ðɪs ɪz/ — A3
though /ðəʊ/ — A8
thought (noun) /θɔ:t/ — A5, D2
thousand /'θaʊzənd/ — E6

throw* /θrəʊ/ — A7, C5, D2
throat /θrəʊt/ — A5
through (preposition) /θru:/ — A3
through: I'll put you through (on telephone) /aɪl 'pʊt ju: 'θru:/ — A3
throughout /θru:'aʊt/ — C5
throw* /θrəʊ/ — C5, D2
ticket /'tɪkɪt/ — E7
till (preposition) /tɪl/ — C3
time: for the first time /fə ðə 'fɜ:st 'taɪm/ — D7
time: in 50 years' time /ɪn 'fɪfti 'jɪəz 'taɪm/ — E3
time: short of time /'ʃɔ:t əv 'taɪm/ — C3
time: the (first) time /ðə ('fɜ:st) 'taɪm/ — A5
timetable /'taɪmteɪbl/ — E7
tip (small end) /tɪp/ — A4
tired: unless you're too tired /'taɪəd/ — C3
to tell you the truth /tə 'tel ju: ðə 'tru:θ/ — B3
to within (e.g. a few pounds) /tə wɪ'ðɪn/ — B3
together /tə'geðə(r)/ — B2
tomorrow: the day after tomorrow /tə'mɒrəʊ/ — C3
ton /tʌn/ — B2
too (+ adjective + infinitive) /tu:/ — C1
tool /tu:l/ — C7
tooth (teeth) /tu:θ (ti:θ)/ — D2
top /tɒp/ — A6, C6
top: at the top /ət ðə 'tɒp/ — A6
top: on top of /ɒn 'tɒp əv/ — B2
towards /tə'wɔ:dz/ — A3
town /taʊn/ — D4
town: market town /'mɑ:kɪt 'taʊn/ — C7
traffic lights /'træfɪk 'laɪts/ — A3
traffic warden /'træfɪk 'wɔ:dn/ — A5
train /treɪn/ — B2
train: take* a train — C2
training /'treɪnɪŋ/ — D3
transfer (transferred) /'trɑ:ns'fɜ:/ — A7
transfer: I'll see if I can transfer you (on telephone) — A3
travel (uncountable) /'trævl/ — A2
travel (travelled) /'trævl/ — A4, E1
triangle /'traɪæŋgl/ — A6
trip /trɪp/ — E1
trouble (uncountable) /'trʌbl/ — A5, E7
trouble: get* into trouble /'get ɪntə 'trʌbl/ — D2
trouble: if it's not too much trouble — E7
true /tru:/ — B4, C6
trunks: swimming trunks /'swɪmɪŋ 'trʌnks/ — E2
trust (noun) /trʌst/ — B8
truth /tru:θ/ — C4
truth: tell* the truth /'tel ðə 'tru:θ/ — C4
truth: to tell you the truth — B3
try on /'traɪ 'ɒn/ — A5
trying to connect you /kə'nekt/ — A3
turn into /'tɜ:n 'ɪntə/ — C8
turn out /'tɜ:n 'aʊt/ — D7, E4
Turn right/left at ... — A3
turn up /'tɜ:n 'ʌp/ — C6
TV aerial /'ti: 'vi: 'eərɪʊl/ — C8
typical /'tɪpɪkl/ — D8
tyre /'taɪə(r)/ — A7
umbrella /ʌm'brelə/ — E2
un- /ʌn/ — D6
unable /'ʌn'eɪbl/ — C4
unattractive /'ʌnə'træktɪv/ — C4
uncomfortable /ʌn'kʌmftəbl/ — C1, C6

under- /'ʌndə(r)/ — D6
unemployed /'ʌnɪm'plɔɪd/ — B4
unemployment /'ʌnɪm'plɔɪmənt/ — A8, D2
unhappy /'ʌn'hæpi/ — C1
uniform /'juːnɪfɔːm/ — A5
uninhabitable /'ʌnɪn'hæbɪtəbl/ — E3
unless /ən'les/ — E2
unless you're too busy/tired
/'bɪzi, 'taɪəd/ — C3
unlikely /'ʌn'laɪkli/ — E3
unsuccessful /'ʌnsək'sesfl/ — D6
up /ʌp/ — C6
up to date /'ʌp tə 'deɪt/ — B8
upbringing /'ʌpbrɪŋɪŋ/ — D3
upset (adjective) /'ʌp'set/ — C1
upset* /'ʌp'set/ — C1
upstairs /ʌp'steəz/ — C6, C8
useful /'juːsfl/ — D3
useless /'juːsləs/ — C6
usual: as usual /əz 'juːʒuːəl/ — E4
valley /'væli/ — D5
variety /və'raɪəti/ — D5
vehicle /'viːɪkl/ — A7
verb /vɜːb/ — B1
vertical /'vɜːtɪkl/ — D5
village /'vɪlɪdʒ/ — C7, D4, D6
violence /'vaɪələns/ — C5
visit (verb) /'vɪzɪt/ — E1
visit: on a visit /ɒn ə 'vɪzɪt/ — B4
vocabulary /və'kæbjələri/ — B1
volunteer /vɒlən'tɪə(r)/ — C7
vowel /'vaʊl/ — B1
wagon /'wægn/ — C7
waist /weɪst/ — E3
wait: I can't wait to ...
/aɪ 'kɑːnt 'weɪt tə/ — D2
waiting-room /'weɪtɪŋ 'ruːm/ — E7
Wales /weɪlz/ — A2
walk: go* for a walk /wɔːk/ — E2
war /wɔː(r)/ — A2, E1
warden: traffic warden
/'træfɪk 'wɔːdn/ — A5
warm /wɔːm/ — C6, D2
warning /'wɔːnɪŋ/ — E3
wash (my) hair /'wɒʃ (maɪ) 'heə(r)/ — C3
washing machine /'wɒʃɪŋ mə'ʃiːn/ — B8
waste (verb) /weɪst/ — B7
way: a long way away
/ə 'lɒŋ 'weɪ ə'weɪ/ — D5
way: in many ways /ɪn 'meni 'weɪz/ — D8
way: in some way /ɪn 'sʌm 'weɪ/ — D2
way: on his way /ɒn hɪz 'weɪ/ — A7
We were/got cut off /'kʌt 'ɒf/ — A3
weak /wiːk/ — D1
wear* /weə(r)/ — A5, D6
wedding /'wedɪŋ/ — B8
wedding anniversary
/'wedɪŋ ænɪ'vɜːsəri/ — C2
weight /weɪt/ — A8, E6
welcome (verb) /'welkəm/ — E1
well (noun) /wel/ — C7
well-dressed /'wel 'drest/ — D1
Well, anyway, ... /'wel 'eniweɪ/ — E7
well informed /'wel ɪn'fɔːmd/ — B3
Well, really! /'wel 'rɪəli/ — E7
Welsh /welʃ/, the Welsh — A2
Welshman/woman
/'welʃmən, womən/ — A2
west /west/ — A4
west: south-west /'saʊθ 'west/ — A4
western /'westən/ — A4
Western Europe /'westən 'jʊərəp/ — A2
wet /wet/ — C6

What about ...? /'wɒt ə'baʊt/ — C3
What do you mean by ...? — D3
What/How about ...ing? — D7
What time? /'wɒt 'taɪm/ — C3
What time were you thinking of? — C3
Where shall we meet?
/'weə ʃəl wi 'miːt/ — C3
Where was I? /'weə 'wɒz 'aɪ/ — E7
whether /'weðə(r)/ — D5, E2
while /waɪl/ — D8
whisper (verb) /'wɪspə(r)/ — B8
white coffee /'waɪt 'kɒfi/ — E2
Who's that? (on telephone)
/'huːz 'ðæt/ — A3
whole /həʊl/ — D2
whole: a whole lot of ...
/ə 'həʊl 'lɒt əv/ — C3
why don't you ...? /'waɪ 'dəʊnt juː/ — D7
why not ...? (+ infinitive without 'to')
/'waɪ 'nɒt/ — D7
wide /waɪd/ — D1
widen /'waɪdn/ — C8
win* /wɪn/ — C6, D4, D6
wind (noun) /wɪnd/ — A4
window frame /'wɪndəʊ 'freɪm/ — C8
window pane /'wɪndəʊ 'peɪn/ — C8
winter /'wɪntə(r)/ — D4
wish (noun and verb) /wɪʃ/ — D2
within /wɪ'ðɪn/ — D4
within: to within (e.g. a few pounds)
/tə wɪ'ðɪn/ — B3
wonder (verb) /'wʌndə(r)/ — D5, D7, E2
wonderful /'wʌndəfl/ — D2, E1
wood /wʊd/ — E8
word: my last word /maɪ 'lɑːst 'wɜːd/ — B3
work: do* work /'duː 'wɜːk/ — C2
work of art /'wɜːk əv 'ɑːt/ — E5
worker: factory worker
/'fæktəri 'wɜːkə(r)/ — C7
working conditions
/'wɜːkɪŋ kən'dɪʃnz/ — B5
working knowledge /'wɜːkɪŋ 'nɒlɪdʒ/ — B1
world /wɜːld/ — C7, D8
World: Third World /'θɜːd 'wɜːld/ — C7
worried /'wʌrɪd/ — C1, D1
worry (verb) /'wʌri/ — A1
worse /wɜːs/ — E4
worth ...ing /'wɜːθ ...ɪŋ/ — C7
would you rather ...?
/wʊd juː 'rɑːðə(r)/ — B5
wound (verb) /wuːnd/ — A8
wreck (verb) /rek/ — A7, A8
writer /'raɪtə(r)/ — E5
wrong /rɒŋ/ — C4, C6
wrong: go* wrong /'gəʊ 'rɒŋ/ — C7
wrong number: I've/You've got the
wrong number /'rɒŋ 'nʌmbə(r)/ — A3
yard (= measure) /jɑːd/ — D4
yard: Go* straight ahead for ...
yards/metres
/'streɪt ə'hed ... 'jɑːdz, 'miːtəz/ — A3
year: 50 years from now — E3
year: by the year 3000 — E3
year: in 50 years' time — E3
yet: not ... yet /'nɒt ... 'jet/ — C3
You can say that again — E7
You can't miss it /juː 'kɑːnt 'mɪs ɪt/ — A3
You know how it is — C3
... you see /juː 'siː/ — E7
young /jʌŋ/ — C6
youth (= time of life) /juːθ/ — E3

130

Acknowledgements

The authors and publishers are grateful to the following copyright owners for permission to reproduce photographs, illustrations, text and music. Every endeavour has been made to contact copyright owners and apologies are expressed for any omissions.

page 16: dialogue adapted from *People, Book 2* by permission of Françoise Houdart and Michael Swan, published by Librairie Hatier, Paris.   page 22: recording for Exercise 2 by permission of GWR-FM Radio.   page 26: *Piper and Drummer* by Albrecht Dürer reproduced by permission of Rheinisches Bildarchiv, Cologne and Wallraf-Richartz-Museum, Cologne.   page 29: *bl* © *The Guardian*. pages 30 and 31: cartoons reproduced by permission of *Punch*.   page 36: article reproduced by permission of *The Sun*; articles from *The Daily Mirror* reproduced by permission of *The Daily Mirror / Syndication International*; article from *The Daily Mail* reproduced by permission of *The Daily Mail / Solo*; articles reproduced from *The Daily Express* and *The Daily Star*.   page 39: extract from *Parkinson's Law* by C. Northcote Parkinson published by John Murray (Publishers) Ltd; extract from *Loneliness* by Jeremy Seabrook, reproduced by permission of the author. pages 42 (recording for Exercise 2) and 118: extracts from *Dandelion Wine* by Ray Bradbury reprinted by permission of Don Congdon Associates, Inc. © 1957, renewed 1987 by Ray Bradbury.   page 45: 'Mini-sagas' © Alan Sutton Publishing / The Sunday Telegraph Ltd.   page 49: cartoons reproduced by permission of *Punch*.   page 71: 'The Star' by Solveig von Schoultz from *Snow and Summers* published by Forest Books.   page 80: extract from *A Nation of Strangers* by Vance Packard published by Random House, Inc.   page 81: extract from *This Book is About Schools* by Satu Repo © 1980 by Random House, Inc. Reprinted by permission of Pantheon Books, a division of Random House, Inc.   page 86 (recordings for Exercises 1–5): distributed under licence by BBC Enterprises. Audio recordings © BBC Enterprises 1974.   page 93: *t* and *c* cartoons reproduced by permission of *Punch*; *b* cartoon reproduced by permission of *Private Eye*.   page 95: extract from *Teaching as a subversive activity* by Neil Postman and Charles Weingartner published by Pitman Publishing. page 99: *t* cartoon reproduced by permission of *The Spectator*; *b* cartoon reproduced by permission of *Punch*. page 100: 'When you are old and grey' © 1953 Tom Lehrer. Copyright renewed. Used by permission. 'Warning' by Jenny Joseph from *Selected Poems* 1992. Permission granted by John Johnson Ltd, London, on behalf of the author. © Jenny Joseph.   page 101: cartoon reproduced by permission of *Punch*.   page 102: extracts from 'Chances of your lives' © *The Observer*.   page 103: cartoon reproduced by permission of *Punch*.   page 104: *t Winter Scene with Skaters* by Hendrick Avercamp reproduced by courtesy of the Trustees, The National Gallery, London; *bl Youth leaning against a tree among roses* by Nicholas Hilliard reproduced by courtesy of the Board of Trustees of the Victoria & Albert Museum; *br Portrait of the journalist Sylvia von Harden* by Otto Dix, reproduced by courtesy of Photographie Musée National d'Art Moderne, Centre Georges Pompidou, Paris.   page 110: *bl* Adapted from 'The Earliest Precursor of Writing' by Denise Schmandt-Besserat. © 1978 by Scientific American, Inc. All rights reserved.   *br* Photographs reproduced by courtesy of the Musée du Louvre, Paris.   page 117: extract from 'Chances of your lives' © *The Observer*.   page 120: definitions adapted from the *Longman Dictionary of Contemporary English* edited by Della Summers, published by Longman Group UK Ltd.   page 118: 'What Shall I Say?' by Peter Tinturin © Chappell & Co. Inc., New York, reproduced by permission of Chappell Music Ltd and International Music Publications. Recording used by permission of Big Bear Records.   'The Riddle Song' by Harry Robinson and Julie Felix © 1965 TRO Essex Music Limited.   page 119: 'What did you learn in school today?', by Tom Paxton. © 1964 Cherry Lane Music Inc. Administered by Harmony Music Ltd, 1A, Farm Place, London W8 7SX.   page 121: 'Trying to Love Two Women' by Sonny Throckmorton © 1979 Cross Keys Publishing Co. Inc., USA. Reproduced by permission of EMI Music Publishing Ltd, London WC2H 0EA.

The songs 'Gold Digger' (Lesson D1, Exercise 1) and 'I will take you there' (Lesson D5, Exercise 5C) were written by Steve Hall. 'Fiddling across the USA' (Revision and fluency practice B, Exercise 8) was written by Jonathan Dykes (words) and Robert Campbell (music). This version of the song 'Logger Lover' (Revision and fluency practice C, Exercise 9) is by Dick Stephenson.

The authors and publishers are grateful to the following illustrators and photographic sources:

David Atkinson, pages 14 and 15.   Kathy Baxendale, pages 9 *tr*, 12 *bl*, 29.   Caroline Bays, pages 86 and 87. Ken Brooks, pages 70, 83.   Peter Byatt, pages 26, 32, 42 *r* and 43, 66 and 67.   John Chamberlain, pages 78 and 79. Tony Coles, page 77.   David Downton, page 41.   Annie Farrall, page 74.   Teri Gower, pages 64 and 65, 82, 99. Amanda Hall, page 76.   Mark Harfield, page 10.   Sue Hillwood Harris, pages 56 and 57.   Joanna Kerr, pages 20 and 21.   Kiki Lewis, page 100.   Joe McEwan, page 33. Edward McLachlan, pages 16 and 17, 54, 55, 61.   Carl Melegari, page 60.   Kaoru Miyake, page 42 *l*.   Mark Peppé, page 111.   Chris Ryley, pages 48, 73, 84. Fletcher Sibthorp, page 106.   Madeleine Thompson, pages 96 and 97.   Kathy Ward, pages 58 and 59.   Rosemary Woods, page 44.   Janet Woolley, pages 108 and 109.

J. Allan Cash Photo Library, page 53.   Adams Picture Library, page 8 *uml*.   Allsport / Denis Boulanger, page 52 *br*.   Art Directors Photo Library, page 88 (*picture 12*). Clive Barda, page 9 *b*.   © 1992 Comstock Inc., page 13 *b*. Greg Evans International, page 8 *umr*.   Hulton Deutsch Collection Limited, page 43, 52 *lml* and *bl*.   The Kobal Collection, page 52 *uml* and *umc* .   Harald Lange / Bruce Coleman Limited, page 88 (*picture 2*).   Nigel Luckhurst, pages 22 and 23 (with thanks to CN-Fm 103 Radio Cambridge).   Pictor International-London, page 12 *t*, 13 *c*. Graham Portlock, pages 12 *b* and *c*, 19 (*pictures 1, 2, 3, 4, 6, 8, 9, 10*), 34 and 35, 36, 64, 73, 115.   Andrew J. Purcell / Bruce Coleman Limited, page 88 (*picture 11*). Rex Features, page 52 *umr*.   Robert Harding Picture Library, page 88 (*picture 4*).   Spectrum Colour Library, pages 8 *b*, 105.   Telegraph Colour Library, pages 8 *lm*, 13 *t*, 88 (*picture 5*).   Tony Stone Worldwide, pages 9 *t* and *m*, 19 (*picture 7*), 52 *t* and *bc*, 83, 88 (*pictures 1 l and br, 9, 13*), 102.   'ZEFA' photo library, pages 8 *t*, 19 (*picture 5*), 52 *lmc* and *lmr*, 88 (*pictures 1 tr, 3, 6, 7, 8, 10, 14*)

Picture research by Sandie Huskinson-Rolfe (PHOTOSEEKERS)

(*t* = top   *b* = bottom   *um* = upper middle   *lm* = lower middle   *c* = centre   *r* =right   *l* = left)

Phonetic symbols

Vowels

symbol	example
/iː/	eat /iːt/
/i/	happy /'hæpi/
/ɪ/	it /ɪt/
/e/	when /wen/
/æ/	cat /kæt/
/ɑː/	hard /hɑːd/
/ɒ/	not /nɒt/
/ɔː/	sort /sɔːt/; all /ɔːl/
/ʊ/	look /lʊk/
/uː/	too /tuː/
/ʌ/	cup /kʌp/
/ɜː/	first /fɜːst/; burn /bɜːn/
/ə/	about /ə'baʊt/; mother /'mʌðə(r)/
/eɪ/	day /deɪ/
/aɪ/	my /maɪ/
/ɔɪ/	boy /bɔɪ/
/aʊ/	now /naʊ/
/əʊ/	go /gəʊ/
/ɪə/	here /hɪə(r)/
/eə/	chair /tʃeə(r)/
/ʊə/	tourist /'tʊərɪst/

Consonants

symbol	example
/p/	pen /pen/
/b/	big /bɪg/
/t/	two /tuː/
/d/	day /deɪ/
/k/	keep /kiːp/; cup /kʌp/
/g/	get /get/
/tʃ/	choose /tʃuːz/
/dʒ/	job /dʒɒb/; average /'ævrɪdʒ/
/f/	fall /fɔːl/
/v/	very /'veri/
/θ/	think /θɪŋk/
/ð/	then /ðen/
/s/	see /siː/
/z/	zoo /zuː/; is /ɪz/
/ʃ/	shop /ʃɒp/; directions /də'rekʃənz/
/ʒ/	pleasure /'pleʒə(r)/; occasionally /ə'keɪʒənli/
/h/	who /huː/; how /haʊ/
/m/	meet /miːt/
/n/	no /nəʊ/
/ŋ/	sing /sɪŋ/; drink /drɪŋk/
/l/	long /lɒŋ/
/r/	right /raɪt/
/j/	yes /jes/
/w/	will /wɪl/

Stress

Stress is shown by a mark (') in front of the stressed syllable.

mother /'mʌðə(r)/   average /'ævrɪdʒ/
about /ə'baʊt/   tonight /tə'naɪt/

Irregular verbs

Infinitive/Present	Simple Past	Participle
be /biː/	was /wəz, wɒz/, were /wə(r), wɜː(r)/	been /bɪn, biːn/
beat /biːt/	beat /biːt/	beaten /'biːtn/
become /bɪ'kʌm/	became /bɪ'keɪm/	become /bɪ'kʌm/
begin /bɪ'gɪn/	began /bɪ'gæn/	begun /bɪ'gʌn/
bend /bend/	bent /bent/	bent /bent/
bet /bet/	bet /bet/	bet /bet/
bite /baɪt/	bit /bɪt/	bitten /'bɪtn/
bleed /bliːd/	bled /bled/	bled /bled/
blow /bləʊ/	blew /bluː/	blown /bləʊn/
break /breɪk/	broke /brəʊk/	broken /'brəʊkn/
bring /brɪŋ/	brought /brɔːt/	brought /brɔːt/
build /bɪld/	built /bɪlt/	built /bɪlt/
burn /bɜːn/	burnt /bɜːnt/	burnt /bɜːnt/
buy /baɪ/	bought /bɔːt/	bought /bɔːt/
can /k(ə)n, kæn/	could /kʊd/	been able /bɪn 'eɪbl/
catch /kætʃ/	caught /kɔːt/	caught /kɔːt/
choose /tʃuːz/	chose /tʃəʊz/	chosen /'tʃəʊzn/
come /kʌm/	came /keɪm/	come /kʌm/, been /bɪn, biːn/
cost /kɒst/	cost /kɒst/	cost /kɒst/
cut /kʌt/	cut /kʌt/	cut /kʌt/
deal /diːl/	dealt /delt/	dealt /delt/
do /dʊ, də, duː/	did /dɪd/	done /dʌn/
draw /drɔː/	drew /druː/	drawn /drɔːn/
dream /driːm/	dreamt /dremt/	dreamt /dremt/
drink /drɪŋk/	drank /dræŋk/	drunk /drʌŋk/
drive /draɪv/	drove /drəʊv/	driven /'drɪvn/
eat /iːt/	ate /et/	eaten /'iːtn/
earn /ɜːn/	earnt /ɜːnt/	earnt /ɜːnt/
fall /fɔːl/	fell /fel/	fallen /'fɔːlən/
feed /fiːd/	fed /fed/	fed /fed/
feel /fiːl/	felt /felt/	felt /felt/
fight /faɪt/	fought /fɔːt/	fought /fɔːt/
find /faɪnd/	found /faʊnd/	found /faʊnd/
fly /flaɪ/	flew /fluː/	flown /fləʊn/
forget /fə'get/	forgot /fə'gɒt/	forgotten /fə'gɒtn/
get /get/	got /gɒt/	got /gɒt/
give /gɪv/	gave /geɪv/	given /'gɪvn/
go /gəʊ/	went /went/	gone /gɒn/, been /bɪn, biːn/
grow /grəʊ/	grew /gruː/	grown /grəʊn/
hang up /'hæŋ 'ʌp/	hung up /'hʌŋ 'ʌp/	hung up /'hʌŋ 'ʌp/
have /(h)əv, hæv/	had /(h)əd, hæd/	had /hæd/
hear /hɪə(r)/	heard /hɜːd/	heard /hɜːd/
hide /haɪd/	hid /hɪd/	hidden /'hɪdn/
hit /hɪt/	hit /hɪt/	hit /hɪt/
hold /həʊld/	held /held/	held /held/
hurt /hɜːt/	hurt /hɜːt/	hurt /hɜːt/
keep /kiːp/	kept /kept/	kept /kept/
know /nəʊ/	knew /njuː/	known /nəʊn/
lead /liːd/	led /led/	led /led/
lean /liːn/	leant /lent/, leaned /liːnd/	leant /lent/, leaned /liːnd/
learn /lɜːn/	learnt /lɜːnt/	learnt /lɜːnt/
leave /liːv/	left /left/	left /left/
lend /lend/	lent /lent/	lent /lent/
let /let/	let /let/	let /let/
lie /laɪ/	lay /leɪ/	lain /leɪn/
lose /luːz/	lost /lɒst/	lost /lɒst/
make /meɪk/	made /meɪd/	made /meɪd/
mean /miːn/	meant /ment/	meant /ment/
meet /miːt/	met /met/	met /met/
must /məst, mʌst/	had to /'hæd tə/	had to /'hæd tə/
overtake /'əʊvə'teɪk/	overtook /'əʊvə'tʊk/	overtaken /'əʊvə'teɪkn/
pay /peɪ/	paid /peɪd/	paid /peɪd/
put /pʊt/	put /pʊt/	put /pʊt/
read /riːd/	read /red/	read /red/

Infinitive/Present	Simple Past	Participle
rebuild /ˈriːˈbɪld/	rebuilt /ˈriːˈbɪlt/	rebuilt /ˈriːˈbɪlt/
repay /rɪˈpeɪ/	repaid /rɪˈpeɪd/	repaid /rɪˈpeɪd/
ride /raɪd/	rode /rəʊd/	ridden /ˈrɪdn/
ring /rɪŋ/	rang /ræŋ/	rung /rʌŋ/
rise /raɪz/	rose /rəʊz/	risen /ˈrɪzn/
run /rʌn/	ran /ræn/	run /rʌn/
say /seɪ/	said /sed/	said /sed/
see /siː/	saw /sɔː/	seen /siːn/
sell /sel/	sold /səʊld/	sold /səʊld/
send /send/	sent /sent/	sent /sent/
set /set/	set /set/	set /set/
shake /ʃeɪk/	shook /ʃʊk/	shaken /ˈʃeɪkn/
shine /ʃaɪn/	shone /ʃɒn/	shone /ʃɒn/
shoot /ʃuːt/	shot /ʃɒt/	shot /ʃɒt/
show /ʃəʊ/	showed /ʃəʊd/	shown /ʃəʊn/
shut /ʃʌt/	shut /ʃʌt/	shut /ʃʌt/
sing /sɪŋ/	sang /sæŋ/	sung /sʌŋ/
sit /sɪt/	sat /sæt/	sat /sæt/
sleep /sliːp/	slept /slept/	slept /slept/
smell /smel/	smelt /smelt/	smelt /smelt/
speak /spiːk/	spoke /spəʊk/	spoken /ˈspəʊkn/
spell /spel/	spelt /spelt/	spelt /spelt/
spend /spend/	spent /spent/	spent /spent/
spit /spɪt/	spat /spæt/	spat /spæt/
split /splɪt/	split /splɪt/	split /splɪt/
stand /stænd/	stood /stʊd/	stood /stʊd/
steal /stiːl/	stole /stəʊl/	stolen /ˈstəʊlən/
strike /straɪk/	struck /strʌk/	struck /strʌk/
swim /swɪm/	swam /swæm/	swum /swʌm/
swing /swɪŋ/	swung /swʌŋ/	swung /swʌŋ/
take /teɪk/	took /tʊk/	taken /ˈteɪkn/
teach /tiːtʃ/	taught /tɔːt/	taught /tɔːt/
tear /teə(r)/	tore /tɔː(r)/	torn /tɔːn/
tell /tel/	told /təʊld/	told /təʊld/
think /θɪŋk/	thought /θɔːt/	thought /θɔːt/
throw /θrəʊ/	threw /θruː/	thrown /θrəʊn/
understand /ʌndəˈstænd/	understood /ʌndəˈstʊd/	understood /ʌndəˈstʊd/
upset /ʌpˈset/	upset /ʌpˈset/	upset /ʌpˈset/
wake up /ˈweɪk ˈʌp/	woke up /ˈwəʊk ˈʌp/	woken up /ˈwəʊkn ˈʌp/
wear /weə(r)/	wore /wɔː(r)/	worn /wɔːn/
will /wɪl/	would /wʊd/	–
win /wɪn/	won /wʌn/	won /wʌn/
write /raɪt/	wrote /rəʊt/	written /ˈrɪtn/